COMPARATIVE LITERATURE:
METHOD AND PERSPECTIVE

COMPARATIVE LITERATURE:

Method and Perspective

EDITED BY

Newton P. Stallknecht *and* Horst Frenz

Southern Illinois University Press   CARBONDALE

ALTHOUGH the essays in this volume may be considered independent contributions, it should be noted that they have been motivated by an interest, common to all the contributors, in the problems and methods the student of comparative literature may encounter. In each essay, the author has undertaken to indicate certain objectives and to characterize certain procedures which he considers essential in approaching his particular problem; and in so doing, he has tried to illustrate theoretical statements by including examples drawn from his own reading and research. As a result these essays may be of considerable assistance in helping the student, whatever his special interests, to find his way in this broad area of study.

Comparative literature is, relatively speaking, a young discipline in this country and accordingly its practitioners are still keenly interested in fixing its objectives and defining its scope. Professor Remak turns his attention to these two aspects and gives us a reasoned interpretation of his own, set against other definitions which are included as background. He has appended to his argument an annotated list of historical and critical studies, bibliographies, and similar reference works, which a student of comparative literature will find indispensable.

Professor Seeber supplements the opening essay by considering in detail certain problems of terminology which all students of comparative literature must face if they hope to speak a language intelligible to one another and to the public. He warns the students that many terms employed in the discussion of literature have changed their meaning from period to period and from area to area and must always be weighed against the background of historical interpretation.

The study of the influence of one writer upon another has long occupied a prominent place in literary research. However, it has seemed to many critics in recent years that such studies have been carried to extremes and that there has been too much speculation about the debt which almost every famous author is said to owe to certain of his predecessors, immediate and remote. The problem here has been to develop a technique for the responsible study of literary influence and literary indebtedness. Professor Shaw undertakes briefly to characterize such a technique and to illustrate its operation with reference to his own study of Anglo-Russian literary relations. As a result, it is possible to make a case in defense of this type of research which, when properly executed, contributes significantly to our understanding and appreciation of certain writers.

While the student of comparative literature should be acquainted with a number of foreign languages, he will still be deeply concerned with the problem of translation. He must, in certain cases, himself depend on the use of translations and he will recognize that translations of important literary works from one language to another constitute a major avenue of literary influence. In recent years, increasing attention has been paid to the many problems faced by the translator. Professor Frenz has discussed these problems emphasizing his belief that translating should be considered an art in itself.

Professor Edel argues that "literature and psychology have come to recognize in our century that they stand upon common ground," and explores the various ways in which this generalization may be supported. The interpretation of human consciousness and behavior springing from the works of Freud and Jung is shown to be relevant to the study of contemporary literature—Continental, British, and American. Mr. Edel defends the proposition that "psychoanalysis has contributed important aids to three facets of literary study: (1) to criticism itself, (2) to the study of the creative process in literature, (3) to the writing of biography."

Professor Stallknecht considers the study of literature in its relation to the history of ideas. He is interested in the way in which philosophical ideas are appropriated or absorbed by creative writers and in the manner in which certain ideas undergo transformation as they pass from one period to another. Mr. Stallknecht's orientation is derived from the writings of the English philosopher R. G. Collingwood and the German critic Erich Auerbach rather than from the work of A. O. Lovejoy. The latter's notion of a "unit-idea" is considered critically.

Literature, like any cultural activity, does not and cannot exist in a vacuum, and we must consider, for example, the relationship between literature and the other arts, especially music and painting. This is as rewarding a study as that of the relationship between the literatures of different periods and different countries. Professor Gaither defends this point of view with a number of illustrations which indicate certain significant connections between literature and the fine arts. In the course of her discussion, Miss Gaither comments on a number of critics who, in the tradition of Lessing's *Laocoön*, consider the several arts in comparison with each other.

What we call "literature" is descended from preliterary forms of expression, when the spoken word constituted virtually the only mode of communication. Professor Thompson considers the persistence of these preliterary forms in modern times and their relation to literature proper. His study ranges from comments on the composition of such epics as the *Iliad* and *Odyssey* to the development and wide diffusion of folk tales in ancient and modern times. The student of comparative literature cannot ignore the relationship of literature to the vast body of "unlettered" myths, epics, and tales studied by the folklorist.

From the time of Aristotle to the present decade, European students have found the interpretation of tragedy one of the most fascinating problems both in the history and the philosophy of literature. The historian, the critic, the moralist, and the student of religion alike recognize in tragedy an area of discussion where their special interests interpenetrate. In considering the development of European tragedy, an important distinction must be drawn between the classical drama of the Greeks and the Roman or Stoic drama of Seneca. Professor Pratt has turned his attention to this contrast, and his essay illustrates these two treatments of the tragic situation. Such a study is important not only for an understanding of the development of tragedy in antiquity but also for adequate interpretation of English and European drama of the sixteenth and seventeenth centuries.

Professor Rey emphasizes the fact that the contents and subject matter of certain Romance epics may be considered as historical in origin. He examines in some detail the blending of history and fiction which is as apparent in the Romance epic as in the modern historical novel.

In a second contribution to this volume, Professor Remak invites us to consider the problem involved in isolating and defining a broad literary movement such as that of European Romanticism. His résumé makes apparent the great complexity in which such discussions become involved. The resulting difficulties are multiplied by the fact that the term

Romanticism, like all similar terms, receives different interpretation in different countries. Mr. Remak summarizes the many connotations that this term has acquired and, by doing so, he helps us avoid much confusion and misunderstanding.

Literary criticism and its history may be approached from the comparative point of view. For instance, the work of an author like Shakespeare has been interpreted by critics of diverse national and cultural background; and a review of such criticism will bring into bold relief many important phases of literary relationship. With this in mind, Professor Weisstein has surveyed the various approaches to Hamlet criticism.

In a volume such as this there is almost no limit to the topics that might be selected, and one may hardly hope to offer an exhaustive or strictly systematic consideration of so wide a field. There must therefore be something arbitrary about the selection of the subjects here treated. Nonetheless, these essays may be said to characterize, though not fully to describe, the field of investigation to which they are directed. They are intended to serve primarily as an introduction or invitation to further discussion. As such the authors hope that this volume will prove to be of some interest to all those who are concerned, either in theory or practice, with the problems and methods of comparative literature.

The authors are grateful to Dr. Gian N. G. Orsini, Professor of Comparative Literature at the University of Wisconsin, for reading this volume in manuscript and making a number of valuable suggestions, which they have been happy to adopt.

NEWTON P. STALLKNECHT

March 29, 1961   *HORST FRENZ*

CONTENTS

COMPARATIVE LITERATURE:
METHOD AND PERSPECTIVE

1

Comparative Literature,
Its Definition and Function

Henry H. H. Remak

COMPARATIVE literature is the study of literature beyond the confines of one particular country, and the study of the relationships between literature on the one hand and other areas of knowledge and belief, such as the arts (e.g., painting, sculpture, architecture, music), philosophy, history, the social sciences (e.g., politics, economics, sociology), the sciences, religion, etc., on the other. In brief, it is the comparison of one literature with another or others, and the comparison of literature with other spheres of human expression.

This definition [1] is probably acceptable to most students of comparative literature in this country, but would be subject to considerable argument among an important segment of comparatists which we shall, for brevity's sake, call the "French school." [2] For the purpose of clarifying these differences of opinion, some rather basic, others more of emphasis, it may be wise to take up the first part of our definition before dealing with the second.

While the American and the French "schools" will both subscribe to this portion of our definition, viz. comparative

---

HENRY H. H. REMAK, Professor of German at Indiana University, has published extensively in the fields of Franco-German literary relations (Goethe and French literature, French Realism in Germany) and principles of comparative literature. He is a corresponding member of the Académie des Sciences, Lettres et Beaux-Arts of Marseille.

literature as the study of literature beyond national boundaries, there are important variations of relative stress in its
practical application. The French are inclined to favor questions which can be solved on the basis of factual evidence
(often involving personal documents). They tend to exclude
literary criticism from the domain of comparative literature.
They look askance at studies which "merely" compare, which
"merely" point out analogies and contrasts. Carré and Guyard even warn against influence studies as being too hazy,
too uncertain, and would have us concentrate on questions of
reception, intermediaries, foreign travel, and attitudes toward a given country in the literature of another country during a certain period. Unlike Van Tieghem, these two scholars
are also chary of vast syntheses of European literature as
courting superficiality, dangerous simplifications and slip-
pery metaphysics.

The positivistic roots of these reservations are clearly
discernible. In our opinion, the French desire for literary
"sécurité" is unfortunate at a time which cries, as Peyre
has pointed out, for more (not less) imagination. To be
sure, the problem of influences is a very delicate one and requires of its devotee more encyclopedic knowledge and more
finesse than has been exhibited in some past endeavors of
this kind. In a good many influence studies, the location of
sources has been given too much attention, rather than such
questions as: what was *retained* and what was *rejected*, and
why, and *how* was the material absorbed and integrated,
and with *what success?* If conducted in this fashion, influence studies contribute not only to our knowledge of literary
history but to our understanding of the creative process and
of the literary work of art.

To the extent that the preoccupation with locating and
proving an influence may overshadow more crucial questions
of artistic interpretation and evaluation, influence studies

may contribute less to the elucidation of the essence of a literary work than studies comparing authors, works, styles, tendencies and literatures in which no influence can or is intended to be shown. Purely comparative subjects constitute an inexhaustible reservoir hardly tapped by contemporary scholars who seem to have forgotten that the name of our discipline is "comparative literature," not "influential literature." Herder and Diderot, Novalis and Chateaubriand, Musset and Heine, Balzac and Dickens, *Moby Dick* and *Faust,* Hawthorne's *Roger Malvin's Burial* and Droste-Hülshoff's *Judenbuche,* Hardy and Hauptmann, Azorín and Anatole France, Baroja and Stendhal, Hamsun and Giono, Thomas Mann and Gide are eminently comparable regardless of whether or how much the one influenced the other.[3]

Carré's and Guyard's disinclination toward large-scale syntheses in comparative literature strikes us likewise as excessively cautious. We *must* have syntheses unless the study of literature wants to condemn itself to eternal fragmentation and isolation. If we have any ambitions of participating in the intellectual and emotional life of the world, we must, now and then, pull together the insights and results achieved by research in literature and make available meaningful conclusions to other disciplines, to the nation and to the world at large. The dangers of hurried generalizations, real as they are, are too often advanced as a shield covering up the all too human temptation of playing it safe. "We must wait till all the data are in." But all the data will never be in, and we know it. Even if a single generation succeeded in assembling all the data on a given author or topic, the same "facts" will and should always be subject to different interpretations by different generations. Scholarship must take reasonable precautions, but it should not be paralyzed by illusory perfectionism.[4]

Fortunately, the French have been far less timid and doctrinaire in actual practice than in theory.[5] To French and French-trained scholars, comparative literature owes a large, probably the largest share of important comparative scholarship. Texte's *Rousseau and the Origins of Literary Cosmopolitanism*, Baldensperger's *Goethe in France* and *The Circulation of Ideas in the French Emigration*, Carré's *Goethe in England*, Hazard's admirable panorama of the Enlightenment throughout Europe are only a few among French syntheses distinguished by a dexterous and sensitive handling of comparisons and influences, by a subtle awareness of literary values and of the fine shadings of the uniquely individual as well as an uncanny ability to direct a myriad of observations into lucid patterns of overall developments. Van Tieghem's and Guyard's French introductions to comparative literature are themselves syntheses of substantial usefulness. American scholars, in their turn, must guard against dismissing lightly certain topics (studies of reception, attitudes, intermediaries, travelers, *Belesenheit*) merely because the French seem to have favored them to the exclusion or neglect of other comparative subjects.[6]

In examining the second part of our definition, viz. the relationship between literature and other fields, we come up against a difference not of emphasis but of basic distinction between the "American" and "French" schools. In the only contemporary surveys of the field of comparative literature written to date in book form, Van Tieghem and Guyard do not discuss or even list the relationship between literature and other areas (art, music, philosophy, politics, etc.). During the many years that the *Revue de littérature comparée* was directed by Baldensperger and Hazard, its quarterly bibliographies did not recognize this category of topics at all. This policy has remained unchanged under succeeding editors. In contrast, American comparative-literature curricula and publications (including bibliographies) generally take in this realm.

The French are certainly interested in such topics as the comparative arts, but they do not think of them as being within the jurisdiction of comparative literature.[7] There are historical reasons for this attitude. Despite the rigidities of academic compartmentalization, comparative literature has been able, for more than half a century, to occupy a distinct and distinguished niche in French universities precisely because it combined a wider coverage *of* literature with a prudent restriction *to* literature. The student and teacher of literature who venture beyond national frontiers already assume an extra burden. The French seem to fear that taking on, in addition, the systematic study of the relationship between literature and any other area of human endeavor invites the accusation of charlatanism and would, at any rate, be detrimental to the acceptance of comparative literature as a respectable and respected academic domain.[8]

A related, more fundamental objection should also be taken into consideration: the lack of logical coherence between comparative literature as the study of literature beyond national boundaries and comparative literature as the study of the ramifications of literature beyond its own boundaries.[9] Furthermore, while the geographical connotations of the term comparative literature are fairly concrete, the generic ramifications implied in the American concept raise serious problems of demarcation which American scholars have not been willing to face squarely.

It is difficult to find firm criteria for selection when one scans the mass of titles in Baldensperger-Friederich's *Bibliography of Comparative Literature,* especially in those portions of Book One covering "Generalities," "Thematology" and "Literary Genres," and in the chapter on "Literary Cur-

rents" in Book Three. We are speaking here only of entries
which are, neither by title nor (upon examination) by contents comparative in the geographical sense (except incidentally), whose inclusion in the *Bibliography* must therefore
have been determined by reasons of subject matter extension.
Under the headings of "Individual Motifs" and "Collective
Motifs," for example, we find a large number of investigations of love, marriage, women, fathers-and-sons, children,
war, professions, etc. *within* a national literature. Can the incorporation of these items in a bibliography of *comparative*
literature be justified on the premise that we are dealing here
with two realms—literature and "motifs"? But motifs are
part and parcel *of* literature; they are intrinsic, not extraneous. Under the headings of "Literary Genres" and "Literary
Currents," we find studies on the American novel, the German *Bildungsroman*, the Spanish Generation of '98, etc. etc.
But accounts of literary genres, movements and generations
in a certain country, even if they are of a general nature, are
not comparative per se. The notions of genres, movements,
"schools," generations etc. are implicit in our idea of literature and literary history; they are inside, not outside of literature. We submit that, with a modicum of rationalizing, almost anything and everything in literary scholarship and
criticism could lay claim to being "comparative literature" if
the ultraelastic criteria of the *Bibliography* are accepted.
Comparative literature as a quasi all-inclusive term would be
close to meaningless.[10]

Granting that there is a twilight zone where a case can be
made pro and con the "comparativeness" of a given topic,
we shall have to be more discriminating in the future about
admitting a topic in this category to comparative literature.
We must make sure that comparisons between literature and
a field other than literature be accepted as "comparative lit-

erature" only if they are *systematic* and if a definitely *separable, coherent discipline* outside of literature is studied as such. We cannot classify scholarly endeavors as "comparative literature" merely because they discuss inherent aspects of life and art that must inevitably be reflected in all literature, for what else can literature be about? A paper on the historical sources of a Shakespearean drama would (unless it concentrates on another country) be "comparative literature" only if historiography and literature were the main poles of the investigation, if historical facts or accounts and their literary adaptations were systematically compared and evaluated, and conclusions arrived at which would bear on the two domains as such. A treatment of the role of money in Balzac's *Père Goriot* would be comparative only if it were principally (not just incidentally) concerned with the literary osmosis of a coherent financial system or set of ideas. An inquiry into the ethical or religious ideas of Hawthorne or Melville could be considered comparative only if it dealt with an organized religious movement (e.g., Calvinism) or set of beliefs. The tracing of a character in a novel by Henry James would be within the scope of comparative literature only if it developed a methodical view of this character in the light of the psychological theories of Freud (or Adler, Jung, etc.).

With this caveat in mind, our preference goes nevertheless to the more inclusive "American" concept of comparative literature. We must, to be sure, strive to achieve and maintain a minimum set of criteria marking off our chosen field; but we must not be so concerned with its theoretical unity as to forget the perhaps more important *functional* aspect of comparative literature. We conceive of comparative literature less as an independent subject which must at all costs set up its own inflexible laws, than as a badly needed auxiliary discipline, a link between smaller segments of parochial literature, a bridge between organically related but physically separated areas of human creativeness. Whatever the disagreements on the theoretical aspects of comparative literature be, there is agreement on its task: to give scholars, teachers, students and last but not least readers a better, more comprehensive understanding of literature as a whole rather than of a departmental fragment or several isolated departmental fragments of literature. It can do so best by not only relating several literatures to each other but by relating literature to other fields of human knowledge and activity, especially artistic and ideological fields; that is, by extending the investigation of literature both geographically and generically.

II

Several areas and terms are contiguous to or seem to overlap with comparative literature: national literature, world literature and general literature. A clarification of their meanings is indispensable for the delimitation of comparative-literature terms.

There is no fundamental difference between methods of research in national literature and comparative literature, between, for example, a comparison of Racine with Corneille and of Racine with Goethe. There are, however, subjects encountered in comparative-literature research which go beyond national-literature scholarship: the contact or collision between different cultures, in general, and the problems connected with translation, in particular. Other topics inherent in the study of national literature occur in somewhat different patterns and tend to occupy a place of greater importance in comparative-literature research: vogue, success, reception, and influence of literature; travel and intermediaries.

Even geographically speaking, an air-tight distinction between national literature and comparative literature is sometimes difficult. What are we to do with authors writing in the same language but belonging to different nations? We should probably not hesitate at all to assign a comparison between George Bernard Shaw and H. L. Mencken, or between Sean O'Casey and Tennessee Williams, to comparative literature, but when we go back to English and American literature of the colonial period the case, as Wellek has suggested, becomes much less clear-cut. Maeterlinck and Verhaeren were Belgians writing in French; would a study of their intimate connections with French Symbolism be classed as comparative literature? What about Irish authors writing in English or Finnish nationals composing in Swedish? Similar difficulties arise in investigations of the Nicaraguan Rubén Darío's place in Spanish literature, or of the eminent positions of the Swiss Gottfried Keller and Conrad Ferdinand Meyer, the Austrians Adalbert Stifter and Hugo von Hofmannsthal in German literature (not to speak of the still more complicated cases of Rilke and Kafka). To what extent should legal naturalization be taken into account? There is surely a difference, in the consequences for their literary work, between the British citizenship of T. S. Eliot and the American citizenship of Thomas Mann.

Inversely, there are authors belonging to the same nation but writing in different languages or dialects. Welsh literature in relation to English, Low German literature in relation to German, Flemish literature in relation to French (in Belgium), Sicilian literature in relation to Italian, Ukrainian literature in relation to Great Russian, Basque and Catalan literature in relation to Spanish or French, raise questions that must be answered from case to case. In general, we may state the rule that a scholar asserting that a transitional topic of this nature is comparative must assume the burden of positive proof that he is dealing with significant differences in language, nationality or tradition.

Most comparatists, while admitting complications and overlapping, will agree that these difficulties are neither frequent nor serious enough to invalidate the distinction between literature studied within and across national boundaries.

Between comparative literature and world literature,[11] there exist differences of degree as well as more fundamental differences. The former comprise elements of space, time, quality and intensity. Comparative literature (geographically speaking) involves, like world literature, an element of space, but frequently, though not necessarily, a more restricted one. Comparative literature often deals with the relationship of only two countries, or two authors of different nationality, or one author and another country (e.g., Franco-German literary relations, Poe-Baudelaire, Italy in the works of Goethe). The more pretentious term "world literature" implies recognition throughout the world, ordinarily the western world.

"World literature" also suggests an element of time. As a rule, the acquisition of world renown takes time, and "world literature" usually deals with literature consecrated as great by the test of time. Contemporary literature is, therefore, somewhat less frequently covered by the term "world literature," whereas comparative literature, at least in theory, may compare anything that is comparable no matter how old or how recent the work(s) may be. It must be readily admitted, however, that in practice many, perhaps most, comparative literature studies do deal with literary figures of the past who have achieved world-wide fame. Much of what we have been and shall be doing is, in effect, comparative world-literature.

World literature deals therefore predominantly with time- and world-honored literary productions of enduring quality (e.g., the *Divine Comedy; Don Quijote; Paradise Lost; Candide; Werther*), or, less markedly, with authors of our own day who have enjoyed very intense applause abroad (e.g. Faulkner, Camus, Thomas Mann), which, in many cases, may prove transitory (Galsworthy, Margaret Mitchell, Moravia, Remarque). Comparative literature is not bound to the same extent by criteria of quality and/or intensity. Illuminating comparative studies have been, and many more could be done on second-rate authors, often more representative of the time-bound features of their age than the great writers. Such investigations would include authors once thought great or known to have been very successful (e.g., Lillo, Gessner, Kotzebue, Dumas father and son, Scribe, Sudermann, Pinero), or even minor authors who never made headway abroad, but whose production might illustrate pan-European trends of literary taste (in Germany alone, such writers as Friedrich de la Motte-Fouqué, Zacharias Werner, Friedrich Spielhagen, Max Kretzer).

In addition, certain first-rate writers not yet acclaimed by world literature are eminently fitted for comparative-literature studies. The latter may actually contribute to their acceptance as figures of world literature. Among the men of letters of the past, just recently "discovered" or resurrected (or in the process of being so) by the western world are Donne, Blake, Hölderlin, Büchner, Gérard de Nerval, Lautréamont, and Melville. Others, equally worthy of international attention, are still waiting for commensurate recognition outside their own countries: Espronceda, Larra, Galdós, Azorín, Baroja (Spain); Herder, Hebbel, Keller, Trakl, Hofmannsthal, Hesse (Germany, Austria and Switzerland); Petöfi (Hungary); Creanga, Eminescu, Sadoveanu (Rumania); Jens Peter Jacobsen and Isak Dinesen (Denmark); Fröding (Sweden), Obstfelder (Norway); Willa Cather— the list is endless. Baltic, Slavic (except Russian) and litera- tures outside the occidental tradition have hardly been touched; they are bound to contain many surprising literary nuggets.

Elements of space, time, quality and intensity provide dif- ferences of degree between world literature and comparative literature. But there are more fundamental distinctions. In the first place, the American concept of comparative litera- ture embraces inquiries into the relationship between litera- ture and other orbits; world literature does not. In the second place, even the more restricted, "French" definition of com- parative literature (where the material to be studied is en- tirely literary, as it is in world literature) specifies a method; world literature does not. Comparative literature requires that a work, author, trend or theme be actually compared with a work, author, trend or theme of another country or sphere; but a collection of essays on, let us say, Turgenev, Hawthorne, Thackeray and Maupassant, under one cover, might very well be called *Figures of World Literature* with- out containing any or perhaps only incidental comparisons. Webster defines "comparative" as "studied systematically by comparison of phenomena . . . as, *comparative* literature."

Many courses devoted to the analysis of literary master- pieces from various countries, mostly read in translation, are now being offered in American colleges, and many antholo- gies designed for such courses have been published. These courses and textbooks should be, and usually are designated by the term "world literature" rather than "comparative literature," since the works read are by and large studied as individual masterpieces, not (at least fairly) systematically compared. It would be up to the instructor or editor to make such a course or book truly comparative, provided the choice of texts lends itself to comparative treatment.

A comparative literature study does not have to be comparative on every page nor even in every chapter, but the overall intent, emphasis and execution must be comparative.[12] The assaying of intent, emphasis and execution requires both objective and subjective judgment. No rigid rules can and should, therefore, be set down beyond these criteria.[13]

The term "general literature" has been used for courses and publications concerned with foreign literature in English translation, or, more loosely yet, for offerings that do not fit into departmental pigeonholes and appear to be of interest to students outside one national literature. Sometimes it refers to literary trends, problems and theories of "general" interest, or to aesthetics. Collections of texts and of critical studies or comments dealing with several literatures have been assigned to this category (e.g., many anthologies and such historical and critical works as Laird [ed.], *The World through Literature,* Shipley [ed.], *Dictionary of World Literature* and *Encyclopedia of Literature.* See Bibliography). It must be remembered that, like the term "world literature," general literature fails to prescribe a comparative method of approach. While "general literature" courses and publications may afford an excellent basis for comparative studies, they are not necessarily comparative in themselves.

The very haziness of the term "general literature" seems to have worked to its advantage in this country. A much more precise definition of "general literature" by the French scholar Paul Van Tieghem (Sorbonne), though not widely accepted beyond France, deserves nevertheless our attention.[14] To him, national literature, comparative literature and general literature represent three consecutive levels. National

literature treats questions confined to one national literature; comparative literature normally deals with problems
involving two different literatures; general literature is devoted to developments in a larger number of countries making up organic units, such as Western Europe, Eastern Europe, Europe, North America, Europe and North America,
Spain and South America, the Orient, etc. Expressed visu-
ally, national literature would be the study of literature within
walls, comparative literature across walls, and general literature above walls.[15] In a comparative-literature study, national
literatures would remain primary factors, serving as anchors
of investigation; in a general-literature study, national literatures would simply provide examples for international trends.
According to van Tieghem, a study of the place of Rousseau's
Nouvelle Héloïse in literature would be part of national literature; a paper on the influence of Richardson on Rousseau's *Nouvelle Héloïse* would belong to comparative literature; a survey of the European sentimental novel would be
general literature. Van Tieghem himself has written a number of works illustrating his ideas of general literature: *Latin
Literature of the Renaissance, Literary History of Europe
and America since the Renaissance, Pre-romanticism, European Romanticism*, and the *Discovery of Shakespeare on the
Continent*. Other syntheses of this kind include Curtius' *European Literature and the Latin Middle Ages*, Farinelli's *Romanticism in the Latin World*, Friederich's *Outline of Comparative Literature*, and Hazard's masterful twin works, *The
European Mind, 1680–1715* and *European Thought in the
XVIIIth century*.

Van Tieghem's definitions raise at least one question. Is
it not arbitrary and mechanical to relegate the term comparative literature, as he has done, to comparative investigations limited to two countries, while studies involving more

than two countries are reserved for general literature? Why should a comparison between Richardson and Rousseau be classified as comparative literature, whereas a comparison between Richardson, Rousseau and Goethe (as undertaken years ago by Erich Schmidt) would be assigned to general literature? Is not the term "comparative literature" sufficient to cover syntheses encompassing any number of countries (as it does in Friederich's *Outline of Comparative Literature*)?

In setting up his distinctive categories, Van Tieghem was probably thinking less of logically coherent units than of a necessary division of labor. The number of creative, historical and critical works to be absorbed by a scholar before he can hope to portray adequately even a limited period or aspect of *one* literature has become so enormous that we cannot expect the same scholar to take on one or more additional literatures. In turn, for reasons of inclination, aptitude and longevity, scholars specializing in comparative literature will, Van Tieghem fears, probably be unable to assemble and integrate the researches of more than two national literatures. A third group of scholars is therefore needed to pull together the findings of national literature and comparative literature and merge them into general literature.

The dangers of such an arrangement, aside from its very hypothetical workability, given the cherished individualism of the scholarly profession, are readily apparent. Comparative-literature and general-literature scholars would have to be content with organizing the findings of others (in itself a Herculean task), an assignment bound to expose them to loss of contact with the literary text, and carrying the seeds of mechanization, superficialization and dehumanization of literature. Van Tieghem's own books certainly have not escaped this peril altogether. On the other hand, Hazard, in his two syntheses, has magnificently succeeded in presenting the spirit of an age (pre-enlightenment and rationalism) without depriving the bones of the flesh.

We are inclined to think that a rigid division of labors between national-literature, comparative-literature and general-literature scholars is neither feasible nor desirable.[16] National-literature scholars should realize and act on their obligation to widen their perspectives, and should be encouraged to undertake, now and then, excursions into other literatures or spheres related to literature. Comparative-literature scholars should return, from time to time, to the more circumscribed areas of a national literature to make sure that at least one foot is firmly planted on the ground. This is precisely what the best scholars in the comparative field, both here and abroad, have consistently done.

III

None of the terms discussed are completely clear-cut. Overlapping exists among all. The definitions of and distinctions between national literature and comparative literature are, however, sufficiently clear to be useful. While we subscribe to the more inclusive American concept of comparative literature, we urge that topics claimed to belong to this field be subjected to closer scrutiny, on the basis of stricter criteria, than heretofore. World literature, in the sense of literature of such outstanding merit or success as to have gained international attention, is a serviceable term, but must not be laxly used as a sort of alternative for comparative literature or general literature. It is to be hoped that the term general literature will be avoided, whenever possible. It means, at least at present, too many different things to too many people. In its place, we should use synonyms for the intended connotation: comparative literature, or world literature, or literature in translation, or western literature, or literary theory, or the structure of literature, or just literature, whichever the case may be.

SELECTIVE BIBLIOGRAPHY

Every effort has been made to compile the most useful, selective yet representative, annotated bibliography on the fundamentals of comparative literature so far available in English. Each item listed has been read and carefully analyzed for its contribution to the central questions discussed in the essay.

It is clear that the subjective factor in a selective bibliography cannot be gainsaid; it is hereby cheerfully acknowledged. To be persuasive a selective bibliography should also include a list of rejected items and a statement of the reasons for their exclusion. If, e.g., Fernand Baldensperger's "Littérature comparée: le mot et la chose" (*Revue de littérature comparée* I – 1921 – 5–29) is not listed, it is partly because of its remote date, partly because it is primarily historical, partly because it does not come sufficiently to grips with the essentials of definition and function of our discipline. For all too obvious reasons, it is not practicable to explain every rejection, but we can be expected to state our general criteria.

We have aimed at providing a *working* bibliography — that is to say, a manageable list of relevant items that would be within relatively comfortable reach of American teachers and scholars. Publications in English, French and German have therefore been given preference, a procedure all the more justified since most (though certainly not all) important contributions to comparative literature have been in these languages. Further preference has been given to *recent* publications, since neither the essay nor the bibliography are historically oriented. Hence the vast majority of items dates from the 1950's, a much smaller number from the late 1940's, and only a handful from an earlier period. Particular care has been taken to have various viewpoints represented.

Surveys of comparative literature studies and facilities here and abroad were included only if the contribution in question is particularly and intentionally illuminating with regard to definition and method. Section 2 (Studies on Basic Aspects of Comparative Literature) is clearly the most complete within the limits set above, for it was felt that a maximum of guidance was needed in this highly disconcerting yet fundamental area. In the other sections, we list only an indispensable minimum of works. Scholarship dealing exclusively with the vast fields of literature and the arts, literature and science, literature and politics, etc. could, for reasons of space, not be included; we refer the reader to the appropriate sections of Baldensperger-Friederich's *Bibliography* and its supplements in *Yearbooks* I, II, IV, VI, VII, and IX. Anthologies of World Literature have also been excluded, and the few entries on "world literature" have been admitted only because they happen to bear directly on the essence of comparative literature. In general, the items listed under the various categories must be viewed as representative samples that will easily lead to additional sources for those desiring a more complete documentation.

Within the individual sections or subsections, items have been listed in chronological order of appearance. This separates, to be sure, certain entries that seem closely related, but a grouping by "sub-problems" or schools of thought would have raised difficult questions of classification and carried the subjective character of the bibliography too far. The chronological arrangement within sections, besides being clear and unequivocal, has the further advantage of reflect-

ing the genetic and simultaneous aspects of the "great debate" and the shifts in the general evolution of opinion.

1 SURVEYS OF COMPARATIVE LITERATURE AS A DISCIPLINE

PETERSEN, JULIUS. "Nationale oder vergleichende Literaturgeschichte?" *Deutsche Vierteljahresschrift für Literaturwissenschaft und Geistesgeschichte,* VI (1928), 36–61. Still a basic,
well annotated investigation into the meaning, limitations and
potentialities of comparative literature in its relationship to national, general, world and universal literature. Conclusions: *1*]
Since the characteristics of a national literature can be brought
out only in comparison with other literatures, every history of
national literature must be comparative. A discipline that does
nothing but compare has, however, no *raison d'être. 2*] Comparative literature studies on themes, motives and problems belong
to literary morphology, criticism and aesthetics, hence to general
literature, but may indirectly be of use to national literature.
3] An international literary history of certain periods must limit
itself to culturally related nations (*Kulturgemeinschaften*). A
history of the universal development of world literature is not
feasible. *4*] Analogies in the evolution of certain national literatures—outside causal connections of cultural community—represent a worthwhile field of study, as yet largely uncultivated. It
requires the cooperation of several disciplines.

STRICH, FRITZ. "Weltliteratur und vergleichende Literaturgeschichte," in Emil Ermatinger (ed.). *Philosophie der Literaturwissenschaft.* Berlin, 1930, pp. 422–41. Fundamental, still
valid considerations on the meaning of world and comparative
literature, to which several paragraphs of our preceding essay
owe much. Short bibliography.

GUÉRARD, ALBERT. "What is World Literature?" in his
Preface to World Literature. New York, 1940, pp. 3–16. A clear,
(too?) simple and interestingly written introduction to the field
which distinguishes between world literature ("works enjoyed
in common, ideally by all mankind, practically by our own Western group of civilization"), comparative literature ("the study

of relations, in the literary field, between different national or linguistic groups") and general literature ("the study of problems common to all literatures").

Poggioli, Renato. "Comparative Literature," in Joseph Shipley (ed.). *Dictionary of World Literature.* New York, 1943, pp. 114–17. Concise but pithy semihistorical, semidescriptive survey of the field.

Warren, Austin, and Wellek, René. *Theory of Literature.* New York, 1948 (second edition, moderately revised, 1956; also available in Harvest paperback edition, 1956). Forceful chapter on "General, Comparative and National Literature" (pp. 38–45) raises crucial questions of definition without necessarily attempting to resolve them. Valuable notes and bibliography.

Van Tieghem, Paul. *La Littérature comparée.* Paris, 1951 (fourth edition, revised). History, theory, problems, methods and results of comparative and general literature. Has selective, useful bibliography of books (only a few articles) almost exclusively limited to publications written in French. First edition in 1931.

Guyard, M.-F. *La Littérature comparée.* Paris, 1951. Concise introduction to the field of comparative literature, organized along the lines of Van Tieghem. Brief but important preface by Jean-Marie Carré. Rudimentary bibliography.

Carré, Jean-Marie. "La Littérature comparée depuis un demi-siècle," *Annales du Centre Universitaire Méditerranéen,* iii (1951), 69–77. Although published in a remote location, important as authoritative statement of the tenets of the French school of comparative literature (see also preceding item, Guyard). Conceives comparative literature as distinct from literary comparison or general literature, is wary of influence studies, encourages work in history of literary voyages and history of literary interpretation of one country by another, and stresses "l'homme."

Porta, Antonio. *La Letteratura comparata nella storia e nella critica.* Milan, 1951. Eloquent and discriminating lectures on comparative literature and literary history, comparative literature and criticism, the literary unity of Europe, the teaching of comparative literature, and the present state of comparative literature studies. Tendency toward rhetoric and generalities. Some rather shocking mistakes in names and titles. Bibliography.

WEHRLI, MAX. *Allgemeine Literaturwissenschaft.* Bern, 1951. Highly competent survey of various critical and historical approaches to literature current since the 1930's. Emphasis on German literature, but important foreign publications are considered. Chapter on world and comparative literature. Index of topics and names. Copious footnotes.

VOISINE, JACQUES. "Les Etudes de Littérature Comparée," *Revue de L'Enseignement Supérieur,* no. 3 (1957), pp. 61–67. Convenient elementary summary of situation of comparative literature in general and French comparatism in particular.

LAIRD, CHARLTON. "Comparative Literature," in *Contemporary Literary Scholarship,* ed. Leary (1958), pp. 339–68. A somewhat loose-jointed and, in details, not wholly reliable but very serviceable introduction to the status quo in the field. Selective annotated bibliography.

BROWN, CALVIN S. "Comparative Literature," *The Georgia Review,* XIII (Summer 1959), 167–89. Sound, spirited and readable introduction to the field of Comparative Literature, the best available to date for the nonspecialist. No bibliography.

2 STUDIES ON BASIC ASPECTS OF THE DEFINITION AND FUNCTION OF COMPARATIVE LITERATURE

HANKISS, JEAN. "Littérature universelle?" *Helicon,* I (1938), 156–71. Analyzes the problem inherent in writing horizontal international literary history as compared to vertical national history, and indicates that the former is less organic than the latter.

WAIS, KURT. "Vergleichende Literaturbetrachtung," in *Forschungsprobleme der Vergleichenden Literaturgeschichte* (ed. Wais), I (1951), 7–11. Difficulty of facing both one's own and foreign literature "objectively." Qualitative differences among national literatures. Need for selectivity and aesthetic judgment in tracing portrait of European literature, for differentiation between reception and influence.

TEESING, H. P. H. "Die Bedeutung der vergleichenden Literaturgeschichte für die literarhistorische Periodisierung," in *Forschungsprobleme der Vergleichenden Literaturgeschichte* (ed. Wais), I (1951), 13–20. Stresses differences between corresponding periods (e.g., Romanticism) in various literatures. Cautiously postulates certain regular sequences in evolution of national literatures. Immanent evolution of national literatures is primary, foreign influences secondary.

AUERBACH, ERICH. "Philologie der Weltliteratur," in *Weltliteratur*. Festgabe für Fritz Strich. Bern, 1952, pp. 39–50. Beautifully written, balanced contribution stressing the necessity, in view of the impending standardization of world literature, for historical syntheses based on studies of the evolution of a concrete phenomenon in world literature (such as Curtius' topoi, specific lines of Dante as interpreted by successive generations, etc.). Rejects syntheses resting on too general, too abstract preformed terms, or on presumed literary periods, or on cooperative efforts.

HÖLLERER, WALTER. "Methoden und Probleme vergleichender Literaturwissenschaft," *Germanisch-Romanische Monatsschrift*, Neue Folge, II (1952), 116–31. Dwells on problems facing (especially German) comparatists: demarcation of the field, terminology, methods, approaches (biographical, epochal, typological, textual, stylistic, formal, structural, conceptual, imagistic). Numerous examples.

HÖLLERER, WALTER. "Die vergleichende Literaturwissenschaft in Deutschland nach dem Kriege," *Rivista di letterature moderne*, III (1952), 285–99. Excellent survey of postwar tendencies in German comparative-literature research. Proposes increased emphasis on comparative interpretations of central portions of poetic works (e.g., Balzac-Büchner, Baudelaire-Nietzsche, Döblin-Sartre) and of symbols and images (tears, laughter, the actor, the city, etc.).

PEYRE, HENRI. "A Glance at Comparative Literature in America," *Yearbook of Comparative and General Literature*, I

(1952), 1–8. Phosphorescent survey of the opportunities and pitfalls of comparative literature in this country. Good general bibliography (pp. 2–3).

GILLIES, ALEXANDER. "Some Thoughts on Comparative Literature," *Yearbook of Comparative and General Literature,* I (1952), 15–25. Sensible observations by a British scholar on the problems of comparative-literature research, followed by three overstated but rousing examples of the effect of literature on history (Shakespeare's reception in Germany, Madame de Staël's vision of Germany, Herder as the father of the Slav Renaissance).

LEVIN, HARRY. "La littérature comparée: point de vue d'outre-Atlantique," *Revue de littérature comparée,* XXVII (1953), 17–26. Stresses desirability of less source, influence and success, and of more analogy, motif, stylistics, genre, movement and tradition studies in comparative literature. Underlines importance of research dealing with the classical tradition, Baroque and Realism.

HÖLLERER, WALTER. "La littérature comparée en Allemagne depuis la guerre," *Revue de littérature comparée,* XXVII (1953), 27–42. While tolerant of various approaches, warns against too limited topics (emitter-receptor-transmitter), cause-and-effect studies, as well as too vast and abstract topics (such as the establishment of general aesthetic "laws" by way of comparative literature or *Geistesgeschichte*). Favors, somewhere between national literature and world literature, cultivation of *European* literary history within certain geographical units and certain periods, using, among other methods, that of confrontation of central portions of comparable works (see above).

RODDIER, HENRI. "La littérature comparée et l'histoire des idées," *Revue de littérature comparée,* XXVII (1953), 43–49. Pleads for transfer to comparative literature of methods used by A. O. Lovejoy to arrive at syntheses in the history of ideas. Argues in favor of cooperative endeavors concerned with semantic clarification and interpretation of central texts. States that the scientifically acceptable coherence of comparative literature as a discipline must be purchased at the price of a self-imposed temporal and geographic limitation to natural groupings of related national cultures (à la Toynbee). This entails increased attention to smaller countries within such units (Holland, Switzerland).

[MUNTEANO, BASIL.] "Conclusion provisoire," in "Orientations en littérature comparée," *Revue de littérature comparée,* XXVII (1953), 50–58. For modest, noble and gently ironic fair-mindedness on the highly controversial question of the orientation of comparative literature, this is a model statement.

WELLEK, RENÉ. "The Concept of Comparative Literature," *Yearbook of Comparative and General Literature,* II (1953), 1–5. Keen refutation of Carré's and Guyard's concepts.

MALONE, DAVID H. "The 'Comparative' in Comparative Literature," *Yearbook of Comparative and General Literature,* II (1954), 13–20. Continued rebuttal of Carré and Guyard. Long overdue rescue of "pure" comparisons in comparative literature.

FRIEDERICH, WERNER P. "Our Common Purpose," *Yearbook of Comparative and General Literature,* IV (1955), 55–59. Plea for tolerance among practicioners of comparative literature.

STRUVE, GLEB. "Comparative Literature in the Soviet Union, Today and Yesterday," *Yearbook of Comparative and General Literature,* IV (1955), 1–20; VI (1957), 7–10; IX (1959), 13–18. Aside from a fascinating account of the repercussions of politics on comparative scholarship, this report calls attention to highly-pertinent, little-known Russian theories (Alexander Veselovsky, Plekhanov, Zhirmunsky) on influences, translations and cultural analogies (stadialism).

RODDIER, HENRI. "Littérature comparée et histoire des idées," in *Littérature générale et histoire des idées.* Actes du premier congrès national de littérature comparée. Paris, 1957, pp. 16–19. Plea for the preparation of a dictionary of ideological terms indispensable for the understanding of the evolution of literature, beginning with a specific period and a limited area. Very brief review of conflicting tendencies in present-day comparative-literature research. See Bémol's comment below (Munteano).

MUNTEANO, BASIL. "Littérature générale et histoire des idées," in *Littérature générale et histoire des idées.* Actes du premier congrès national de littérature comparée. Paris, 1957, pp. 20–30. In this lively, searching and challenging paper, a curious mixture of old and new, Munteano proposes complementary synthesis of horizontal "general literature" and vertical "history of ideas." Restricts literary history and comparative literature to *actual, conscious* contacts. Follows essentially Van Tieghem in assigning to "General Literature" assemblage of vaster, mutually relevant data and currents. General literature would also cover relationship between literature and other arts. Sees philosophy of history as ultimate synthesis. In the ensuing discussion, Bémol demands that artistic nature of literature be recognized along with its ideological importance.

ETIEMBLE, RENÉ. "Littérature comparée, ou comparaison n'est pas raison," in *Savoir et Goût,* vol. III of *Hygiène des Lettres.* Paris, 1958, pp. 154–73. Argues for emphasis on *literature* (structure, style, intrinsic values) as well as *comparison* (including pure parallelisms between Oriental and Western literatures which may enable us to arrive at literary invariables) without abandoning historical studies. Criticizes conservatism, provincialism and even nationalism in French concepts of comparative literature; calls for more intensive study of Oriental, Slavic, Semitic, Finno-Ugrian etc. literatures. Seems unaware of Malone's article (see above) and makes no effort to differentiate between comparative literature, general literature and world literature.

GILLET, J. "Cosmopolitisme et littérature comparée," in *Les Flandres dans les mouvements romantique et symboliste.* Actes du second congrès national de littérature comparée. Paris, 1958, pp. 45–51. In rejecting Höllerer's "vague assimilation between Comparative Literature and Cosmopolitanism," Gillet objects to comparative study of "some works detached from their national context" as a sort of "exercise in virtuosity." He argues that the comparatist must start from historically and geographically restricted, concrete cases within a national framework, but need not necessarily stop there.

VAN DER LEE, A. "Zur Komparatistik im niederländischen Sprachraum," in *Forschungsprobleme der Vergleichenden Litera-*

turgeschichte (ed. Ernst and Wais), Tübingen, II (1958), pp. 173–77. Sketch of the status quo in the Dutch-Flemish speaking areas with emphasis on questions of definition and function (particularly Baur's quadripartition of comparative literature into crenology, doxology, genology and thematology, the perfecting of which leads to a historical-aesthetic synthesis).

FRIEDERICH, WERNER PAUL. "Zur Vergleichenden Literaturgeschichte in den Vereinigten Staaten," in *Forschungsprobleme der Vergleichenden Literaturgeschichte* (ed. Ernst and Wais), Tübingen, II (1958), pp. 179–91. Outlines the positions of the three main components of comparative literature in the United States (world literature and great books courses, the "French school" and the "American school"), and offers to reconcile them.

GUÉRARD, ALBERT. "Comparative Literature?" *Yearbook of Comparative and General Literature*, VII (1958), 1–6. In this more vivacious than circumspect paper, Professor Guérard argues that comparative literature is a makeshift term needed only as long as "the nationalistic heresy has not been extirpated" and should soon be in a position to commit a triumphant suicide.

BLOCK, HASKELL M. "The concept of influence in Comparative Literature," *Yearbook of Comparative and General Literature*, VII (1958), 30–37. Balanced and persuasive plea for the rehabilitation of the term "influence" in comparative literature as "an intrinsic part of literary experience."

HANKISS, JANOS. "Théorie de la littérature et littérature comparée," in *Comparative Literature*. Proceedings of the Second Congress of the International Comparative Literature Association, Chapel Hill. Vol. I, 1959, pp. 98–112. Affirms essential unity of national literary history, comparative literature and the theory of literature.

RODDIER, HENRI. "De l'emploi de la méthode génétique en littérature comparée," in *Comparative Literature*. Proceedings of the Second Congress. I, 113–24. A spirited French reaction to the dangers of "abstract . . . simplistic . . . intransigeant . . . sterilizing . . . formalism" inherent in too sweeping an application of the New Criticism to comparative literature. Likens the

New Criticism to a study of the qualities of the violin without worrying about the violinist. Proposes an extension of the genetic method so fruitful in biographies to literary genres, themes, types, myths etc., culminating in the juxtaposition of vertical histories of particular literatures resting on systematic researches about the circumstances that have contributed to the uniqueness of this literature, that have limited its possibilities of evolution, with special stress on the language. Such a cooperative endeavor would elucidate the national variations of labels applied to European literature such as *the* Renaissance, *the* Reformation, *the* classicism, etc., but would also show characteristics common to several national literatures.

MUNTEANO, BASIL. "Situation de la littérature comparée. Sa portée humaine et sa légitimité," in *Comparative Literature*. Proceedings of the Second Congress. I, 124–42. Far-reaching diagnosis of the "crisis" in comparative literature. Rejects the "myth" of the literary work as an absolute self-contained unit and the stringent separation between "extrinsic" and "intrinsic" (Wellek), the task of interpretation being precisely the reconstruction of the transmutation from extrinsic *to* intrinsic. Defends intelligent use of the search for sources, influences and affinities. Comparison is by necessity dialectic. Considers comparative literature as practical, convenient, necessary subdivision of general science of comparison: dialectic comparatism.

WELLEK, RENÉ. "The Crisis of Comparative Literature," in *Comparative Literature*. Proceedings of the Second Congress. I, 149–59. Vigorous, even more outspoken and less conciliatory restatement of the critiques leveled previously by Wellek against prevailing comparative-literature research, notably against "an artificial demarcation of subject matter and methodology, a mechanistic concept of sources and influences, (and) a motivation by cultural nationalism, however generous."

LA DRIÈRE, J. CRAIG. "The Comparative Method in the Study of Prosody," in *Comparative Literature*. Proceedings of the Second Congress. I, 160–75. Elucidates the comparative method in literary studies from his experiences with the comparative method in the study of prosody. Argues for necessity of variety in comparative studies, that theory, history and criticism are distinct, though not unrelated, and that, in line with Baldensperger, Hankiss and Van Tieghem, comparative literature be viewed as an intermediate step between national and general literature. Advocates collaborative projects in solving comparative questions beyond the reach of any individual scholars.

GUILLÉN, CLAUDIO. "The Aesthetics of Influence Studies in Comparative Literature," in *Comparative Literature.* Proceedings of the Second Congress. I, 175–92. Aesthetic-genetic theory and classification of influence studies, distinguishing between genuinely genetic "sources vécues," conventions and techniques, and parallelisms. Representative bibliography.

PEYRE, HENRI. "Seventy-five Years of Comparative Literature. A backward and a forward glance," *Yearbook of Comparative and General Literature,* VIII (1959), 18–26. Urges more attention to human values.

WILL, FREDERIC. "Comparative Literature and the Challenge of Modern Criticism," *Yearbook of Comparative and General Literature,* IX (1960), 29–31. Plea that the comparatist recognize the inaccessibility of the literary work as a private entity, but exploit its public features.

REMAK, HENRY H. H. "Comparative Literature at the crossroads: diagnosis, therapy, and prognosis," *Yearbook of Comparative and General Literature,* IX (1960), 1–28. Survey and evaluation of the great debate on the essence, function and purpose of Comparative Literature during the last decade. Bibliography.

3 COMPREHENSIVE INTERNATIONAL HISTORIES OF LITERATURE AND CRITICISM

Among the many studies of literary history and criticism from the international angle, we have selected only two kinds: histories of literature and criticism spanning vast geographic areas through several centuries, and works furnishing a picture of the totality of the foreign literary relations of a particular country.

VAN TIEGHEM, PAUL. *Histoire littéraire de l'Europe et de l'Amérique de la Renaissance à nos jours.* Paris, 1946 (first printed in 1941). An expanded and revised version of his *Précis de l'Histoire Littéraire de l'Europe depuis la Renaissance,* Paris, 1925, translated into English as *Outline of the Literary History of Europe since the Renaissance,* New York, 1930. In contrast to many so-called comparative histories of literature which are juxtapositions of separate national histories under one cover, this is a genuinely international history organized not by countries but by periods and genres. The mass of names and titles and the impossibility of delving into any one author make this (like the Friederich-Malone) a valuable reference work rather than a readable, connected history.

FRIEDERICH, WERNER P., and MALONE, DAVID H. *Outline of Comparative Literature from Dante to O'Neill.* Chapel Hill, 1954. A supranational, truly comparative history of literature, stressing influences, parallels and contrasts. Index of names and topics, but no bibliography.

WELLEK, RENÉ. *A History of Modern Criticism, 1750–1950.* New Haven, 1955. *Volume* I: The Later Eighteenth Century. *Volume* II: The Romantic Age. *Volume* III (not yet published): The Later Nineteenth Century. *Volume* IV (not yet published): The Twentieth Century. Indispensable. Primary stress on literary theory, secondary stress on literary taste. First two volumes cover England, France, Germany and Italy. Last two will also include Russia, Spain, and the United States. Quotations in English, with original texts in notes. Selective and descriptive bibliography, notes, chronological tables, index of names, topics and terms in each volume.

WIMSATT, WILLIAM K., and BROOKS, CLEANTH. *Literary Criticism. A short History.* New York, 1957. A biased, brilliant, brash, uneven and exceedingly stimulating history of criticism from Socrates to Jung. Many references. Index.

MOMIGLIANO, ATTILIO (ed.). *Letterature comparate.* Milan, 1948. Collection of surveys by various scholars covering the relations between Italian literature and classical (Sorbelli), French (Pellegrini), Spanish (A. Croce), English (Praz), German and Scandinavian (Santoli), dialect (Sansone) and troubadour (Viscardi) literature. Each survey followed by extensive bibliography.

KOHLSCHMIDT, WERNER, and MOHR, WOLFGANG (eds.). *Reallexikon der deutschen Literaturgeschichte.* Berlin, 1955——(2nd ed.). Contains succinct, comprehensive, amply annotated accounts of foreign influences (American, English, Finnish, etc.) on German literature.

STAMMLER, WOLFGANG (ed.). *Deutsche Philologie im Aufriss.* Berlin, 1957 (2nd ed., vol. III). Provides, in separate studies, systematic coverage of foreign influences on German literature (Nordic, Finnish, English, American, Dutch, French, Italian, Spanish, Hungarian, Oriental, Indian, East Asian, Russian, Czech, Yugoslav). Bibliographies.

Although I have not included in this section of my essay bibliographies of national literatures that contain chapters on their foreign relations, the very inadequate attention that Spanish literature has received from non-Hispanists prompts me to mention the substantial comparative section in José Simón Diaz, *Bibliografía de la literatura hispánica* (Madrid, 1950), I, 469–517. I owe this reference to the kindness of Professor G. N. G. Orsini.

4 COMPARATIVE CHRONOLOGICAL TABLES

VAN TIEGHEM, PAUL (ed.). *Répertoire chronologique des littératures modernes.* Paris, 1935. Lists by years (1455 to 1900), subdivided by languages, important works and related facts of all European (except Turkish) and American literatures. Alphabetical index of authors and works.

SPEMANN, ADOLF. *Vergleichende Zeittafel der Weltliteratur.* Stuttgart, 1951. Less elaborate parallel to van Tieghem's *Répertoire,* but covers, in addition, the years 1150 to 1455 (briefly) and 1900 to 1939 (very extensively). Helpful alphabetical index of all authors mentioned, with titles and dates of their works.

BRETT-JAMES, ANTONY. *The Triple Stream. Four centuries of English, French and German literature. 1531–1930.*

Cambridge, England, 1953; Philadelphia, 1954. Juxtaposed tabulation, by years, of literary names (birth and death dates) and titles from English, French and German literature, including Belgium, Austria and Switzerland. Some nonliterary dates pertinent to literature are listed. Practically no references to translations and intermediaries. Some choices of dates dubious. Index of all authors. (See also Bompiani entry under 7)

5 BIBLIOGRAPHIES OF COMPARATIVE LITERATURE

BALDENSPERGER, FERNAND, and FRIEDERICH, WERNER P. *Bibliography of Comparative Literature.* Chapel Hill, 1950. Indispensable, (too?) comprehensive reference work. Ingenious organization, though not perspicuous at first glance. Stresses emitter. No descriptive or evaluative comments. Lists very few reviews. Addition of index would augment usefulness of work considerably. Supplements, published annually since 1952 in *Yearbook of Comparative and General Literature,* include since 1954 some descriptive remarks.

Bibliographie générale de littérature comparée (published with the aid of UNESCO). Paris, vol. I (1949–50), II (1951–52), III (1953–54), IV (1955–56), and V (1957–58) published so far. Quarterly bibliographies of the *Revue de littérature comparée* collected in annual volumes. Sections on bibliography, theory, style, literary genres, themes and types, general relations, intermediaries, currents, movements and epochs, "ambiances," influences (the latter arranged by emitting nations). Nondescriptive, noncritical. Some reviews listed. Index.

ROSENBERG, RALPH P. "Bibliographies," *Comparative Literature,* II (1950), 189–90. Check-list of bibliographies pertaining, in whole or in part, to Comparative Literature, which appear periodically in American publications.

FISHER, JOHN H. "Serial Bibliographies in the Modern Languages and Literatures," *PMLA,* LXVI (1951), 138–56. Invaluable noncritical survey, although somewhat dated. Has a special section on "Bibliographies of Comparative Literature" (150–51), but some comparative-literature bibliographies are listed under other headings in the survey. Subject index and index of bibliographers. The annual bibliographies and "Research in Progress" (the latter published intermittently) in *PMLA* contain a special section on comparative literature and references to comparative-literature items under different headings.

Comparatistische Bibliografie (Comparative Bibliography). Edited by the Instituut voor Vergelijkend Literatuuronderzok (Institute for Comparative Literature). University of Utrecht, 1955——. Bibliographical cards (about four hundred per year), comprising all significant Dutch, Flemish and Afrikaans publications, books as well as articles, on comparative literature or important for comparative literature. Each card contains a catchword in Dutch, German and French or English (depending upon the linguistic preference of the subscriber) referring to the contents of the publication.

Regesten (Register of the acquisitions of the Institute for Comparative Literature). University of Utrecht, 1956——. Contains many brief reviews in Dutch, much more descriptive than critical, of recent literary studies in various languages acquired by the Institute. A good many items, though not always the majority, are comparative. Four issues per year.

6 PERIODICALS

Only those periodicals exclusively devoted to Comparative Literature and currently published are covered.

Revue de littérature comparée, 1921——. Scholarly articles and reviews with marked preference for problems of literary history. Extensive bibliographies. News and notes. Quarterly.

Comparative Literature, 1949——. Scholarly articles and reviews, inclined toward problems of literary criticism. Lists of "Books received." Brief announcements. Quarterly.

Yearbook of Comparative and General Literature, 1952——. Articles on teaching and organizational aspects of comparative literature. Biographical sketches of great comparatists. Broad questions of definition. Comparative literature activities here and abroad. Reviews of professional works (for teaching purposes), of translations and editions. Supplements to Friederich-Baldensperger's *Bibliography of Comparative Literature.*

7 OTHER USEFUL REFERENCE WORKS

SHIPLEY, JOSEPH T. (ed.). *Dictionary of World Literature.* New York, 1943 (2nd revised ed., New York, 1953). Encyclopedia of literary terms, forms, techniques, methods, problems, schools, and criticism (only exceptionally authors and critics). Signed contributions of considerable originality. Both editions should be consulted.

SHIPLEY, JOSEPH T. (ed.). *Encyclopedia of Literature.* New York, 1946 (two vols.). Condensed surveys of the literary history of the nations of the world, arranged alphabetically according to names of nations. Each survey followed by a bibliography of pertinent literary histories. Biographical notices about most important writers at the end of the second volume.

SMITH, HORATIO (ed.). *Columbia Dictionary of Modern European Literature.* New York, 1947. Signed, informative and refreshingly written articles on authors, national literatures (thirty-one), critics and movements (uneven coverage) from about 1870 to date of publication. Great Britain and Ireland are excluded. English translations, and English (including American) criticism of continental literature (in the concise bibliography following each article) given particular attention.

EPPELSHEIMER, HANNS W. *Handbuch der Weltliteratur.* Frankfurt, 1947–50 (2nd ed.). Volume I: to the end of the eighteenth century; Volume II: nineteenth and twentieth centuries. Covers oriental, classical, medieval and modern literature. Organized by great epochs subdivided by countries, genres or movements. Brief descriptive introduction to epochs, genres, works, writers followed by bibliography accompanied by numerous short but helpful descriptive and/or critical remarks. Concise biography for main authors. Each volume has index of names, terms and anonymous works. Volume II contains general bibliographies pertaining to literary scholarship, national literatures and genres, forms, themes and problems of literature; also errata and addenda. Handy reference, despite shortcomings.

Dizionario letterario Bompiani. Milan, 1947–50. Comprehensive, rich, and magnificently illustrated reference work on world literature in nine volumes, arranged alphabetically within its main sections (artistic movements, works, persons appearing in works, and index). Comparative chronological tables from Ancient Greece to 1914 in vol. IX (1950).

Index Translationum. International Bibliography of Translations. Published by UNESCO. Paris, since 1949. Appears annually, covering the literature of the preceding year. Contains also alphabetical list of authors, and (but only until vol. VI, 1954, for 1953) of translators and publishers by country. From volume IV (1952, for 1951) on, supplements for previous years. Last volume published: 1960, for 1958.

LEACH, MARIA (ed.). *Dictionary of Folklore, Mythology and Legend.* New York, 1949–50. Volume I (A-I), Volume II (J-Z). Standard reference work. In addition to articles on some 8,000 folklore terms, contains surveys of American, Basque, French, German, etc. folklore, and biographies of important folklorists.

LAIRD, CHARLTON (ed.). *The World Through Literature.* New York, 1951. Generally competent, well-written surveys of Primitive (Radin), Far Eastern (Chinese by Shao Chang Lee, Japanese by Younghill Kang and John Morrison), Indian (Buck), Near Eastern (Koran by Calverley, Arabic by Jurji), Hebrew (Silberschlag), Greek and Latin (Benham), Italian (Prezzolini), French (Huse), Spanish and Portuguese (Schevill), German (Morgan), Scandinavian (Benson), Slavic (almost exclusively Russian, by Posin) and Latin American (Nichols) literatures. Bibliography, often with descriptive and critical comments, is appended to each essay. Index of names and titles.

PEI, MARIO A., and GAYNOR, FRANK (eds.). *Liberal Arts Dictionary.* New York, 1952. Definition of artistic, literary and philosophical terms, with corresponding French, German and Spanish terms. Comprehensive index of the foreign language words.

STEINBERG, S. H. (ed.). Cassell's *Encyclopedia of World Literature.* New York, 1954. First published as Cassell's *Ency-*

clopedia of Literature, London, 1953. Two volumes. Volume I, part 1: histories of the literatures of the world from oral traditions to the present. Articles on literary forms, literary schools, contemporary trends, special subjects, and particular aspects of literature throughout all times and countries. Volume I, part 2: biographies of writers from earliest times to 1914 (A-H). Volume II, part 2: same, (I-Z). Volume II, part 3: biographies of contemporary writers, 1914 to present (A-Z). Articles and biographies written in a lively individualistic style. Entries followed by selective bibliographies.

ROBLES, F. C. SAINZ. *Ensayo de un Diccionario de la literatura.* Madrid, 1953–56 (2nd ed.). Covers general aspects and terms (volume 1, 1954), Spanish and Spanish-American authors (volume 2, 1953) and foreign authors (volume 3, 1956). Descriptive and (moderately) critical. Gives primary and secondary sources.

Dictionnaire des Oeuvres de tous les temps et de tous les pays (eds. Laffont and Bompiani), in five volumes, 2nd edition, Paris, 1955. Contains an analysis of and commentary on more than twenty thousand works, with the stress on world literature. Profusely illustrated. Last volume contains indices of authors and illustrations, and synoptic chronological tables.

Dictionnaire biographique des auteurs de tous les temps et de tous les pays (eds. Laffont and Bompiani), in two volumes, Paris, 1957–58. Contains surprisingly extensive, interesting appreciations of (particularly literary) authors of all times and countries, the more ambitious ones signed by reputable scholars. Many illustrations, references to sources, and significant quotations on these authors.

2

On Defining Terms

Edward D. Seeber

M OST TERMS commonly encountered in traditional literary history and criticism—for example the French *bal-
lade* or "dramatic irony"—are adequately defined in various
reference works,[1] and present no special problems of interpretation. At the same time there are many others, often de-
ceptively simple, that are not susceptible of such facile definition, and it is to this more complicated order that attention is
here directed by means of a few examples, practical suggestions, and illustrative references.

In specific contexts, terms may demand close study for different reasons; indeed, they sometimes must be considered
simultaneously in more than one of the following categories:

 1] *Terms that may undergo a change of meaning in different eras.* The adjective "Gothic" had, in the seventeenth century, a pejorative sense suggesting the phrase "of
the time of the Goths"; it commonly meant "archaic," "un-
couth," "barbarous," "ugly," even "formidable" (as in "a
Gothic alp"). It was applied with similar connotation to
Gothic architecture. These meanings carry over, in both
France and England, well into the eighteenth century: Dide-

EDWARD D. SEEBER is a Professor of French at Indiana University and a
corresponding member of the Académie des Sciences, Lettres et Beaux-
Arts of Marseille. His numerous publications in the area of eighteenth-
century French and comparative literature include a study of French anti-
slavery opinion, annotated translations of two early French travelers to
the United States, and an edition of rare Huguenot manuscripts. With
Professor Remak he edited the works of Charles-Michel Campion.

rot in 1750 spoke of the "Gothic committee" that condemned the *Encyclopédie,* and Shenstone, alluding to the
intrusion of art into nature, used the phrase "otherwise night,
gothicism, confusion, and absolute chaos are come again." [2]
But in the same century the term also becomes tempered; it
means "that which is not practiced by fashionable people"
or "old-fashioned," and is eventually associated with melancholy and nostalgia. This change reflects the growing interest
in olden times and the so-called Gothic Revival, when many
popular authors with marked antiquarian interests (Blair,
the Wartons, Young, Mather Lewis, Ann Radcliffe, etc.)
stirred public appreciation of a hitherto despised architec-
tural style, and transformed Gothicism into a much cultivated
aspect of Romantic literature.

Similarly "nature" meant quite different things to Rabelais, Pascal, Rousseau, and Balzac, just as the bald precept
"follow nature" was persistently followed, but variously con-
strued, by successive generations of English poets.

2] *Terms that may mean different things within the
same era.* In his *Essay on Criticism* Alexander Pope
equated nature with common sense, reason, the universal,
and the rules of classical composition:

> *Learn hence for ancient rules a just esteem;*
> *To copy Nature, is to copy them.*
>
> . . . .
>
> *These rules of old discover'd, not devis'd,*
> *Are Nature still, but Nature methodis'd.*

Within the same era, needless to say, "follow nature" and
terms like "reason" and "imitation" were interpreted differently by the Classicists and the Romanticists. Another example is the term "natural religion" which had two disparate
meanings in the eighteenth century: it was applied to similar-

ities with Christian practices discovered by early explorers and travelers among primitive peoples, and at the same time it was, for freethinkers, a synonym of deism or religion according to nature.

3] *Terms that may have different meanings in different countries.* Such terms cannot be discussed here in detail. Suffice it to recall the differences between the Italian and English sonnet form or the English and French ballad, and the sense of Romanticism in, say, France and Germany.

4] *Terms that may mean different things to the same writer using them.* Some terms used repeatedly by an author must be studied carefully to detect variations in meaning or even contradictions in usage. Striking examples are "virtue" and "natural goodness," so common in the writings of Rousseau.

The use of "Romanticism" suggests that a certain number of everyday terms are by nature so complex as to defy specific and adequate definition—although this has been attempted repeatedly. Obviously a movement marked by sharp differences in method, subject matter, and personalities, in which one encounters, as in English Romanticism, such varied components as external nature, the Lyric Revival, medievalism, subjectivity, humanitarianism, melancholy, orientalism—to name only a few—precludes a simple definition.

Two other good examples are "Classicism" and "Baroque." The full sense of Classicism depends, among other things, on a knowledge of the meaning attached to "reason," which is in turn associated with the concept of "common sense," "the universal," and "nature." At this point one is confronted with terms requiring further definition as well as the understanding of several basic assumptions which appealed to the neoclassic mind. One must account for other terms, for example "imitation" and "creation" as opposed to "invention," and even the derivative term "original genius" —that which is above all rules and a Romantic tendency. Terms, then, must often be studied both in their context of a given moment, and also in their changing and altered meanings; and it must be remembered not only that Classicists and Romanticists sometimes used a given term in different ways, but also that both Classical and Romantic traits often coexisted in the same writer, as they did in Balzac.[3]

"Baroque," another term widely discussed in recent times, began as a relatively simple concept and then expanded to a considerable degree; and its close study is now yielding a broader understanding of its meaning with respect to eras, authors, and literary productions. Comprehension of difficult terms may sometimes be hastened by an examination of other, related terms: Havens found, for example, that Rousseau's "natural goodness" is better understood in reference to its opposite, "natural perversity."

In attempting an historical approach, we may in some cases turn profitably to the older language dictionaries for knowledge of literary terms at a given period, and their subsequent alterations of meaning. For example, *pittoresque* is not found in the 1734 edition of the *Dictionnaire de Trévoux,* though it appears in the 1771 edition as a term applied to painting—something invented by, or imagined by, the artist, relating to the disposition or attitude of his figures, their unusual or original expressions, etc. The same sources give curious and confused definitions of the novel, reflecting the reputation of this genre before Rousseau's day. According to the 1734 edition, novels are "livres fabuleux" containing stories or adventures of love and chivalry, invented to divert and amuse. "Novels are prose-poems" (Fontenelle); "novels are lies in the guise of probability, and ingenious fictions written to occupy the time of decent lazy folk . . . [the reading of which] inspires indolence and love" (Huet). Bourdaloue's sermon on worldly pastimes is cited for its fine passage condemning novel-reading. The expanded article of 1771 declares that "novels ruin the taste of young people who come to prefer their extravagant, wondrous elements to the natural simplicity of truth."

But caution is needed in using such works. The *Dictionnaire de Trévoux* was a Jesuit publication and, in many respects, merely a continuation of earlier dictionaries, notably that of Furetière; therefore one cannot assume that the articles are uniformly unbiased or even up-to-date. Similarly the eighteenth-century dictionaries which bore the name of Pierre Richelet, compiler of the *Dictionnaire français* of 1680, are unreliable sources for usage at that time. And the dictionary of the French Academy is notoriously slow in admitting new words: Balzac's coinage *humanitarisme*, of 1838, did not appear until 1931. One must remember that many concepts and abstractions have not, in the past, become matters of lexicographical record until long after they were well known or even commonplace. Gas, for example, was certainly known before the term was invented by Helmont in the seventeenth century, and humanitarianism was a familiar sentiment before the word itself came into being in the mid-nineteenth. Similarly, a feeling for the picturesque did not wait upon the dictionaries to give it approbation and currency, and its history is best studied elsewhere.[4]

It follows that one must cultivate not only the practice of scanning original texts, but also the ability to recognize a concept that may not be labeled by a familiar term. Thus a prose passage may reveal characteristics of the "prose-poem," as in the case of Rousseau's *La Nouvelle Héloïse* (Part VI, Letter 7), where textual alterations were deliberately made to affect the rhythm, resulting in ornaments like the Alexandrine "Malheureux qui se livre à ton calme trompeur." One must be able to distinguish the Gothic in lines like these, from the *Faerie Queene:*

> *Low in a hollow cave,*
> *Far underneath a craggy cliff ypight,*
> *Darke, doleful, dreary, like a greedy grave,*
> *That still for carrion carcasses doth crave,*
> *On top whereof there dwelt the ghastly Owle*
> *Shrieking his baleful note . . .*

and, in the following passage from the first chapter of Samuel Johnson's *Rasselas,* the neoclassic feeling for the universal, for "nature" which is everywhere and at all times the same, as opposed to the individualistic, the particular, and the eccentric:

From the mountains on every side, rivulets descended, that filled all the valley with verdure and fertility, and formed a lake in the middle, inhabited by fish of every species, and frequented by every fowl whom nature has taught to dip the wing in water. This lake discharged its superfluities by a stream which fell with dreadful noise from precipice to precipice till it was heard no more.

The sides of the mountains were covered with trees, the banks of the brooks were diversified with flowers; every blast shook spices from the rocks, and every month dripped fruits upon the ground. All animals that bite the grass or browse the shrub, whether wild or tame, wandered in this extensive circuit, secured from beasts of prey by the mountains which confined them.

Let us now examine in greater detail some aspects of the literature of melancholy in England and in France, in relation to problems of identification, provenance, shift of meaning, and reconciling of terms. Around 1728, following a sojourn in England, Voltaire wrote an amusing account of his return to a tavern where he had met on the previous day a group of gay and affable Englishmen; now, gloomy and taciturn, their laconic remarks turned to the subject of suicide and the baleful effect of the east wind. Most contemporary French readers would have recognized in this scene the ravages of that common English affliction known as the spleen — although the term was not yet current on the continent.

In 1621 Robert Burton had published his *Anatomy of Melancholy*, a scholarly and exhaustive compendium of earlier views on the kinds, causes, and cures of those "black humours" that plague mankind. "Melancholy" is Burton's common term, subdivided into types such as "flegmatick melancholy," "head melancholy," "love melancholy," and "religious melancholy." Older writers, he says, referred to it variously as "a bad and pievish disease," "a commotion of the mind," "a perpetual anguish of the soul," "a kind of dotage without fever," etc.:

The most received division is into three kinds. The first proceeds from the sole fault of the *brain*, and is called *head melancholy:* the second sympathetically proceeds from the *whole body*, when the whole temperature is melancholy: the third ariseth from the bowels, liver, spleen, or membrane called *mesenterium*, named *hypochondriacal* or *windy melancholy*, which Laurentius subdivides into three parts, from those three members, *hepatick, splenetick, mesaraick.*[5]

The physiological connection between disorders of the spleen (or vapors arising therefrom) and human behavior was a matter of longstanding concern: the term "spleen," it will be recalled, was used by Shakespeare to denote a whim or caprice, hot temper, high spirit, or violent ill-nature. Sometime during the seventeenth century, "spleen" superseded "melancholy" and other terms as the common name for the "English distemper." "Only some fumes from his heart, Madam, makes his head addle," wrote Killigrew in *Pandora* (1664). " 'Tis called the spleen of late, and much in fashion."

In 1653 Sir William Denny had labeled this affliction "the Dumps" and "a melancholy Fitt"; and thereafter, even when "spleen" was the well-established term, synonyms were numerous: on through the eighteenth century we find "black jaundice," "a wise distemper" (or "disease"), "vapors" or "hysteric disorders" (in women), "hypochondriacism," "hypochondriack malice," "the hipp," "fits of chagrin," an "infection," "tyrannical distemper," "perturbation of mind," "the disease," "the dumps" or "dumbs," "a fit of the sullens," "the mopes," and *taedium vitae.*

In France also the particular type of hypochondria issuing from *la rate* (the spleen) was recognized; indeed, the Latin adjective *spleneticus* had become French *splénique* as early as the sixteenth century, and Molière later cites "les vapeurs de la rate" and "le *parenchyme splénique*, c'est-à-dire la rate." [6] But the term "spleen," for the affliction itself, was slow in passing into the French vocabulary, in spite of numerous travelers and other continental writers who, by 1725, had widely publicized the "English malady." Its first appearance, as a borrowed substantive, was probably in the abbé Leblanc's *Lettres d'un François* (La Haye, 1745), which made several important contributions to the current of eighteenth-century Anglomania. The word soon became popular in the many plays and novels that depicted the typical melancholy *milord,* and with Voltaire and Diderot (who used the form *splin*).

As in England, synonyms and paraphrases are also found, such as "la maladie anglaise," "mélancolie hypocondriaque," "affection vaporeuse," and, especially, "vapeurs," in both males and females. Among the more interesting terms identified with spleen is "consomption," defined by Guérineau de Saint-Péravi in his *Epître sur la consomption* (1761) as the English equivalent of French "vapeurs." Caylus, a contemporary, says in his story *Les Deux Anglois* that the English "sont sujets à une noire mélancolie qui dégénère en un mal incurable qu'ils appellent *consomption.*" Diderot's *Encyclopédie*, article "Phtisie" (1765), defines "phtisie hypocondriaque ou hystérique" (also called "phtisie nervuse" and "vapeurs") as a *"consomption* of the whole body, without fever, cough, or difficulty of respiration," and adds that the disease is prevalent in England "in recent times," as in France.

During the first half of the nineteenth century, the terms "spleen," "consomption," "vapeurs," and "melancholia anglica" are very common; Vigny and later Flaubert use the English term "blue devils" (female vapors), and medical treatises introduce special and related terms like "lypémanie" and "mélancolie suicidique intermittente."

The frequent allusions to spleen in French literature of the eighteenth century concerned in part the English, and, especially after 1750, the French themselves; for they eventually acknowledged its inroads as a baneful effect of Anglomania, even blaming it for their supposedly increasing rate of suicides. It was with genuine anxiety that the abbé Gérard wrote in *Le Comte de Valmont* (1774): "What have we gained from this Anglomania, so contagious and so universal in our day? Spleen, consumption, disgust with life . . . [and] suicide, that barbaric craze which has become a system and a principle. . . . Fine presents, indeed!"

The unprecedented outpouring of melancholy literature from the end of the French Revolution through the Romantic period invites speculation concerning the persistence of "spleen." Its identification is both complicated and obscured by that convenient label *mal du siècle* which we now relate specifically to the pernicious *maladie morale* (Burton's "head melancholy") that infected the generation born or maturing in the midst of the disquieting events of 1793 and 1814 and influenced unquestionably the lives and works of Chateaubriand, Senancour, Musset, Constant, and others.

At the same time, other strains of melancholy were pervading French literature and creating new terms: "le youngisme," from Edward Young's *Night Thoughts;* "le mal de René," from Chateaubriand (which, Sainte-Beuve said, merely superseded "le mal de Rousseau"); "le byronisme," from the poet whom Musset called "the great prophet of melancholy"; and "le werthérisme," from Goethe's novel. But anyone familiar with the frequent discussions, in eighteenth-century England and France, of the various causes, symptoms, and cures of the "English malady," can easily trace its robust survival in the first half of the nineteenth century.

For example, there is no plainer case of acute spleen than that of Chateaubriand's René (both in *Les Natchez* and in the later story). This is apparent from his oppressive melancholy and *taedium vitae*, his attempted cure by traveling (a commonplace for more than a century), his hypersensitivity to sights and sounds, his visions and involuntary cries, and his determination in the fall of the year (when suicides in England were allegedly at their peak) to end his life. Indeed, Chateaubriand's own René-like childhood and English influences, as reported in his *Mémoires d'Outre-Tombe*, are revealing: He studied English in his youth, composed his *René* largely in England, and returned to France "English in manners, in taste, and, to a certain point, in opinions." His early melancholy led to the most extravagant behavior, visions, and exaltation; he attempted suicide, and exclaimed on at least one occasion: "I have the spleen."

Sainte-Beuve remarked in an essay on Senancour (1832) that *Obermann* (1804) reflects this author's "psychology, melancholy disposition, and ennui," and that this ennui constituted, in part, the *mal du siècle*.[7] It is generally agreed that Senancour's melancholy was, indeed, personal, sincere, and intellectual. Yet the influence of Sterne, Young, and Goethe has been remarked;[8] Senancour's "stupor, apathy, and torpor" contributing to his "great misery" have been described as a neurosis inherited from his parents,[9] and in 1837 George Sand actually referred to his "spleen."[10] Young Obermann, it will be noted, is in some respects a conventional splenetic type: Consumed with boredom, melancholy, and suicidal impulses, he attempts a cure by traveling to Switzerland; his neighbors take him to be either a lunatic or a splenetic Englishman, and expect him momentarily to add another "beau suicide" to the village annals.

Raphaël, in Balzac's *La Peau de chagrin* (1831), is plainly splenetic, as is the hero of Lamartine's *Raphaël* (1849) with his dejection, desire to travel, and thoughts of suicide; George Sand refers repeatedly to her own "terrible disposition au spleen" in her letters and autobiographical works;[11] and many other writers occupy themselves with this affliction down to Baudelaire, whose poem "Spleen" (first published in *Fleurs du mal,* 1857) begins with the lines

> *Quand le ciel bas et lourd pèse comme un couvercle*
> *Sur l'esprit gémissant en proie aux longs ennuis,*

introducing the familiar detail of climatic influence, long blamed as a prime cause of English spleen.

We may conclude that the popular term "mal du siècle," though quite properly associated with certain Romantic sensibilities discomposed by events growing out of the Revolution, may easily obscure and underrate other important aspects of melancholy. This *mal* had larger implications: If "la jeunesse a besoin de pleurer" [12] during the early nineteenth century, it is equally true that many youths assiduously cultivated *la mode romantique,* just as their forebears had made of spleen a "fashionable disease." [13] André Monglond not only refers astutely to Mme du Deffand, who died in 1780, as a writer who "offers us an early case of the *mal du siècle,*" but finds its "first form" much earlier in Prévost's novel *Cleveland* (1732); [14] and as early as 1827 Antoine Caillot recognized the broad implications of this term in an epitome of the *mal du siècle.* Certain conditions, he said, have produced in many individuals

a sad, morose nature which makes them impervious to all that gentle and consoling emotions can communicate to the heart. Nothing pleases these unfortunates; everything, on the contrary, is for them a source of ennui and disgust. Unbearable to themselves, as to others, they seek continually to be avoided and to flee from themselves; but their imagination endeavors in vain to wander from object to object; always coming back to itself, it finds there only the same images which sadden it. They love only solitude, and solitude only adds to their black melancholy, the burden of which they drag about with them everywhere. . . . For a few years they drink from the cup of bitterness; and when it is almost empty, they throw themselves with barbaric joy into the arms of a voluntary death. This malady, which the English call *spleen,* and the French *consomption,* has become, since the Revolution, commoner than people think, and is possibly, in our land, the principal cause of suicides.[15]

In conclusion, these remarks support the view that the nineteenth century, with its striking new patterns of literature, is the crowning point of the involved and progressive history of the melancholy genre, in which two centuries of preoccupation with the spleen—often encountered under the guise of innumerable terms—play a large part.

The language of aesthetics and literary criticism, which now and then suffers from obscurity and fuzziness, can benefit greatly from a cultivated and respectful caution in the use and interpretation of specific literary terms, and from the avoidance of doctrinaire generalizations. Some aspects of its problems appear in the present contention over the term "Baroque," and again in the need for the *Glossary of the New Criticism* (Chicago, 1949), "partly a glossary, partly a concordance, partly a work in speculative aesthetics," in which William Elton exhibits over one hundred terms in the basic vocabulary of the new criticism. More recently the same author has published, under the title *Aesthetics and Language* (Oxford, 1954), several chapters by different writers emphasizing the need for scrupulous attention to critical language; and reference to similar works [16] will serve to exemplify the truth of the statement: "When words are used as words should be used, they are tools of thought. When the proper usage is neglected, they tend to become the masters of thought." [17]

A LIST OF SPECIMEN WORD STUDIES and related works by modern authors, readily expansible with the aid of various bibliographies, is here appended to provide instructive examples. Among these a good point of departure is Logan P. Smith's "Four Words," cited under the caption "Creative."

BAROQUE

CATTAUI, GEORGES. "Baroque et rococo," *Critique,* no. 122 (1957), 613–34.

GAXOTTE, PIERRE. "Qu'est-ce donc que le baroque?" *Figaro littéraire,* Sept. 7, 1957, pp. 1, 4.

GILMAN, STEPHEN. "An Introduction to the Ideology of the Baroque in Spain," *Symposium,* I (1947), 82–107.

HATZFELD, HELMUT. "Baroque Style: Ideology and the Arts," *Bucknell Review,* VII (1957), 71–79.

———. "A Clarification of the Baroque Problem in the Romance Literatures," *CL,* I (1949), 133–39.

———. "A Critical Survey of Recent Baroque Theories," *Bol. del Inst. Caro y Cuervo,* IV (1949), 461–91.

Journal of Aesthetics & Art Criticism. General bibliography, V (1946); several articles, XIV (1955).

MUELLER, JOHN H. "Baroque: Is it Datum, Hypothesis, or Tautology?" *JAAC,* XII (1954), 421–37.

NELSON, LOWRY, JR. "Góngora and Milton: Toward a Definition of the Baroque," *CL,* VI (1954), 53–63.

ROUSSET, JEAN. *La Littérature de l'âge baroque en France.* Paris, 1953.

WADSWORTH, PHILIP A. "New Views of French Classicism, in Relation to the Baroque," *FR,* XXV (1952), 173–81.

WELLEK, RENÉ. "The Concept of Baroque in Literary Scholarship," *JAAC,* V (1946), 77–109.

CLASSICISM

GIRAUD, VICTOR. "Qu'est-ce qu'un classique?" *RDM,* Jan. 1, 1931, pp. 119–38.

MOREAU, PIERRE. *Le Classicisme des romantiques.* Paris, 1932.

PEYRE, HENRI. *Le Classicisme français.* New York, 1942.

———. *Qu'est-ce que le classicisme?* Paris, 1933.

RANSOM, JOHN C. "Classical and Romantic," *Sat. Rev. of Lit.,* Sept. 14, 1929, pp. 125–27.

SEILLIÈRE, ERNEST. "Qu'est-ce que le classique?" *Nouvelle Revue critique,* Dec. 1933, pp. 529–54.

VAN TIEGHEM, PAUL. "Classique," *Rev. de synthèse historique,* XLI (1931), 238–41.

CONCEIT

POTTER, G. R. "Protest Against the Term 'Conceit,'" *PQ*, xx (1941), 474–83.

CREATIVE

SMITH, LOGAN PEARSALL. "Four Words," *Society for Pure English*, Tract no. XVII (1924); reprinted in his *Words and Idioms*. London, 1948.

ENTHUSIASM

BABCOCK, R. W. "A Note on Genius, Imagination and Enthusiasm in Some Late Eighteenth-Century Periodicals," *N & Q*, CXCII (1947), 93–95.

ELTON, O. "Reason and Enthusiasm in the Eighteenth Century," in *Essays and Studies by Members of the English Association*. Vol. x. Oxford, 1924.

FANCY

BULLITT, JOHN, and W. JACKSON BATE. "Distinctions Between Fancy and Imagination in Eighteenth-Century English Criticism," *MLN*, LX (1945), 8–15.

BUNDY, MURRAY W. *Theory and Imagination in Classical and Medieval Thought*. Urbana, 1927.

KALLICH, MARTIN. "The Association of Ideas and Critical Theory: Hobbs, Locke, and Addison," *ELH*, XII (1945), 290–315.

GENIUS; ORIGINAL GENIUS

BABCOCK, R. W. (see under Enthusiasm).

KAUFMAN, PAUL. *Essays in Memory of Barrett Wendell*. Cambridge, Mass., 1926.

SMITH, L. P. (see under Creative).

GOTHIC

CLARK, KENNETH. *The Gothic Revival. An Essay in the History of Taste*. New York, 1929.

HOLBROOK, WILLIAM C. "The Adjective *Gothique* in the XVIIIth Century," *MLN*, LVI (1941), 498–503.

KAUFMAN, PAUL (see under Genius).

KLIGER, SAMUEL. "The 'Goths' in England: An Introduction to the Gothic Vogue in Eighteenth-Century Aesthetic Discussion," *MP*, XLIII (1945), 107–17.

LONGUEIL, ALFRED E. "The Word 'Gothic' in Eighteenth-Century Criticism," *MLN*, XXXVIII (1923), 453–60.

IMAGINATION

BABCOCK, R. W. (see under Enthusiasm).

BOND, DONALD F. " 'Distrust' of Imagination in English Neo-Classicism," *PQ*, XIV (1935), 54–69.

———. "The Neo-Classic Psychology of the Imagination," *ELH*, IV (1937), 245–64.

BULLITT, JOHN, and W. JACKSON BATE (see under Fancy).

BUNDY, MURRAY W. "Invention and Imagination in the Renaissance," *JEGP*, XXIX (1930), 535–45 (see also under Fancy).

HAMM, V. M. "The Imagination in English Neo-Classical Thought and Literature (1650–1780)," *Harvard University . . . Summaries of Theses.* Cambridge, 1932.

IMITATION

BULLITT, JOHN, and W. JACKSON BATE (see under Fancy).

CARAPETYAN, ARMEN. "The Concept of the *imitazione della natura* in the Sixteenth Century," *Jl. of Renaissance and Baroque Music*, I (1946), 47–67.

CLEMENTS, ROBERT J. "Michelangelo and the Doctrine of Imitation," *Italica*, XXIII (1946), 90–99.

INFLUENCE

HASSAN, IHAB H. "The Problem of Influence in Literary History: Notes Towards a Definition," *JAAC*, XIV (1955), 66–76.

INVENTION

BUNDY, MURRAY W. (see under Imagination).

KALLICH, MARTIN (see under Fancy).

METAPHYSICAL POETS

NETHERCOT, ARTHUR H. "The Term 'Metaphysical Poets' before Johnson," *MLN*, XXXVII (1922), 11–17.

MYTH

DOUGLAS, WALLACE W. "The Meaning of 'Myth' in Modern Criticism," *MP*, L (1953), 232–42.

NATURAL GOODNESS

HAVENS, GEORGE R. "Rousseau's Doctrine of Goodness According to Nature," *PMLA*, XLIV (1929), 1239–45.

———. "La Théorie de la bonté naturelle de l'homme chez J.-J. Rousseau," *RHL*, XXXI (1924), 629–42; XXXII (1925), 24–37, 212–25.

———. "The Theory of 'Natural Goodness' in Rousseau's *Confessions*," *MLN*, XXXVIII (1923), 257–66.

———. "The Theory of 'Natural Goodness' in Rousseau's *Nouvelle Héloïse*," *MLN*, XXXVI (1921), 385–94.

NATURALISM

BEUCHAT, CHARLES. *Histoire du naturalisme français.* Paris, 1949.

COGNY, PIERRE. *Le Naturalisme.* Paris, 1953.

DUMESNIL, RENÉ. *L'Epoque réaliste et naturaliste.* Paris, 1945.

———. *Le Réalisme et le naturalisme.* Paris, 1955.

LINDEN, WALTHER. *Naturalismus.* Leipzig, 1936.

MARTINO, PIERRE. *Le Naturalisme français (1870–1895).* Paris, 1945.

WALCUTT, CHARLES C. "From Scientific Theory to Aesthetic Fact: the 'Naturalistic' Novel," *Quarterly Rev. of Lit.,* III (1946), 167–79.

NATURE

LOVEJOY, ARTHUR O. " 'Nature' as Aesthetic Norm," *MLN,* XLII (1927), 444–50.

PRIESTLEY, F. E. L. "Newton and the Romantic Concept of Nature," *Univ. of Toronto Quarterly,* XVII (1948), 323–36.

SCHINZ, ALBERT. "The Concept of Nature in Philosophy and Literature; a Consideration of Recent Discussion," *Proceedings of the American Philosophical Society,* LXVIII (1929), 207–25.

NOVEL

GRANT, DOUGLAS. "The Novel and its Critical Terms," *Essays in Criticism,* I (1951), 421–29.

ORIGINALITY

SMITH, LOGAN P. (see under Creative).

PICTURESQUE

HUSSEY, CHRISTOPHER. *The Picturesque.* London and New York, 1927.

PRE-RAPHAELITISM

DE ARMOND, ANNA. "What is Pre-Raphaelitism in Poetry?" *Delaware Notes,* 19th Series (1946), 67–86.

PROGRESS

BURY, J. B. *The Idea of Progress.* London, 1920.

REALISM

BECKER, GEORGE J. "Realism: An Essay in Definition," *MLQ,* X (1949), 184–97.

DUMESNIL, RENÉ. *Le Réalisme.* Paris, 1936 (see also under Naturalism).

LEVIN, HARRY. "What is Realism?" *CL*, III (1951), 193–99.

LUKÁCS, GYÖRGY. *Studies in European Realism*. Trans. by Edith Bone. London, 1950.

SPENDER, STEPHEN. *The New Realism, a Discussion*. London, 1939.

REASON

ELTON, O. (see under Enthusiasm).

MICHÉA, R. "Les Variations de la raison au XVIIe siècle. Essai sur la valeur du langage employé en histoire littéraire," *Revue philosophique*, CXXVI (1938), 183–201.

RELATIVISM

HEYL, BERNARD C. "Relativism Again," *JAAC*, V (1946), 54–61.

ROCOCO

KIMBALL, SIDNEY F. *Le Style Louis XV: origine et évolution du rococo*. Paris, 1949.

SENSE

KRAPP, ROBERT M. "Class Analysis of a Literary Controversy: Wit and Sense in Seventeenth-Century English Literature," *Science & Society*, X (1946), 80–92.

SITUATION

LANCASTER, H. C. " 'Situation' as a Term in Literary Criticism," *MLN*, LIX (1944), 392–95.

STREAM OF CONSCIOUSNESS

BOWLING, L. E. "What is the Stream of Consciousness Technique?" *PMLA*, LXV (1950), 333–45.

SUBLIME

MONK, S. H. *The Sublime: A Study of Critical Theories in Eighteenth-Century England*. New York, 1935.

SYMBOL

MISCHEL, THEODORE. "The Meaning of 'Symbol' in Literature," *Arizona Quarterly*, VIII (1952), 69–79.

TASTE

ARONSON, A. "The Anatomy of Taste. A Note on Eighteenth-Century Periodical Literature," *MLN*, LXI (1946), 228–36.

HAVENS, RAYMOND D. "Changing Taste in the Eighteenth Century," *PMLA*, XLIV (1929), 501–36.

HOOKER, EDWARD N. "The Discussion of Taste, from 1750 to 1770, and the New Trends in Literary Criticism," *PMLA*, XLIX (1934), 577–92.

UT PICTURA POESIS

FOLKIERSKI, WLADYSLAW. *"Ut pictura poesis:* ou l'étrange fortune du *De arte graphica* de Du Fresnoy en Angleterre," *RLC*, XXVII (1953), 385–402.

HAGSTRUM, JEAN H. *The Sister Arts.* Chicago, 1958.

HAIGHT, ELIZABETH H. "Horace on Art: *ut pictura poesis,*" *Classical Journal*, XLVII (1952), 157–62.

HOWARD, WILLIAM G. *"Ut pictura poesis,"* *PMLA*, XXIV (1909), 44–123.

VIRTUE

SCHINZ, ALBERT. "La Notion de vertu dans le *Premier Discours* de J.-J. Rousseau," *Mercure de France*, XCVII (1912), 532–55.

WIT

KALLICH, MARTIN (see under Fancy).

KRAPP, ROBERT M. (see under Sense).

3

Literary Indebtedness and
Comparative Literary Studies

J. T. Shaw

T HE study of literary indebtedness has never given up its
place as an important branch of literary research within
particular literatures, and especially in comparative literature. However, its value and validity have been so questioned [1] that it has recently been on the defensive. Source
hunting has been deprecated as having been too frequently
practiced incautiously and as an end in itself. The study
of literary influence has been under attack from several directions. Some consider the concept of influence "positivistic" and reject it on that ground.[2] Other, deterministic schools
have rejected it: One contends that meaningful determinism
is national-social-economic rather than international and
literary; [3] another, arguing for determinism in purely literary matters, has maintained that the study of literature should
be merely of the craft as such and that "historical necessity"
in a native literary tradition determines all within it, including any foreign importations, and that hence the concept of
foreign influence is meaningless.[4] Another recent interpretation insists that influence may properly be considered only
with regard to the personality and psychology of the author

JOSEPH T. SHAW, Professor of Slavic Languages at the University of Wisconsin and editor of the *Slavic and East European Journal,* is preparing a
two-volume edition of Pushkin's letters and has written on Byron's relation with Russian literature.

as a person, but that his literary works are properly studied only in terms of the literary tradition, considered as largely autonomous.[5]

At the same time, studies of direct literary relationships and indebtedness continue to provide a staple of literary scholarship, and their place in comparative literature has hardly diminished, as any bibliography of recent literary studies will show.[6] Suggested substitute fields of research, whether of study of parallel manifestations, or of the "isms," or artistic analysis of particular works, or studies of themes and their treatment in various times and literatures do not remove the *raison d'être* of studies of direct literary relationships. Any serious study or analysis of any author includes consideration of the component parts of his work, their meaning and relationship, how they were suggested to the author, and what they mean to him and to his work. No one who has deprecated study of sources or influences has suggested that it is not of interest and value to know how Shakespeare transmutes materials taken from Boccaccio or from Holinshed. No one has argued that the popularity of Shakespeare, Byron, and Scott in Europe in the nineteenth century was not followed in various literatures by the production of works which it is difficult—to put it mildly—to imagine having been written as they were, either in form or content, if these English authors had not written or had not become known. Questions of biographical or social development or of literary genre or tradition simply do not adequately account for such relationships as those between *Don Quixote* and the novels of Henry Fielding.[7]

Some scholars and critics, including many who have studied literary indebtedness, seem to feel that to suggest an author's literary debts diminishes his originality. But originality should not be understood in terms of innovation. Many great authors have not been ashamed to admit that others have influenced them, and many have even paraded their indebtedness to others. They seem to have felt that originality consists, not exclusively or even primarily in innovations in materials or of style and manner, but in the genuineness and effectiveness of the artistic moving power of the creative work. The innovation which does not move aesthetically is of interest only to the formalist. What genuinely moves the reader aesthetically and produces an independent artistic effect has artistic originality, whatever its debts. The *original* author is not necessarily the innovator or the most inventive, but rather the one who succeeds in making all his own, in subordinating what he takes from others to the new complex of his own artistic work.

Direct interrelationships between literatures exist in a context of the reception and popularity of an author or authors of one country in another. The reception of foreign authors in a particular literature and time forms a direct and integral part of the literary taste and hence the shaping of an audience for a native author, as well as the native author's own artistic and critical consciousness. Elaborate and still usable methods of studying reception and popularity have been developed.[8] It can be traced through critical and other comment in newspapers, journals, diaries, and by mentions and allusions in literary works. It can be partially measured by the sales of an author's works, by the number and size of the editions published, and by translations.

One aspect of popularity and reception may be insufficiently taken into account—the availability of an author's works in a language understood in a particular country. For example, English literature can be directly received by Americans, and vice versa. Similarly, French literature could be directly received in Russia during the eighteenth and nineteenth centuries, and authors who wrote in still other languages were made accessible through French translations to the Russian public interested in literature. Thus English, German, and Italian literature were known to Russian cultivated society in the nineteenth century largely through French translations. An intermediate language—and consideration of what works may have been translated into that language, and of what changes works may have undergone in these translations—must often enter into the study of reception.

Particular authors or even literary movements may produce a non or extraliterary effect upon a whole society or a significant part of it. For example, Voltairean, Byronic, or Tolstoyan modes of thought, action, or even dress may have a broad reflection in various societies of their own and later times. And this social action may contribute to forming the social consciousness of a writer who may then embody it in literature, whether or not there is a direct connection between his works and the foreign author's.

One author's reception may lead to that of much of a whole literature in another country. Bryon's popularity in Europe had something to do with that of Thomas Moore and other writers of his time, and perhaps indirectly, in various countries, even contributed to the cult of Shakespeare in the nineteenth century. Turgenev's acceptance in the West led to that of Tolstoy, Dostoevsky, and of modern Russian literature as a whole. One may seek answers to the fascinating question why some authors are exportable while others are not—why Byron was so much better received abroad than any of his English contemporaries. At the same time, reception of an author or his works by an individual or national culture must be sharply differentiated from literary influence, though to be sure it may provide the impetus or intermediaries through which an influence may come to operate. An author could be quite popular in another country but produce no noteworthy effect within its literature.

Curiously enough, there seems to be no readily available juxtaposition of the various terms which may indicate literary indebtedness, with an attempt to define them and discriminate among them. The terms which most need such definition and discussion appear to be translations, imitations, stylizations, borrowings, sources, parallels, and influence.

Translation is itself a creative act; the translator brings into his contemporary native literary tradition a work written in another language and often at a different time. Translations have perhaps been insufficiently studied as literary works in their own right because of the modern translator's usual attempt to give himself up entirely to the form and matter of the original work and to reproduce it to the best of his ability in the new language. Nevertheless, any translator to a greater or lesser degree adapts the translated work to the taste of his own time, and he modernizes the older work he undertakes to translate. Old theory and practice of translation admitted relative freedom of excision, addition, paraphrase, and change of form and often of style. And in any case the selection of a work for translation, if not the execution, is likely to reflect what Professor Poggioli has called the elective affinity of the translator for the work.[9] Thus translations belong not only to the study of the reception of a foreign author in a particular literature, but to the study of the literature itself. They provide the best intermediaries between the work of the foreign and native authors, and it is often the form and content of its transmuted, translated form which has the greatest effect upon the native literature, for in this form it is directly assimilable into, and indeed already a part of, the literary tradition.

In the case of *imitations* the author gives up, to the degree he can, his creative personality to that of another author, and usually a particular work, while at the same time being freed from the detailed fidelity expected in translation. Imitations have often been used as a pedagogic device in an artist's development. They have often been contemned by scholars and critics, but they may have independent aesthetic merit of their own. As Pushkin points out, imitations do not necessarily indicate "intellectual poverty," but they may show a "noble trust in one's own strength, the hope of discovering new worlds, following in the footsteps of a genius, or a feeling in its humility even more elevated, the desire to master one's model and give it a second life." [10] An imitation may be of an entire work or a part; occasionally it may be in the general style and manner of another writer, without specific debts.

Related to an imitation but perhaps best considered separately is a *stylization,* in which an author suggests for an artistic purpose another author or literary work, or even the style of an entire period, by a combination of style and materials. For example, Pushkin often stylizes to convey a particular mood or background. He slightly stylizes after the eighteen-century heroic manner to present Peter the Great in *Poltava.* Pushkin's only poetic epitaph for Byron is in his "To the Sea," where he in part celebrates Byron by having a passage suggestive of him, though the entire poem is quite un-Byronic and though Pushkin had by this time modified his early admiration for his English contemporary.

In the case of *borrowings,* the writer helps himself to materials or methods, especially to aphorisms, images, figures of speech, motifs, plot elements. One may discover the *source* of a borrowing in newspapers, reported conversations, in critical reviews, as well as within artistic works. A borrowing may be an *allusion*, more or less clearly pointing to the literary source; it may or may not be *stylized*. Many sophisticated authors—ancient and modern—have assumed that their readers will read them in literary contexts. The critic's and scholar's task with borrowings is to discover the relationships of the use of the material in the new work to that of the old—the artistic use to which the borrowing is put.

The term *source* is perhaps most frequently used to indicate the place from which a borrowing is taken; it would seem that in literary scholarship this use of "source" should be clearly distinguished from "source" in the sense of a work providing the materials or the basic part of the materials —especially the plot—for a particular work. The source in this sense may or may not provide or even suggest the form for a particular work. In the usual case the source materials and the form involved are quite separate. The source of Pushkin's *Boris Godunov* is Karamzin's *History*, and Shakespeare found sources in Holinshed and Boccaccio, but in each case the artistic use of the materials came from elsewhere.

The various terms cited above all indicate a direct connection between literary works. *Parallels* provide a further subject of interest and value. In cases where there may be some question of the direct source of borrowings, because of comparable materials being present in several available works, a definite source may be determined when there are sufficient exclusive parallels, as Professor Zhirmunsky has argued in demonstrating that Pushkin's use of the genre of the Byronic or romantic verse tale was taken directly from Byron.[11] In addition to this type of parallel, there are comparable manifestations in form or content in different authors, literatures, and perhaps at different times, and with no demonstrable direct relationship to each other. Juxtaposition of comparable works may have great interest and value in the criticism of each of them. These parallels may or may not go back to a common source. Often they are involved in literary movements and may be produced apparently by different literatures operating on the basis largely if not entirely of their own literary tradition, as in the case of Dickens and Gogol. The value of the study of parallels, as with other literary phenomena, is in the light they cast on the qualities and merit of the individual works; they may also be of interest in indicating similarities and differences in national literary traditions. When one studies parallels in this sense he nevertheless should consider the possibility of direct relationships. The author of a recent comparative study of Lermontov's *Demon* and Vigny's *Éloa* failed even to consider whether Lermontov was acquainted with Vigny's work, and hence whether similarities or differences indicate conscious reactions.[12]

An author may be considered to have been *influenced* by a foreign author when something from without can be demonstrated to have produced upon him and/or his artistic works an effect his native literary tradition and personal development do not explain. In contrast to imitation, influence shows the influenced author producing work which is essentially his own. Influence is not confined to individual details or images or borrowings or even sources—though it may include them —but is something pervasive, something organically involved in and presented through artistic works. In the case of Pushkin's *Boris Godunov,* again, the principal influence is not the source—Karamzin's *History*—but Shakespeare's handling of characterization, action, and the dramatic form. Literary influence on an author will result in his literary works as such having pervasive, organic qualities in their essential inspiration or artistic presentation which they otherwise would not have had, either in this form or at this stage

of his development. The seed of literary influence must fall
on fallow land. The author and the tradition must be ready
to accept, transmute, react to the influence. Many seeds from
various possible influences may fall, but only the ones for
which the soil is ready will germinate, and each will be affected by the particular quality of the soil and climate where
it takes root, or, to shift the image, to the shoot to which it is
grafted.

Literary influence appears to be most frequent and most
fruitful at the times of emergence of national literatures and
of radical change of direction of a particular literary tradition in a given literature. In addition, it may accompany or
follow social or political movements or, especially, upheav-
als. Thus, like all literary phenomena, it has a social and often also a meaningful political context, in addition to the
literary one. When literary forms and aesthetics appear to
be outworn, earlier manifestations within the same literature
may provide an answer to authors' present needs, or they
may discover abroad what exemplifies or satisfies their inclinations. In the case of emerging national literatures, authors may seek in form or ideology that which they can adapt
or transmute for their own consciousness, time, and nation.
Usually there will be conflicting domestic and foreign literary
movements and figures; there will usually be foreign influences of varying kinds available for assimilation. For example, French, German, and English authors and literatures in
turn and even concurrently influenced Russian authors and
literary traditions of the eighteenth and nineteenth centuries.

Influence, to be meaningful, must be manifested in an intrinsic form, upon or within the literary works themselves.
It may be shown in style, images, characters, themes, man-
nerisms, and it may also be shown in content, thought, ideas,
the general *Weltanschauung* presented by particular works.

Of course it is necessary to adduce satisfactory external evidence that the hypothetically influenced author *could* have been influenced by the influencing author; for this purpose, mentions, allusions, quotations, diaries, the evidence of contemporaries, and evidences of an author's reading must be used. But the essential test must be within the works themselves. Whether particular borrowings are interpreted as showing influence depends upon their effect and importance in the new work; but influence need not include any specific borrowings. Influence study can be particularly interesting when it can be traced through an author's development, as when Pushkin, at various stages of his career, acclimatized and adapted and later developed in his own way the genre of the romantic verse tale from Byron, the chronicle-play-tragedy from Shakespeare, and the form of the historical novel from Scott. Influence may occur within or across genre lines. There may be a juxtaposition of influences in a particular work, as when Dostoevsky in *The Brothers Karamazov* uses Schiller for the characterization of Dmitri, Goethe for Ivan, and *The Wanderings of the Monk Parfeny* for Father Zosima; but the total work is completely his own, enriched by the influences utilized.

The influence of literary works upon literary works is perhaps the most convincingly demonstrable type, and perhaps aesthetically the most interesting. In addition, there is influence upon the writer as a man. Here the influence may be from a literary or nonliterary man; it will usually be upon content, rather than directly upon genre and style, upon *Weltanschauung* rather than upon artistic form. As Truman Capote recently pointed out to an audience of Russian writers, a nonliterary man, Freud, has been one of the most potent influences on modern Western literature. Philosophers and thinkers have often exerted influence upon writers, from Plato and

Aristotle, to Thomas Aquinas, Hegel, Alfred North White-head, and Karl Marx. Personal and literary influence may coincide, as in the case of Mallarmé and Valéry.[13] The international fame and influence of particular authors may to a considerable extent depend upon answers they provide— or are interpreted as providing—to the *Weltanschauung,* as well as to the literary tradition within a particular country and time.

One of the most complex problems in the study of literary influence is that of direct and indirect influence. An author may introduce the influence of a foreign author into a literary tradition, and then, as in the case of the Byronic tradition in Russia, it may proceed largely from the influence of the native author. But as the tradition continues, it may be enriched by another native author going back to the foreign author for materials or tonalities or images or effects which were not adopted by the first author. Thus Lermontov was influenced by the Byronic verse tale of Pushkin and other Russian authors, but then went directly to Byron for qualities which Pushkin had omitted or modified.[14]

Literary influence has a number of aspects which have particular manifestations in comparative literature. The first of these has to do with translations, which we have already discussed, but to which we must return. Even when there is a general public which can read a foreign work in the original or some intermediate language, the work does not really belong to the native tradition until it has been translated—until appropriate style, form, and diction have been found for it within the native tradition. Thus translations, not only in the conscious changes of a literary work which they often produce, but in the adaptation which any translation provides, play a special role in the inception and the transmission of literary influences. The direct influence is often produced by the translation rather than the original work. And in any case they may emphasize certain works of an author, certain sides of his creative personality, to the exclusion or at least deprecation of others. For example, that the first verse translations of Byron were Zhukovsky's version of *The Prisoner of Chillon* and Kozlov's of *The Bride of Abydos* had great importance in the further development of the Byronic tradition in Russia.

The question of the influence of literary diction and style across languages has hitherto been perhaps insufficiently studied. Each age creates its own literary language, partly in furtherance of the native literary tradition, and partly in opposition to it. In imitating or translating a foreign author, an author gives himself the task of adapting directly the author's style and language to the needs of his own time, language, and literary tradition. In this adapting, the translator or imitator often brings something new into his literary tradition, not only in genre and content, but also in style and diction. Phrase, metaphor, similes, and general style and diction cannot simply be borrowed from another language, but must be reshaped to fit them into the native literary tradition.

A special problem of influence in comparative literature has to do with the time of reception and influence. In the nineteenth century Shakespeare influenced English literature as well as many foreign literatures, and there may be common points of contact in the appreciation and reinterpretation which resulted in this influence. Nevertheless, the influence of Shakespeare in France or in Russia in the nineteenth century was quite different from that in England, because Shakespeare had always been known and exerted a measure of influence in his native land. Revaluation is not discovery. Shakespeare fitted quite differently into nine-

teenth-century English literary tradition from the way he
fitted into the traditions of other countries. The influencing
author must be studied in relationship to the literary traditions where he wrote and where he exerts an influence.
The literary background of each age and country varies, and
hence the influence exerted by an author or literature will
vary in accordance with what a given age feels it needs. A
new element in a literature is qualitatively different from one
that has been there and known, but has been relatively in-
active.

I trust this brief survey of literary relationships has shown
that there is still need for study of reception and popularity
and for all the varieties of direct literary indebtedness including literary influence. With proper caution and safe-
guards, illumination can be cast upon authors, works, and
literary movements. Perhaps the most fruitful immediate
fields for further study are those of the recently or presently
emerging national literatures. Sufficient data may become
available, as has been recently suggested, to push these
studies further back into the past; it has been rightly asked
why such studies usually begin only with the Renaissance or
even later.[15]

It seems to me that even the best studies of literary indebtedness have all too often paid insufficient attention to
detailed study of the interrelationships between particular
works. For example, Estève's monumental study of Byron
in France, certainly one of the best comparative studies of
reception and influence—with its excellent account of Byron's reception in France and its intelligent discussion of
which aspects of Byron were influential upon what French
authors—is nevertheless far less satisfying when one wishes
to discover the relationships between individual works,
when one wishes to evaluate or analyze the French work in-

fluenced.[16] In even the most frequently studied literary contacts, the general conclusions may prove accurate, but many valuable insights remain to be discovered.

The influences upon an author or a literature should be studied, for understanding both. Such studies should take into account what qualities were taken, what were transmuted, what were rejected. The center of interest should be what the borrowing or influenced author does with what he takes, what effect it has upon the finished literary work. The study of direct literary relationships and literary indebtedness can be indispensible to understanding and evaluating the individual work of art, not only for placing it in the literary tradition, but also for defining what it is and what it essentially attempts and for determining wherein it succeeds.

4

The Art of Translation

Horst Frenz

T HROUGHOUT the centuries grave doubts have been raised over the feasibility of translations of literary works. Again and again it has been maintained that it is not possible for anyone to combine in another language the thoughts, the emotions, the style, and the form of an epic, a lyric poem, a poetic drama, or even a prose novel. Yet the fact remains that the art of translation has been practiced everywhere in the world. Through this art many of the literary achievements of one country have found a hearing and even become "naturalized" in other countries. Their people have been able to share the experiences and emotions expressed in foreign works, and men of letters have been stimulated and even profoundly influenced by them.

Most readers must depend upon the translator if they are to know and appreciate the literature of the world. His role is more important than is often realized. One of the most striking illustrations is probably the case of the German Shakespeare translation commonly referred to as the

Professor of English and Chairman of the Comparative Literature Program at Indiana University, HORST FRENZ has been Visiting Professor at Wisconsin, New York University, and Hamburg. He has published *Die Entwicklung des Sozialen Dramas in England* and *Whitman and Rolleston* and translated Gerhart Hauptmann's plays into English for the Rinehart Editions. He has been associate editor and recently became editor in chief of the *Yearbook of Comparative and General Literature.* Professor Frenz is chairman of the Comparative Literature Committee of the National Council of Teachers of English.

Schlegel-Tieck translation. Between 1797 and 1810 August Wilhelm Schlegel published seventeen of Shakespeare's plays, and the remaining ones were translated by Count von Baudissin and Dorothea Tieck under supervision and with the cooperation of her father, Ludwig Tieck. The principle on which these translations were based was faithfulness. Schlegel, realizing the importance of Shakespeare's fondness for mixing poetic and prose elements, preserved Shakespeare's verse forms; he differentiated between rhetorical and conversational prose and attempted in many other ways to reproduce the original.

The Schlegel-Tieck version transformed Shakespeare into a German classic poet who was read, played, and quoted as widely as the German masters themselves. In his lecture on "Shakespeare and Germany," [1] Alois Brandl cited as one of the qualities of this version that "the obsolete words and the quaint meanings of words which often puzzle his English readers, and sometimes even demand comment, are replaced by current phrases." "In our classical translation by Schlegel-Tieck," Brandl continues, "the meaning is put forth so clearly that, when I had to reprint it in a popular edition, there was sometimes not even one passage to be explained in a whole play—so perfectly had the Tudor words been recast in lucid and up-to-date German." Thus, a German reader and spectator might come closer to an understanding of Shakespeare than "a Londoner, who has no other choice than to take him in the original." Schlegel's poetic gift produced a work of art which, while it was faithful to the original, could stand on its own as an original work. He was an "Umdichter," a poet able to use his imaginative powers freely and at the same time willing to accept the Englishman as his master.

It must be kept in mind that Schlegel was the disciple of a

great poet, Goethe, and the representative of an important movement, Romanticism. The romanticists worshipped Shakespeare, for they found in him a universality not only of content but also of form. The time was ripe for a complete transmission of Shakespeare's work to Germany, and Schlegel was the ideal translator to accomplish the task. Here was an act of cooperation—Goethe's extension of the German language, the romanticists' interest in the Englishman, and Schlegel's talent as a translator. The Schlegel-Tieck version captured the German mind so thoroughly and satisfyingly that no other translation has been able to take its place. Many of those who have since tried their hand at translating Shakespeare into German have either used this "standard" translation as a point of departure or have limited themselves to improving the Tieck contributions.[2]

Today the name of the American poet Bayard Taylor is known more for his translation of Goethe's *Faust* than for his own writings. A true disciple of the German poet he undertook the tremendous task of rendering both parts of *Faust* into English and was the first American to try his hand at translating the second part. In order to do justice to the original, he delved into the mysteries of early Greek mythology, studied certain geological theories, and extended his research to editions and critical works throughout the world. Understanding clearly the relationships between the two parts of *Faust* he delighted in the second part because of "its wealth of illustration, and the almost inexhaustible variety and beauty of its rhythmical forms." [3] Taylor, like Schlegel before him, believed in utter fidelity to the sense of the original work of art, in reproducing the verse forms and even, as far as possible, the rhythm and rhyme. A poet in his own right, he was willing to subordinate his poetic powers to the work of his master and thus created a standard work which has lasted far beyond his own time. His *Faust* translation was not only recognized as a significant literary production at the time of its publication but also became the model for many later versions.

Miss Anna Swanwick thought it necessary to revise and improve her first translation of *Faust* by introducing feminine rhymes.[4] In the preface to his rendition Professor van der Smissen acknowledged his indebtedness to Anna Swanwick and Bayard Taylor for often "suggesting a rhyme or a turn of phrase, or pointing the way out of an apparently hopeless impasse."[5] In more than one respect van der Smissen followed the method employed by Taylor, and in the problems dealing with the art of translating he agreed with Taylor. He, like Taylor, saw the task in reproducing the original text, both as to the substance and form, "with utmost fidelity to the sense, rhythm, metre and rhyme, as far as is possible in transferring from one language to another within the narrow limits prescribed by a line of verse."[6] In the recent translation of the complete *Faust* George Madison Priest has adhered to Taylor's principle and preserved the metrical and rhyming schemes of the original. Based upon the conviction that Goethe cannot be improved upon, Priest's aim was "to change nothing, to omit nothing, and above all, to add nothing."[7] Taylor's influence is also noticeable in Alice Raphael's *Faust* translation (1930). After she had written at first in loose and rhymeless verses, her deeper penetration into the masterpiece seemed to dictate the use of rhyme and of Goethe's original meter. In the foreword to her revised translation of 1955,[8] she points out that she "learned to meet the demands established once for all time by Bayard Taylor," namely, neither to add nor omit lines, to maintain "the strictest discipline . . . in wrestling with the essential meaning of words," and to follow the original meters as closely as possible. Yet at the same time she proposes to go beyond Taylor by producing a "version that would meet the demands both of the modern reader and of the modern stage."

Just as Schlegel's Shakespeare translations contain for some modern Germans too much of the Romantic, Taylor's *Faust* has been found by modern Americans to be too Victorian in the use of idiom and rhetoric. However, both men have done invaluable service in presenting a great foreign literary figure to their countrymen. Their translations are still alive today, even if, as particularly in Taylor's case, only as an inspiration to new attempts at translation in the light of recent scholarship and new insights.

In England, too, a number of translations have found a permanent place and exerted their influence throughout the ages. Besides the Authorized Version of the Bible might be mentioned Chapman's Homeric poems, Pope's *Iliad*, Dryden's Vergil, and in the nineteenth century Edward Fitz-Gerald's *Rubaiyyat*. The last work is particularly interesting, for in this case an obscure Persian poet was brought to the attention of the English-speaking world. FitzGerald's important place in the development of English literature has been secured not through any of his original works but through this translation, which, in the opinion of one authority, is "probably quoted more frequently than any other work in English literature." [9] In this country Charles Eliot Norton, editor of the *North American Review*, first recognized the quality of FitzGerald's work—without actually knowing the identity of the translator. He spoke of the "poetic transfusion of a poetic spirit from one language to another, and the re-presentation of the ideas and images of the original in a form not altogether diverse from their own, but perfectly adapted to the new conditions of time, place, custom, and habit of mind in which they reappear." He called the *Rubaiyyat* "the work of a poet inspired by the work of a poet; not a copy, but a reproduction, not a translation, but the redelivery of a poetic inspiration," and concluded that "there is probably nothing in the mass of English translations or reproductions of the poetry of the East to be compared with this little volume in point of value as *English* poetry." [10]

FitzGerald concerned himself little with theological or philosophical problems but found in the epigrammatic stanzas of the Persian poet some answers to his own feelings of doubt, to his questions concerning life after death, and to the complexities of modern life. The consensus of recent scholarly opinion is that most of FitzGerald's quatrains were either "faithful . . . paraphrases" or "composite" stanzas "traceable to more than one quatrain" and that the English poet after the first two editions eliminated most of those quatrains for which there had been no particular ones in the original.[11] He selected from Omar, regrouped the quatrains, and thus gave a certain form to the whole. Even if he created a somewhat different mood, as some critics maintain, there is no justification in going so far as to conclude that the *Rubaiyyat* is no more than "an English poem with Persian allusions." [12] Whatever changes FitzGerald made in transferring the *Rubaiyyat* from Persia to England and whatever method of translating he used to convey the ideas and the emotions of the Oriental poet the fact remains that he has succeeded in making this work known not only in England but also in the whole Western world.

These three examples cited at random reveal some interesting similarities. In each case, a poet attempted to translate another poet's work and made a great success of it. All three—Schlegel, Taylor, and FitzGerald—became well-known figures in world literature largely because of their work as translators. All three did a great deal of preliminary or supplementary labor in connection with the work they were translating. While the first two transplanted two giants of literature, FitzGerald brought a little known writer of the East to the attention of his countrymen and proved how effectively the translator can open new lanes in the literary world traffic. Furthermore, these illustrations are by no means exceptional. Translation has flourished during many of the great epochs of literature, and there seems to be general agreement that the Elizabethan age, for instance, "was also the first great age of translation in England." [13] A host of writers owe their standing in world literature to international fame which they have gained through translation, at times in spite of an insecure foothold in their own literature. The foreign reputation of Heine has kept him respected in Germany, even if sometimes rather reluctantly; it is abroad that the literary rank of Edgar Allen Poe has been established beyond doubt.

To be sure, some countries have depended on translation more than others. It is perhaps true that "German is a language into which others . . . can be more faithfully and successfully translated than into any other"; [14] and that "l'Allemagne est le plus grand pays traducteur du monde." [15] But in many other countries the novels of Cooper, Scott and Dickens, for instance, were more popular than any contemporaneous local fiction. The novels of Balzac and Zola almost immediately became the expression of the "modern" Western world, to the degree of making in many a country the growth of an indigenous *cosmopolitan* fiction supernumerary. Ibsen's fame in Germany and Europe had to silence the opposition at home; and the world-wide popularity of other Scandinavians such as Strindberg, Jacobsen, Lagerlöf, Undset, Hamsun, to what else can it be attributed than to the potency of translation? The case of the great Russian novelists is particularly revealing. Long before Russian was widely understood, Turgeniev, Tolstoy, and finally Dostoevsky outranked native novelists in some highly literary countries.

The twentieth century is far from reversing the trend. "Le xxe siècle, l'âge de la traduction par excellence," a French authority maintains.[16] Even in France, so long notoriously self-sufficient in literary matters, translation now exceeds ten per cent of the total printed production. It is hardly an exaggeration to assert that the "monde moderne apparaît comme une immense machine à traduire." [17] The task of the translator is increasing in importance and he is contributing in a large measure to a one-world concept.

One must also admit that the translator may do a great deal of harm in several ways. First, he may translate the wrong works, that is unknowingly or intentionally ignore certain literary achievements which are worthy of becoming better known. Here fads and fashions play a role, too, and a translator may submit to them in selecting his subjects. It has been claimed again and again that great literary works have a way of attracting attention abroad, but it is very doubtful that this optimistic point of view can be applied to literatures in less well-known languages or in culturally and politically less important areas. Also, ideological curtains of all kinds, political and economic barriers, and racial prejudices are formidable enough to interfere with the task of the translator which should be, above all, to acquaint his own country with the best literature that has been produced in foreign languages.

Then, there is the harm that can be done by a translator who distorts a literary work and thus becomes responsible for presenting an idea or a point of view or a mood which was actually not expressed by the foreign writer. Rabelais, for instance, has become known in the English-speaking world as "a bibulous, gormandizing 'philosopher' shaking his sides in laughter at the follies of humankind and the essential vanity of life" [18] as the result of Sir Thomas Urquhart's translation. By injecting an "amiable scepticism," by implying erotic undertones where there were none in the original, Urquhart created, according to Samuel Putnam, "a false or grossly distorted conception of Rabelais." Urquhart's difficult seventeenth-century style helped to obscure the real Rabelais whose works, after all, were best sellers enjoyed "alike by the learned and the unlearned of his time," whose sentence structure is "prevailingly short, simple, and direct." It was the style of the English translator which prevented many from reading Rabelais and encouraged a "cult on the part of a select few." [19] An aura was created which the original never had.

While in the case just mentioned it cannot be said that the translator intentionally distorted the original, there are other instances in which the translator is fully aware of what he is doing. When the German version of the American war play, *What Price Glory?* (German title: *Rivalen*), by Maxwell Anderson and Laurence Stallings was presented in Berlin in 1929, it did not, as most critics seemed to think, preserve the American point of view. Instead, it had become a play which used the Americans' plot as a vehicle for Carl Zuckmayer's own feelings against militarism, to express his ideas of the "Etappe," to give his conception of the experiences in the front lines, and to portray French and Jewish characters according to his own whims. Zuckmayer did the two playwrights a disservice by introducing his own ideas into the American war play. Interestingly enough, it never had the success that the British war play, *Journey's End*, experienced in Germany at about the same time; that play had been trans-

lated very faithfully. One may venture the conjecture that the
German audiences found nothing in the American play they
could not find in their own war plays.[20]

In the past, it has often been common practice for translators to delete from or add to a work indiscriminately, in
line with their own religious bias or because they were
shocked and embarrassed by statements which struck them
as immoral or obscene. Peter Motteux, who continued the
Rabelais translation begun by Sir Thomas Urquhart, was a
"rabid Protestant" and showed his religious bias when he
simply deleted a significant passage which shows the Cal-
vinists in an unfavorable light.[21] In Edith Wharton's translation of Sudermann's play, *Es lebe das Leben*, a nobleman's
line, "Wenn ich mit einer gesunden Kuhmagd Kinder zeugen
dürfte," becomes "If only I could marry a healthy dairy-
maid." The suggestion of marriage to a dairy-maid is made,
I assume, out of moral consideration; it hardly conveys the
caste concept of the nobility expressed in the original statement.[22]

Such changes for religious or moral reasons have been
somewhat less frequent in recent times, but the history of
the last few decades has shown many cases of distortions
arising out of political considerations. I need only refer to the
Russian translations of Eugene O'Neill's *All God's Chillun
Got Wings* and *The Hairy Ape* in which certain changes were
made in order to bring the plays more in line with the current
social thinking of the Soviet Union. Thus, in the former play,
the racial and economic implications were stressed at the
expense of the emotional impact. In *The Hairy Ape*, the lack
of concerted labor action rather than his own inner upheaval
was made responsible for Yank's downfall.[23] It goes without
saying that this kind of editing or "improving" is hardly
justifiable.

Likewise, plain mistranslations made either out of ignorance of the foreign language or out of carelessness cannot be condoned. The recent translation of Herrmann Hesse's *Das Glassperlenspiel* by Mervyn Savill (English title: *Magister Ludi*) contains so many errors that frequently the meaning of a sentence or a thought is completely distorted. At the end of the introductory chapter, for example, the relationship of the bead game and religion is discussed, and Hesse tells us that the game was very much like a religious service, "während es sich jeder eigenen Theologie enthielt," which is exactly the opposite of the statement found in the translation that "it contained its own theology." And any translator should know that "eine Spielsprache" is a "game-language" and not "a game of speech." [24]

In his version of *What Price Glory?*, Zuckmayer obviously shows ignorance of an American colloquialism when he renders the sentence, "parks his dogs in Flagg's bed" literally as "lässt seine Hunde in Flaggs Bett liegen" instead of realizing that "dogs" is slang for "feet." In this case, the result is amusing, but at times a mistranslation can have rather serious consequences. Instead of being a means of bringing two nations together, a wrong translation may have the opposite effect, may tear them apart. Aesthetically, wrong as well as bad translations do harm to the original author and to his and his country's reputation. As Gilbert Highet put it, "A badly written book is only a blunder. A bad translation of a good book is a crime." [25]

Perhaps it should be added that the real dangers of translation do not arise from mere ignorance or incompetence, that they lie not so much in the translator as in translation itself. The very prophets of translation made it plain that theirs was a problematical job. The author of the translation that has been read more than any other book in the world, St. Jerome's Vulgate, said "Non verbum e verbo, sed sensum exprimere de sensu," enunciating thereby the principle of nonliteralness which has been accepted for all higher translation. And one of the most powerful of all translators, Martin Luther, in stating "Man muss . . . dem gemeinen Mann aufs Maul sehen," found the principle most widely claimed as guide and goal: to arrive at the living common language of the day. Both principles have created more problems than they have settled. The main questions have always been: how far away from literalness can a good translation go? How far can the transposition into current speech be carried? These are the questions which every age has answered differently; but the most important answers for us must be those given in our own age.

Since in recent years English and American translations of the world classics have been appearing at an accelerated pace, it seems appropriate to study the comments of modern translators on the problems of translating into English. Fortunately, most modern translators feel impelled to justify their efforts and thus have created a substantial body of critical material. Let us therefore examine the various principles for the most widely used translations of the present, largely college, popular, or paperback editions—and the gigantic scale on which translations have invaded the colleges and drugstore counters may well be a very important phenomenon of our present cultural life.

Considerable agreement exists that poetry should be translated into poetic form, but there is less agreement on the question whether or not the same verse form, rhyme scheme, etc. should be used in the translation. Edna St. Vincent Millay in her introduction to George Dillon's and her own translations of Baudelaire,[26] feels very strongly that it should, pointing out that to most poets the shape of a poem is of real significance: "To many poets, the physical characters of their poem, its rhythm, its rhyme, its music, the way it looks on the page, is quite as important as the thing they wish to say; to some it is vastly more important." Therefore she feels it is unfair to force a foreign poet into a different meter or form just because the translator may be more familiar with that particular form.

Likewise, Dorothy Sayers for her Dante version chooses the original *terza rima* in spite of certain objections to it, simply because she feels that blank verse, "with its insidious temptation to be literal at the expense of the verse, has little advantage over prose and, though easier to write badly, is far more difficult to write well." Miss Sayers accepts Maurice Hewlett's contention that the translator of Dante can only choose between "*terza rima* or nothing." [27]

John Ciardi, on the other hand, does not follow Dante's complicated rhyme scheme, for he finds he might be able to preserve either the rhyme or "the tone of the language, but not both." His decision is based on the argument that English does not lend itself to rhyme as easily as Italian and that consequently "the language must be inverted, distorted, padded, and made unspeakable in order to force the line to come out on that third all-consuming rhyme." Although Ciardi departs from the *terza rima* and at times uses "deficient" rhymes—in order not to force "an exact rhyme" at the expense of naturalness—he keeps the three-line stanza with the first and third lines rhyming. [28]

However, Rolfe Humphries, in his translation of the *Aeneid*, does not hesitate to change Vergil's meter, for he finds that a loose iambic pentameter would be "the most convenient medium" to take the place of the Latin hexameter. [29] C. Day Lewis, another translator of the *Aeneid*, seems to show equally small concern for meter and form as long as the epic form is in verse which, he contends, will move a translator a little closer to the original. [30]

Theodore Howard Banks, who in translating Sophocles' *The Theban Plays* for stage presentation is particularly concerned with catching "the idioms and cadences of spoken, rather than written, language," [31] writes most of the dialogue in blank verse, while for some parts of it he employs "heroic couplet, heroic quatrains, or irregular rhymed stanzas" in order to indicate a change of meter in the original. On the other hand, the choruses and a number of lyric passages in the dialogue are reproduced in pairs of rhymed stanzas. The choruses, Banks explains, "are distinguished from the dialogue in two other ways. Because they are lyric poems, in which people are not so much speaking as singing, their vocabulary is somewhat fuller and more elaborate. Also, in them, the translation is of necessity less close, since the thought must be paraphrased or expanded to provide rhymes. Rhymed stanzas contrast sharply with the dialogue, however, and this contrast provides an aesthetic effect comparable to that of the Greek." Philip Vellacott, translator of Euripides' plays, tries "to represent faithfully, by one device or another, every idea, image, and association expressed in the poet's original words," [32] and yet he does not attempt the same meters Euripides had employed; rather he alternates between prose and verse, for instance, to make clear the distinction between dialogue and lyric passages or indicates a change in Greek meters by a change from rhymed to unrhymed lines. Similarly, F. Kinchen Smith in his stage version of *Antigone,* chooses prose for the dialogue—partly because he thinks that prose would give "greater faithfulness to the original"—and renders the choral passages into free verse.[33] Stating that their purpose is "to reach—and, if possible, to render precisely—the emotional and sensible meaning in every speech in the play," Dudley Fitts and Robert Fitzgerald, the translators of *Alcestis* and *Antigone,* find occasionally "the best English equivalent in a literalness which extended to the texture and rhythm of the Greek phrasing." However, they would "not follow the Greek word for word, when to do so would have been weak and therefore false." And so they feel justified in using "a more or less free paraphrase" to allow "alterations, suppressions, and expansions." [34]

Almost all authorities maintain that faithfulness should be adhered to in the process of translating, but they do not always mean the same thing by faithfulness. They agree that faithfulness does not imply word-by-word translation, but there the agreement ends. It has already been pointed out that some, like Edna St. Vincent Millay and Dorothy Sayers, insist on preserving the original meter and form of a poem while others find it sufficient to translate into whatever verse form may seem most appropriate. Humphries maintains that he has tried "to be faithful to the meaning of the poem" as he understands it and "to make it sound" to the reader "the way it feels" to him. That does not prevent Humphries from taking "all kinds of liberties" such as transposing lines, cutting "proper names and allusions where . . . they would excessively slow down reader interest," substituting "the general for the specific or the specific for the general." [35]

The translators of *The Song of God: Bhagavad-Gita,* Swami Prabhavananda and Christopher Isherwood, too, maintain that their work is not a paraphrase, that "except in a very few difficult passages, it faithfully follows the original." And yet they admit freely that, without finding any particular justification for such a procedure in the original text, they have "translated the Gita in a variety of styles, partly prose, partly verse" and that "the transitions from one style to another are quite arbitrary." [36]

"To translate poetry into prose, no matter how faithfully and even subtly the words are reproduced, is to betray the poem." [37] This verdict by Miss Millay is interesting in the light of some significant recent attempts at rendering Greek epic poetry into English prose. W. H. D. Rouse, E. V. Rieu, and T. E. Lawrence, three significant translators of *The Odyssey*, have advocated or implied that prose is the appropriate vehicle for the classical epic, since the modern prose novel has taken over the place in literature once held by the epic. Maintaining that most translations of Homer "are filled with affections and attempts at poetic language which Homer himself is quite free from," Rouse feels that a translator must speak just as "naturally" as Homer did: "In these dialogues, and in most of the narrative, I have used Homer's words. I have left something out, but if you read the Greek words without prejudice, you will see that they are as natural and simple as mine. There is absolutely nothing of poetic embellishment in the words; they are the same words which ordinary human beings would use in these conditions . . . in the simplest English the same nobility and beauty is found when the thing said is noble and beautiful." [38] When Rouse claims that he wants to have his version judged "simply as a story," [39] he gives basically the same reason for using prose as did Lawrence and Rieu. *The Odyssey* is considered as a novel, "the first novel of Europe" (Lawrence) [40] and Homer is looked upon as "the world's best story-teller" (Rieu). [41]

While there is some justification for rendering classical epic poetry into English prose, it is more difficult to accept Rieu's contention, expressed in the preface to his translation of Vergil's *Pastoral Poems*, that more is lost than gained "by squeezing Virgil into the mould of alien design" and that the result would have been "less like Virgil" if he had "laboured to render the music of his hexameters in some traditional form of English verse." [42] H. R. Huse, prose translator of Dante's *The Divine Comedy*, does not think that the loss of rhyme and meter is very important and suggests that "rhyme and the division into a certain number of syllables (the meter) are less vital than the style or rhythm of the phrases." [43]

Most of those who favor the translation of poetry into prose do it in an attempt to get at the meaning of the original work. Bayard Quincy Morgan believes that the important message Goethe presents in *Faust* deserves a translation "which should endeavor to focus the reader's attention exclusively, or as nearly as the English language will permit, upon the meaning of the text." A prose version, he suggests, could combine fidelity to the sense with freedom of style while a verse translation is likely to misrepresent "the thought of the original" with the result that "in crucial passages . . . an actual falsification of the poet's intent" may occur. [44]

So far we have spoken only of the rendering of poetry into another language. What about prose literature? Are there no problems involved in the transmission of prose works? George Bull, translator of Benvenuto Cellini's *Autobiography*, speaks of "the extravagance of the original and its frequent changes in tempo and emphasis" and quotes finally the statement by Cellini's French translator, Eugene Plon, who spoke of Cellini's language as "the dialect of the Florentine people, so pure, so original, and so witty, that it defies translation." [45] Rex Warner finds Thucydides' *The Peloponnesian War* difficult—and at the same time pleasurable—to translate into English because of his "style which, in its sudden illuminations and in its abrupt strength, can never, I think, be reproduced in English." [46] Warner thinks that Plato would be easier to translate. H. D. P. Lee, however, in translating Plato's *Republic* faces the problem of "preserving the conversational atmosphere of the original

dialogue" particularly in the very long passages. He encounters difficulties in translating Plato's terminology. Since
a literal translation of moral and abstract terms might well be
misleading or at least clumsy, he feels that a translator
"must go behind what Plato said and discover what he
means" and then express the thought as it "would be expressed today." [47]

Samuel Putnam saw two basic problems facing the translator of *Don Quixote:* "that of attaining a style which, like
the original, shall be free of affectation—colloquial and
modern without being flagrantly 'modernized'; and that of
combining textual and linguistic fidelity with a readable
prose." He maintains that an antiquated style and vocabulary
should be avoided in a modern translation of Cervantes just
as much as "any modernism that would be out of place and
savor of flippancy." And while he, in his translation of
Rabelais, intends to give "as faithful as possible a presentation of Rabelais' writings," he objects, here also, to "an un-
duly modernized version." He feels present-day slang
expressions and colloquialisms would be out of keeping with
the spirit of the work and would too quickly make the
translation obsolete; at the same time, he rejects "unneces-
sary archaisms employed merely for the sake of effect." [48]
John Butt, the translator of *Candide,* holds "the difference of
economy and rhythm between French and English" responsible for some of the difficulties in translating. He finds
that Voltaire's style needs to be expanded here and there so
that it may not "offend an English ear by its very baldness"
and continues: "Voltaire's economy in ligatures has an important effect on his rhythm. It allows him to vary the number
of clauses and sentences which could be linked together in a
rhythmical period. A literal rendering would sound harsh,
and a translator must therefore abandon something of Vol-

taire's rhythm in the effort to make him speak modern English." [49]

Even a modern prose writer such as Balzac poses certain difficulties because, as his translator Marion Ayton Crawford points out, his long sentences are so "packed with meaning, crammed with metaphor and allusion" that they "require to be disentangled and unwound into even longer English sentences." Thus the conclusion is drawn that "a word for word translation of Balzac would be even more incomprehensible than *most* word for word translations" of other writers. [50]

What then is the primary intent of present-day English and American translators? It is, it seems to me, to present to their readers modern versions of the world classics, modern simply meaning easily readable and intelligible to the English or American reader. As J. M. Cohen puts it, the translator's task lies in "reconciling faithfulness to Cervantes with the writing of contemporary English." [51] Ciardi wants to write "idiomatic English." [52] Thomas G. Bergin's aim is "readability." [53] Rieu intends "to present the modern reader with a rendering of the *Odyssey* which he may understand with ease and read with appreciation." And as he explains in another passage, when he speaks of modern readers, he thinks primarily of "those who are unfamiliar with the Greek world." [54] Michael Grant, in his preface to the translation of *The Annals of Imperial Rome*, thinks the first task of the translator is to render the meaning of a literary text, "to convey, as faithfully as possible, the essential thought and significance of what Tacitus wrote." Then he adds that a translator should also attempt to reproduce "expression"— in the case of Tacitus to bring out the conciseness of his style —but that it is most important that the translation be readable. He sees no point in imitating Tacitus' style, if it should result in an "unreadable translation." [55]

Una Ellis-Fermer writes in the introduction to the translation of three Ibsen plays that her "volume attempts the impossible task of pretending that Ibsen wrote his plays in the English of 1950." [56] And L. W. Tancock, who espouses "the principle of fidelity to the *tone* of the original," goes one step further when he states that it is "the duty of a translator to try to reproduce on English readers the effect which the original had upon its readers when it was published." [57] Since it is in some cases very difficult to ascertain what the effect of a poem has been on its readers, this is hardly a criterion that can seriously be considered. Nevertheless it seems clear that what is meant is simply that the translated work should stand as a modern work, with modern vocabulary and word order, in the idiom of our time, and should *not* read like a translation.

If this survey of contemporary opinions held by the best practitioners seems confusing and often contradictory, it only mirrors the true state of affairs. Still, it is not quite the final word on our subject. The theory of translation seems to have come of age in the very last few years. Three books may be singled out as representative: Edmond Cary's *La Traduction dans le monde moderne* appeared in Switzerland in 1956; Theodore Savory's *The Art of Translation* was published in London in 1957; and a symposium *On Translation* was edited by R. A. Brower and published by the Harvard University Press in 1959. The French author starts out with the sentence "Il n'existe pas d'ouvrage d'ensemble consacré à la traduction." Fortunately, this is the only completely erroneous statement in an otherwise very well documented and most practical volume, which gives much attention to nonliterary fields of translation, as it behooves the Ecole d'Interprètes of Geneva. In his preface, the English author warns that "the student of the process of translation is unlikely to come upon a couple of dozen . . . appraisals of the art of the translator" and eventually lists a bibliography of three dozen such treatises. But the American symposium concludes with "A Critical Bibliography of Works on Translation" (by B. Q. Morgan) which quotes from some two hundred items and is in itself the most comprehensive historical treatise on translation.

In Savory's book one finds an altogether reasonable and scholarly exposition of especially the literary problems involved. Of particular interest is the page (49) where the author sets forth six instructions and their *opposites*, "because the only people qualified to formulate them have never agreed among themselves." Two of the contrasting points read as follows: "A translation should read like an original work." "A translation should read like a translation." "A translation of verse should be in prose." "A translation of verse should be in verse." Mr. Savory is extremely liberal in allowing for *all* the contradictions and justifying them all by the needs of different kinds of readers.

This rather unprincipled principle, namely that a good translation is the one which the contemporary reader expects and accepts, is also shared by the majority of contributors to the American symposium. It is not an evasion. It is the necessary latitude within a field which the good translators have created for themselves. Moreover, it is only the profession as a whole which seems to enjoy it, not the individual translator. From all the heated controversies of past and present the fact emerges that the individual translator can translate one work only in one way, his best way, and that his best way is always a tension between the precise idiom of the original and the very personal idiom of the translator. The loving rivalry between the original and the new idiom can never be eliminated, nor can the tension between imitation and reproduction, between closeness and naturalness, between form and meaning, between poetry and prose. These things represent divergent ideals, but in translation they have to be reconciled, for translation is a matter of compromise.

It is not true, however, that the happy medium is the one and only solution. Even in this field one-sided ideals have produced fine results, although it has generally been true that the freest translations have won the widest popularity, while the closest are appreciated most by those who are able to go to the originals themselves. Moreover, the present trend towards the naturalized and the vernacular is not necessarily a perennial one. The most "contemporary" versions may well age the quickest. In general, translations date more quickly than their original. But apart from this, the natural revolution of taste should cause a future generation to prefer translations that transmit a maximum of the historic, or the exotic, to relish the strange originalness (Ezra Pound excels in this type) rather than the slick naturalization.

The last few years have seen the study of translation become aware of its historical antecedents, but also of the complexity of its theories. Perhaps Dryden would even today be right to complain "that there is so little Praise and so small Encouragement for so considerable a part of Learning." But the theoretical attention has certainly increased enormously, in quantity, and this development is by no means confined to the West.[58] As with everything in the field of the arts, there is no straight progress in quality. It would take a good deal of complacency to proclaim that our age is producing the best translations. It would hardly be more safe to maintain that it has reached new clarity or new validity in formulating its theories. The impression is rather that of a greater diversity and greater tolerance of viewpoints. Thus it is very fitting that the last word on the subject so far should be, not the opinion of one authority, but a symposium of twenty different voices and viewpoints.

In conclusion, let us ask if there is any justification for calling translating an art. It is clear that a translator must bring sympathy and understanding to the work he is to translate. He must be the original author's most intimate, most exact, in short, his best reader. But he must do more than read. He must attempt to see what the author saw, to hear what he heard, to dig into his own life in order to experience anew what the author experienced. No nation sees even a simple incident in the same way as another and thus a translator has to express a phrase, an event, a situation as it should be said in his own language. At times he may be able to stay close to the foreign word, but what is more important is that he be able to imagine the situation—that he understand what a German translator has called the "lebendige Zusammenhang." [59] The translator as well as the writer must be sensitive to the mythological, historical, and social traditions reflected in a language and must use words to convey not only sounds but also rhythm, gesture, expression, melody, color, and association.

However, it should be pointed out that translating is neither a creative art nor an imitative art, but stands somewhere between the two. It is not creative because it does not follow the inspirations of the translator, but rather undertakes to create in the manner of another that which is already created. But neither is it an imitative art, for it must not only convey the idea of the work translated, but must also transform it. [60] The translator must be creative, a "maker"; at the same time, he must submit to the reality of the writer whom he is translating. Thus translating is a matter of continuous subconscious association with the original, a matter of meditation. Two spheres of languages move closer together through the medium of the translator to fuse at the moment of the contact into a new form, a new *Gestalt*. Here we recognize signs of an artistic process. The fact that the perfect fusion is not always reached should not prevent us from calling translating an art. After all, in the other arts there are amateurs, craftsmen, and masters, too.

André Gide has expressed the point of view that every creative writer owes it to his country to translate at least one foreign work, to which his talent and his temperament are particularly suited, and thus to enrich his own literature.[61] Let us hope that our present writers will feel obligated to follow this dictum. Only then will the position of the translator become more respected, will the quality of translations improve, and we will be less hesitant to speak of translating as an art.

5

Literature and Psychology

Leon Edel

LITERATURE and psychology—and in particular psychoanalysis—have come to recognize in our century that they stand upon common ground. Both are concerned with human motivations and behavior and with man's capacity to create and use symbols. In this process, both have become involved in the study of the subjective side of man. With the incorporation of psychoanalysis into psychology, that is the study of the unconscious from the symbols it projects, literature has found itself calling increasingly upon the knowledge derived from Sigmund Freud's explorations of the psyche at the turn of the century. Any examination of literature and psychology must concern itself alike with the direct fertilization of imaginative writing by psychoanalysis and the use which literary criticism and biography have made of the psychological and psychoanalytical tools.

Man's observation of his inner self and his emotions is as old as Aristotle. But it was not until the Romantic Movement that creative artists showed a deeper awareness of the existence of an unconscious dream-making faculty in the poet. Rousseau, in seeking to recover and examine his early ex-

LEON EDEL, biographer and critic, Professor of English at New York University, has devoted much attention to inter-disciplinary study of literature and psychology. In addition to biographies of Henry James and Willa Cather, he is author of *The Modern Psychological Novel* and *Literary Biography*. He has been visiting professor at Harvard, Princeton, Indiana and Hawaii.

perience; Goethe in his belief that fiction must occupy itself
with the inner thoughts of man; Coleridge, in perceiving
man's involuntary "flights of lawless speculation"—that is
day-dream as well as night-dream—and his "modes of in-
most being"—all these writers found themselves by this
process engaged in psychological exploration. German romantic critics, such as Friedrich Schlegel or Jean Paul, in
searching for the laws of man's nature which result in the
writing of poetry, were pursuing, on a critical level, similar
ends. Balzac, in his introduction to the *Comédie Humaine,*
recognized that there existed "phenomena of brain and
nerves which prove the existence of an undiscovered world of
psychology," and in this country Hawthorne spoke of the
"topsy-turvy commonwealth of sleep." The American novelist expressed the belief that modern psychology would reduce the dream worlds to a system "instead of rejecting them
as altogether fabulous." During the nineteenth century the
works of Dostoevsky, Strindberg, Ibsen and Henry James,
showed a profound awareness of unconscious motivation in
human beings akin to the insights of Coleridge. But it was not
until 1900, with the publication of Sigmund Freud's *The
Interpretation of Dreams,* that students of literature began to
recognize the similarity between the poet's dream-work and
his actual creativity.

In subsequent years, Freud's writings on certain nonliterary problems served to illuminate such questions as wit
and its relation to the Unconscious, the concept of wish-ful-
filment, the problems of neurosis and the associative character of symbols—all applicable to literary study. Even
more important for literary criticism and biography were his
actual writings on the nature of art and the artist (collected in
1924 under the title *Psychoanalytische Studien an Werken
der Dichtung und Kunst*). These included his psychoanalytic

study of a minor novel by Wilhelm Jensen, *Gradiva*, his essay on Leonardo da Vinci, with its profound observations on biographical speculation and the relation of a biographer to his subject, and his study "Dostoevsky and Parricide." Freud held that art represents an attempt to gratify certain wishes in the artist, and that the audience finds similar gratification in what the artist has created, thus extending our understanding of what Aristotle had explained as katharsis. Freud conceived of art as "an intermediate territory between the wish-denying reality and the wish-fulfilling world of fantasy." He held that the content of an artist's work, like the manifest content of a dream, may reveal what were the unconscious wishes of the creator. However, he recognized always that psychoanalysis cannot explain the genesis of the artistic talent, and that there were mysteries of the creative intelligence and imagination concerning which psychoanalysis could at best only speculate without hope of scientific answer.

As early as 1910 Wilhelm Stekel in *Dichtung und Neurose* began the application of Freud's ideas to the study of artistic creativity. In the ensuing years a whole library of books was written concerning the specific relations between literature and psychoanalysis. Notable exponents of "applied psychoanalysis" have been C. G. Jung, Otto Rank, Ernest Jones, Hanns Sachs, Oskar Pfister, Ernst Kris, Franz Alexander and Erich Fromm, while in the camp of literature are to be found such diverse figures as Louis Cazamian, Charles Badouin, Gaston Bachelard, Robert Graves, Edmund Wilson, Lionel Trilling, Maud Bodkin and others.

Parallel to the early Freudian explorations of the inner consciousness of man in this century we find analogous explorations undertaken, wholly on the ground of literature, by the so-called "stream of consciousness" or "internal

monologue" writers—certain novelists in various countries
who tried to tell their stories "from the inside" by lodging the
reader within the consciousness of the character. The reader
was thus made a direct participant in the mental and sensory
experience of the fictitious personality.

This represented, in the novel, an extraordinary revolution
in narrative technique: Time becomes vertical instead of
being horizontal, since the reader is always experiencing the
thoughts of the character at the very moment of experience,
that is in present time—a situation not unlike the experience
of the spectator at the cinema. The material, moreover, is
presented without the order or chronology of the conventional novel, the data being given in the disordered state in
which they come into consciousness through the operation of
sensory stimuli, memory, association. The result, in terms of
narration, was the removal of the omniscient author from the
actual work. The reader is required to deduce the story and
the characters from the mental and emotional data furnished,
without the author's seeming directly to assist in the progress
of the story. The novel of subjectivity stemmed in part from
the writings of Henri Bergson in the late nineteenth century
and notably his exploration of human time (as distinct from
mechanical time) and the processes of memory. In the
United States, William James's *Principles of Psychology*
offered certain illuminating pages on the psychology of
thought and it was he who first employed the metaphor
"stream of consciousness." While these philosophical and
psychological observations and theories were being advanced, the French and German symbolists, stimulated by
the use of the thematic material in the Wagnerian operas,
had attempted to use language associatively and evocatively
in order to give verbal representation of what might be
termed the thematic material of the consciousness, including

the operation of the senses. This resulted in many literary attempts to capture momentary experience and to frame and preserve these moments in language. The difference between "stream of consciousness" or "internal monologue" and the soliloquies of the classic dramas was that the conventional monologue was wholly intellectual and given in a logical and ordered sequence, whereas the Symbolists and their successors sought to convey the actual flow of experience in the human consciousness, and to create the illusion of thought and the impingement of external stimuli upon the inner man —in its unsorted condition: the flotsam and jetsam as it might be found in the stream of consciousness.

The earliest attempt to tell a story wholly "from within" is now regarded to have been made by Édouard Dujardin in his 1888 experiment, *Les lauriers sont coupés,* a work which he said was inspired by Richard Wagner's use of the leitmotiv in his music. So, in thought, he explained, themes occur and recur and these can be set down in a language designed to capture the innermost thoughts, those which he believed to be closest to the unconscious. In his seminal essay on the art of fiction (1884), Henry James echoed the ideas of Goethe and urged upon novelists the recreation of the "atmosphere of the mind." In this he pointed the way to his own novels written just after the turn of the century in which he foreshadowed the modern novel of subjectivity by his unremitting efforts to maintain a "point of view" and an "angle of vision"—committing the reader to an interior view of experience and the solipsistic universe of the individual character. However, he did not actually seek to recreate the illusion of a flow of thought or of a consciousness upon which perceptual experience is impinging.

In England, on the eve of the First World War, Dorothy M. Richardson began writing a long subjective novel which she entitled *Pilgrimage.* She arranged it in twelve parts, each published separately between 1915 and 1938, and then brought out the entire work in four volumes. In this long novel the reader, if he can translate himself into the mind of the protagonist, is posted wholly in the consciousness of a woman named Miriam Henderson whose pilgrimage, mental and emotional, takes her from her adolescence to her middle years. Miss Richardson's effort, less searching and imaginative, yet of unfailing realism, paralleled that of Marcel Proust in France. His novel, however, was not so much stream of consciousness or internal monologue as a continual probing of memory and association and their relation to human time—carried out by a first-person narrator.

The fountainhead of the subjective movement in fiction was James Joyce, the Irish novelist, whose *A Portrait of the Artist as a Young Man* projected the developing mind and consciousness of the artist on five distinct levels: sensation, emotion, physical passion, religious passion and finally the level of intellectual awareness. Told with a remarkable symbolic use of language, this novel represented a turning point in modern English fiction. It was followed by *Ulysses* in 1922 in which Joyce's verbal mastery enabled him to create a series of streams of consciousness of certain individuals in Dublin during a single day. At the same time he used the Odyssey myth to represent modern man's voyage and adventures during the one day in the one city. The book had a profound influence upon such writers as Virginia Woolf and William Faulkner during the late 1920's. Joyce's final work, *Finnegans Wake* in 1939, derived from the Jungian hypothesis of racial memory and the "collective unconscious." It is an attempt to suggest the cyclical nature of history, building upon the postulates of Giambattista Vico, and the role of myth and symbol as an ever-recurring and repetitive phenomenon in human life. *Finnegans Wake* is the only work of fiction—and it might be argued whether it can actually be called a novel—in the whole of literature in which its four principal characters, H. C. Earwicker (Here Comes Everybody), his wife and two children, are asleep from beginning to end. Around their sleeping figures is the swirl of all time and all history; the Liffey river at their doorstep is in reality all rivers, and they are also Adam and Eve and Cain and Abel, the family eternal. In this way James Joyce produced a book which is a kind of composite of all time and that portion of eternity in which thinking man, historically aware, functions. By that token the book is poem-epic-drama-novel rolled into one, like its characters and the time-stuff of its texture.

While the novel of the "inner vision" achieved its particular technical development at the hands of Joyce, analogous experiments had been carried out in other literatures. In Vienna, Arthur Schnitzler had experimented with a modified internal monologue and in his *Fraulein Else*, both in its technique and the substance of the story, unravels a psychotic episode through the inner vision of the person who suffers it. Alfred Döblin, in *Alexanderplatz*, was the chief exponent in Germany of the Joycean experiments; and imitators have been legion during the succeeding decades.

This "inward turning" in literature, in its first phase, must be recognized as having occurred largely without the benefit of psychoanalysis. It paralleled rather than derived from the Freudian development and influence. But there came a moment after the First World War when literature and psychology increasingly erased the boundaries between them, and psychoanalysis began directly to fertilize imaginative writing. Thus Italo Svevo's *La Coscienza di Zeno* written in Trieste (Svevo was a personal friend of James

Joyce) is an account of a psychoanalysis undergone by the protagonist. There are signs in the novels of William Faulkner of his direct exposure to certain psychological ideas. In *Light in August,* we have what might be considered a textbook account of the protagonist's "conditioning"—the way in which Joe Christmas, whipped every hour on the hour because he would not learn his catechism, learns how to adapt himself to cruelty but not to kindness. During the 1920's one of the most successful plays produced in New York was *Strange Interlude* in which the characters, through continual soliloquizing, reveal to us their inner thoughts. O'Neill followed this with a distinctly Freudian play, *Mourning Becomes Electra,* which explored Oedipal problems in a New England family, and which showed also, as much of O'Neill's work did, exposure to the psychological plays of a pre-Freudian dramatist, August Strindberg.

More directly, the work of Thomas Mann derived much from Freud. The German master acknowledged his debt in an essay "Freud and the Future" published in 1936 in which he discussed certain of the ideas and themes used by him in the Joseph novels which stemmed from the psychoanalytic movement. But where Mann used Freud as illumination of the romantic self-discovery of man, Franz Kafka found in him the means of constructing eerie writings which contain some of the macabre qualities of a Poe and the grotesqueries of a Gogol. Kafka hit upon the idea of treating subjective material as if it were wholly objective: his narratives of dream states are told as if the dream had actually occurred in reality. The result is the creation of an often terrible sense of day-nightmare, rendered acutely vivid by the matter-of-fact method of narration.

It would be a large undertaking to chronicle the full impact of the psychoanalytic movement upon contemporary literature. Few writers of any eminence have escaped being exposed directly or indirectly to some of its ideas. Certain writers have actually had the experience of analysis; most, however, have imbibed psychoanalytic ideas by reading the leading theorists and the numerous commentaries and popularizations.

Psychoanalysis has contributed important aids to three facets of literary study: 1] to criticism itself, 2] to the study of the creative process in literature, and 3] to the writing of biography. In addition it is helping to illuminate a tangential literary problem which belongs essentially to the field of aesthetics: the relation of the reader to the work.

1] *Psychology and criticism.* Two notable approaches exist in literary criticism, and both are used a great deal today in exegesis of a given text, a] the study of psychological elements within the work itself, without relating these in any way to the origin or history of the work; b] the study of possible myth and archetypal patterns in the work.

A] A large part of Ernest Jones's essay on *Oedipus and Hamlet* consists of an examination of the motivation and behavior of the characters in Shakespeare's play, a close scrutiny of all of Hamlet's soliloquies for evidence of what they disclose about his inner life, a study of his attitudes toward the significant persons in his family setting—his mother and stepfather—and in general an attempt to speculate more closely than ever before, in the light of psychoanalysis, on what in other times was discussed as the classic question of Hamlet's sanity. Jones sees no madness in the Prince of Denmark's behavior, but studies the ambiguities within his constituted personality in the light of Freud's hypothesis of the Oedipus complex. Building upon a hint from Freud, Jones presumes Hamlet's tergiversation to spring from his parricidal fantasies. Since, in his unconscious, he has sought to obliterate his father—as the Oedipal complex posits—he identifies himself (again unconsciously) with his uncle who has actually murdered his father and married his mother. The uncle therefore is, in his fantasy, the prototype of Hamlet, and represents for him the embodiment of his own unconscious guilt over fantasied incest and obliteration of the father. But to kill the uncle, Jones argues, would thus be for Hamlet the equivalent of killing himself, and for this reason Hamlet hesitates. His conflict does not permit him to act.

B] Perhaps the most important critic to consider the Jungian theory of myth and archetype has been Maud Bodkin and her book, *Archetypal Patterns in Poetry,* has had a profound influence since its publication in 1934. Her hypothesis is that archetypal patterns or images are "present within the experience communicated through poetry, and may be discovered there by reflective analysis." She likens these patterns to the culture patterns studied by anthropologists. The patterns, she observes, may be "described as organizations of emotional tendencies, determined partly through the distinctive experience of the race or community within whose history the theme has arisen." Among the archetypes or patterns she studies are the "Paradise-Hades or Rebirth" archetype; or the archetypes of devil, hero, god; or the various forms which the image of woman has taken in folklore and literature. While Miss Bodkin took her point of departure from Jung she has also derived from Sir James Frazer's *The Golden Bough* and various other studies in mythology. Her work illuminates the relation between many myths and poetry as well as seeking to show a relation between patterns of religion and "poetic faith." The criticism of her work, and of those who have followed her, has been that in seeking underlying myths and archetypes within a given literary work, the study of the individual qualities of that work is obscured in favor of universal patterns. The critical observation and exegesis become so general, it is argued, as to be virtually without meaning since it is applicable to so many other works as well. The individual writer, in such a process, is submerged by the critic in his race and in endless time.

Directing his attention to universal symbols rather than archetypal forms, a French physicist-philosopher, Gaston Bachelard, has in recent years produced a series of studies on what he calls *l'imagination matérielle:* the thematic use made by poets and novelists of air, water, fire, earth. His *Psychanalyse du feu* was written as early as 1937 and was followed by *L'eau et les rêves* (1942), *L'air et les songes* (1943), and *La terre et les rêveries du repos* (1948). These also, to a degree, take their inspiration in Jungian thought. They constitute a valuable contribution to the literature of dream symbolism as manifested in works of the imagination.

2] *Psychology and the creative process.* Much literary scholarship in the pre-Freudian period was devoted to tracking down the sources, both biographical and literary, of a given work. A vast literature exists in which the books read by certain writers and the events of their lives have been explored to demonstrate how these influenced the works created. Since the advent of psychoanalysis, criticism has turned from such primitive attempts to penetrate the artistic consciousness, and has sought a more systematic study of the imaginative process, that is the nature of the artist's fantasies and the underlying patterns these take in his work, whether poetry, drama or prose. It is now increasingly recognized that most creative writers do not live in a library; if they are bookish men, the books they read serve largely as stimulus to their imaginative faculty—that it is this faculty and not the food it feeds upon which is all-important. If literary sources are discovered today, and the methods of psychoanalysis are applied to them, the scholar seeks to determine how these sources melted together in the creative consciousness to produce the new work of art. The psychoanalytic approach searches out why a given writer attaches himself to certain sources rather than to others. The study of the creative process inevitably involves looking into biographical material; but it involves certain larger questions which have preoccupied many literary critics as well as psychoanalytical theorists. Thus certain literary critics have pointed out that when psychoanalysts study literary works and their creators they nearly always end up with a description of the neurotic character of the artist. They make art seem the product of certain infantilisms lingering in the artist's consciousness.

There exists for instance a study of Robert Louis Stevenson which shows the "feeding problems" of his infancy and which tries to prove from this his attachment to his mother, the subsequent difficulties apparent in his relations with women as well as the possible psychogenic origin of his tuberculosis, and the extraordinary "orality" from which he suffered. From this is deduced the hypothesis that Stevenson wrote stories reflecting the imagination of an arrested adolescent. But all this, it can be argued, tends to reduce Stevenson to a diagnosis more suited for the clinic than for literary criticism. The diagnosis may be completely accurate in terms of psychoanalysis, but it is wholly "reductive" in character where the study of the literary personality is involved: The emphasis would seem to be misplaced from the mystery and beauty of creation—from such remarkable fantasies as *Dr. Jekyll and Mr. Hyde* and *Treasure Island* —to matters wholly clinical.

It is to this type of study that Lionel Trilling alludes in his

essay on "Art and Neurosis" in which he reaches the conclusion that the artist "whatever elements of neurosis he has
in common with his fellow-mortals" is nevertheless healthy
"by any conceivable definition of health," in that he is given
the power to plan, to work and to bring his work to a conclusion. Applied to the study of the creative process in literature, psychoanalysis can best be employed in showing precisely, as Charles Lamb put it in an essay on the sanity of
genius, that "the true poet dreams being awake. He is not
possessed by his subject but has dominion over it." The
psychoanalytic critic might be inclined to modify this to the
statement that the artist is usually possessed by his subject
but is capable of gaining possession over it.

Certain psychoanalysts, in developing their studies of ego
psychology—notably Ernst Kris—have helped to modify
in recent years the trend toward "reductive" analysis. While
the revelation of unconscious processes in art has largely
interested the psychoanalysts who have used "applied psychoanalysis" to diagnose the personality of the artist, most
literary critics and biographers who have used it have been
concerned with the actual fabric of the artist's creation, the
means by which his verbal imagination gives form and structure to his materials.

3] *Psychology and Biography.* The tendencies discussed
above under the heading of "creative process" apply inevitably in the writing of biographies of men who were themselves writers. There have been biographies of writers by
professional psychoanalysts, such as Marie Bonaparte's
Edgar Poe or Phyllis Greenacre's study of Swift, which are
more clinical than literary studies, preoccupied with deducing
the workings of the unconscious from the writings and the
biographical evidence. Literary biographers have tended,
when using psychoanalytical theories, to concern themselves

with the gaining of certain insights capable of being assimilated within their own rather than the psychoanalytic discipline. Thus the biographer may learn from a slip of the pen in a manuscript or letter much about the subject under study; but where the psychoanalytically trained writer would use the slip as guide to the unconscious, the literary biographer would be inclined to apply this particular slip to the revelation of verifiable facts. The use of psychoanalytic concepts in biography can enable the biographer to escape from the web of his subject's rationalizations; and it can help to explain his predilection for certain subjects and themes. The psychologically-oriented biographer also can catch the small and seemingly insignificant detail, which in the past would have been discarded, and use it to illuminate personality. Above all, such a biographer differs from his predecessors by grasping the contradictions and ambiguities within the subject where the old-time biographer sought to efface contradiction and to make his figure more consistent—that is less ambivalent—then people really are. Betty Miller's portrait of Robert Browning or this writer's life of Henry James exemplify the use of psychoanalytical tools so employed as to submerge the clinical aspect and keep in the forefront the living personality in terms of common literary reference. An unique example of psychoanalytical biography —unique because its subject was the founder of psychoanalysis and because it was written by his co-worker—is Ernest Jones's biography of Sigmund Freud. This is remarkable both as biography and as a lucid explanation of Freud's inner life and its relation to the genesis and history of the psychoanalytic movement. But it suffers, in part, from being written in the language of the profession.

A notable early venture into psychoanalytic biography of great breadth and imaginative scope was the series of portraits which Stefan Zweig projected as *Die Baumeister der Welt, Versuch einer Typologie des Geistes.* Zweig grouped the types he chose in four volumes: "master builders" such as Balzac, Dickens, Dostoevsky; the demoniacal genius represented by Hölderlin, Kleist and Nietzsche, figures exalted to creation but driven to self-destruction; adepts at self-portraiture, Casanova, Stendhal, and Tolstoy; and finally mental healers such as Mesmer, Mary Baker Eddy, and Freud. These are not always successful in their analysis, and are outdated in terms of psychoanalytic thinking of recent years; but the literary gift possessed by Zweig gives the portraits vividness nevertheless, and they will be read as pioneering attempts to bring to biography the illumination of psychoanalysis.

The reader and the work. — Here psychology and criticism come together on ground which belongs to the study of aesthetics. The question of reader and work goes back to the beginnings of literature. Even in Homer may be discerned the devices by which the poet sought to keep his listeners attentive and engaged. In modern times we can find in Proust a close and analytical discussion of how a reader becomes subjectively involved in the novel he is reading and his process of identification with certain characters and scenes in the story. In his ghostly tale, "The Turn of the Screw," Henry James deliberately created certain ambiguities which, he explained, were so many blanks which the reader's imagination would fill in. Each reader thus brings to the story's ambiguities his own particular and private data. In clinical psychology valuable experiments have been carried out from which the literary critic may derive considerable guidance: These involve using "unstructured" material, such as the ink blots of the Rorschach test, or highly structured materials such as works of art, in order to study the effect of their stimulus upon the viewer—as related to the viewer's specific needs and his character structure.

Notable critical studies have been the works of I. A. Richards and also of the semanticists, disciples of Alfred Korzybski. Richards, in collaboration with C. K. Ogden, published as early as 1923 *The Meaning of Meaning,* a study of language designed to link criticism more closely to verbal meaning. In *The Principles of Literary Criticism* (1924) and *Science and Poetry* (1926) Richards developed certain ideas which have had a profound effect on contemporary criticism in the Anglo-American world. He focused his search upon the nature and value of poetry, investigating what occurs within a poem and the way in which a reader may be affected by it. His approach was perforce on the ground of psychology, and his method was descriptive. Richards believed that readers can be trained to read properly and when trained can then appreciate works otherwise generally incommunicable or "difficult." This line of reasoning, pursued by other critics, has led to widespread insistence, particularly in America, upon the importance of explication of text as the primary function of the critical act. It has led, also, to a great deal of "fantasy-reading" of texts.

In general it may be said that while there is a great—and ever-growing—awareness of the illumination offered by psychoanalysis in studying human behavior and the mental processes, the relations between this discipline and the disciplines of literary study are still blurred and uncharted. There is a natural resistance among men of letters, and the Academies, to "psychologizing," a strong feeling that human perception into the psyche, already so profound in the works of the master writers, requires no further aid, especially of scientifically-oriented psychological exploration. It is further argued that the divergences among the psychoanalytic schools in themselves are sufficiently contradictory to call for great caution—and may render ambiguous and highly arbitrary the uses to which a given theory is put in literature.

The use of symbolism by the Freudians in a fixed and rigid manner has been much criticized, most students of literature knowing that while symbols are often universal they have particular associative meanings for every individual. Otto Rank's theory of anxiety as resultant of the birth trauma offers little to literary study, and the "inferiority complex" school of Alfred Adler has much more to do with therapeutic problems than with offering any particular ground of interest for the literary scholar, save in the valuable light Adler cast on the human struggle for power. The Jungians have supplied, as indicated above, much material for literary study because of their orientation toward religion and mysticism and their belief in the "collective unconscious," which they hold contains man's "racial memories." Of greater significance, in the view of some, has been the American school of Harry Stack Sullivan which sees the individual as a product of "interpersonal relations" and argues that the pattern of a child's early and not specifically sexual relationship with significant figures plays a major role in the individual's personality formation. Because the novel deals in great measure with interpersonal relations, this school has much to offer to the literary student. Also valuable have been some of the approaches of Karen Horney and Eric Fromm, who draw upon sociological and anthropological thought in formulating their theories. They emphasize the immediate— and the cultural—problems in the life of an individual rather than the biological instinctual emphasis of Freud.

There is little doubt that much of the literary use of psychoanalysis has been to date rather crude and primitive, tending to simplify material highly complex and to make stereotypes of creative personality. It has tended to imitate psycho-analytic use of literary material rather that adapting psycho-analytic insights and methods to literary usage. The cross-fertilization of the disciplines has been inevitably richest in the case of those writers who have a thorough grounding in both disciplines—and largely in the fields of criticism and biography. There is little evidence today that imaginative writers, relying upon their own observation and feeling, have been able to integrate in a satisfactory fashion the theoretical concepts of psychoanalysis. Where this has been done, the results have been mechanical, unless they have been used by creative writers not so much for the psychoanalytic process it-self as for certain broad insights, as T. S. Eliot has done in his poems and plays. The number of literary critics and biographers thoroughly familiar with psychoanalysis is small; and the result is that only a few works, among the many published, can be said to have anything more than an ephemeral and most often a superficial value. The literary scholar who "gets up" his psychoanalytic knowledge from books will have highly theoretical concepts and perhaps an *intellectual* grasp of the psychoanalytic tool, but is not likely to understand sufficiently well—as Freud warned—the role of the unconscious, and in particular its relation to that of the emotions. The difference might be described as analogous to the difference between the novels of a writer like André Gide, which are all intelligence and rationality, and the work of Proust, which is all association and emotion.

One distinct advantage which those critics and biographers who have first hand experience of the psychoanalytic process enjoy is that they are less likely to project ideas and fan-tasies from their own psyche into the work or the life they are writing. In this respect they have an attitude of self-observation similar to that which the psychoanalyst himself must have in order to deal objectively with his patients.

In sum, psychology has already shown that in literature it can find many fertile examples of the creative imagination which illustrates the psychology of thought and the workings of the unconscious. Literature on its side is still absorbing and learning to use the psychological tool and in particular the concepts of psychoanalysis. The problem for literature has been in part one of terminology, the technical terms of psychoanalysis being ill-adapted to the needs of literary criticism. The most successful users of psychoanalysis in the study of literature have been those biographers and critics who have found ways of *translating* the specialized terms into the more familiar vocabulary of their own discipline.

What may be expected in the future will be a further clarification of the respective roles of the two disciplines and a better definition of the uses to which psychoanalysis may be put in literature. As the very word "analysis" suggests, it will be most useful on the critical-analytic level. And it will quite likely have its greatest usefulness in the continued study of the creative process and therefore in the writing of biography: that is, in that part of literary study which relates the work to the man and treats the work as a part of the creating mind which put it forth into the world.

BIBLIOGRAPHICAL NOTE

For applications of psychoanalysis to literature see the studies in applied psychoanalysis to be found in the works of Sigmund Freud, C. G. Jung, Ernest Jones and other leading explorers of the psyche. The various journals of the psychoanalytic movement, in different countries, yield a wide range of articles dealing with literature. Basic to the study of literature and psy-

chology are Freud's books on the interpretation of dreams and
his study of wit and its relation to the unconscious. Other works
to consult are Wilhelm Stekel's *Dichtung und Neurose* (Wiesba-
den, 1909) and Otto Rank's *Das Inzest-Motiv in Dichtung und
Sage* (Leipzig, 1926) and *Art and the Artist* (New York, 1932);
I. D. Suttie, *The Origins of Love and Hate* (London, 1935);
W. Muschg, *Psychoanalyse und Literaturwissenschaft* (Berlin,
1930); F. L. Sack, *Die Psychoanalyse im modernen englishen
Roman* (Zürich, 1930); Louis Cazamian, *Études de Psychologie
Littéraire* (Paris, 1913); and Charles Baudouin, *Psychoanalysis
and Aesthetics* (New York, 1924).

In more recent years some of the significant works have
been Edmund Wilson's *The Wound and the Bow* (Boston,
1941); Mario Praz, *The Romantic Agony* (London, 1933);
W. H. Auden, *The Enchafèd Flood* (New York, 1950); Ernst
Kris, *Psychoanalytical Explorations in Art* (New York, 1952);
Lionel Trilling, *Freud and the Crisis of Our Culture* (Boston,
1955); Joseph Campbell, *The Hero with the Thousand Faces*
(New York, 1949); Herbert Marcuse, *Eros and Civilization*
(Boston, 1955); Leon Edel, *The Modern Psychological Novel*
(New York, 1955) and *Literary Biography* (London, 1957);
Louis Fraiberg, *Psychoanalysis and American Literary Criticism*
(Detroit, 1960); Frederick J. Hoffmann, *Freudianism and the
Literary Mind* (Baton Rouge, 1957); and Simon O. Lesser, *Fic-
tion and the Unconscious* (Boston, 1957). The quarterly bulletin
of the "Literature and Psychology Group" of the Modern Lan-
guage Association has for some years published a continuing
bibliography of works relating to the two disciplines.

6

Ideas and Literature

Newton P. Stallknecht

T HE late R. G. Collingwood, a philosopher whose work has proved helpful to many students of literature, once wrote

We are all, though many of us are snobbish enough to wish to deny it, in far closer sympathy with the art of the music-hall and picture-palace than with Chaucer and Cimabue, or even Shakespeare and Titian. By an effort of historical sympathy we can cast our minds back into the art of a remote past or an alien present, and enjoy the carvings of cavemen and Japanese colourprints; but the possibility of this effort is bound up with that development of historical thought which is the greatest achievement of our civilization in the last two centuries, and it is utterly impossible to people in whom this development has not taken place. The natural and primary aesthetic attitude is to enjoy contemporary art, to despise and dislike the art of the recent past, and wholly to ignore everything else.[1]

One might argue that the ultimate purpose of literary scholarship is to correct this spontaneous provincialism that is likely to obscure the horizons of the general public, of the newspaper critic, and of the creative artist himself. There

Director of the School of Letters and Professor of Philosophy at Indiana, NEWTON P. STALLKNECHT has studied the relationship of philosophy and literature both from a historical and a critical point of view. He is author of *Strange Seas of Thought: Studies in William Wordsworth's Philosophy of Man and Nature* and has also written on Wallace Stevens and George Eliott. He is past president and counselor of the Metaphysical Society of America and has contributed frequently to literary and philosophical journals.

results a study of literature freed from the tyranny of the contemporary. Such study may take many forms. The study of ideas in literature is one of these. Of course, it goes without saying that no student of ideas can justifiably ignore the contemporary scene. He will frequently return to it. The continuities, contrasts, and similarities discernible when past and present are surveyed together are inexhaustible and the one is often understood through the other.

When we assert the value of such study, we find ourselves committed to an important assumption. Most students of literature, whether they call themselves scholars or critics, are ready to argue that it is possible to understand literary works as well as to enjoy them. Many will add that we may find our enjoyment heightened by our understanding. This understanding, of course, may in its turn take many forms and some of these—especially those most interesting to the student of comparative literature—are essentially historical. But the historian of literature need not confine his attention to biography or to stylistic questions of form, "texture," or technique. He may also consider ideas. It is true that this distinction between style and idea often approaches the arbitrary since in the end we must admit that style and content frequently influence or interpenetrate one another and sometimes appear as expressions of the same insight. But, in general, we may argue that the student can direct the primary emphasis of his attention toward one or the other.

At this point a working definition of *idea* is in order, although our first definition will have to be qualified somewhat as we proceed. The term *idea* refers to our more reflective or thoughtful consciousness as opposed to the immediacies of sensuous or emotional experience. It is through such reflection that literature approaches philosophy. An idea, let us say, may be roughtly defined as a theme or topic with which our reflection may be concerned. In this essay, we are, along with most historians, interested in the more general or more inclusive ideas, that are so to speak "writ large" in history of literature where they recur continually. Outstanding among these is the idea of human nature itself, including the many definitions that have been advanced over the centuries; also secondary notions such as the perfectibility of man, the depravity of man, and the dignity of man. One might, indeed, argue that the history of ideas, in so far as it includes the literatures, must center on characterizations of human nature and that the great periods of literary achievement may be distinguished from one another by reference to the images of human nature that they succeed in fashioning.

We need not, to be sure, expect to find such ideas in every piece of literature. An idea, of the sort that we have in mind, although of necessity readily available to imagination, is more general in connotation than most poetic or literary images, especially those appearing in lyric poems that seek to capture a moment of personal experience. Thus Burns's

> *My love is like a red, red rose*

and Hopkins'

> *The thunder-purple sea-beach, pluméd purple of thunder*

although clearly intelligible in content, hardly present ideas of the sort with which we are here concerned. On the other hand, Arnold's

> *The unplumbed, salt, estranging sea,*

taken in its context, certainly does so.

Understanding a work of art involves recognition of the

ideas that it reflects or embodies. Thus the student of literature may sometimes find it helpful to classify a poem or an
essay as being in idea or in ideal content or subject matter
typical or atypical of its period. Again, he may discover embodied within its texture a theme or idea that has been
presented elsewhere and at other times in various ways. Our
understanding will very probably require both these commentaries. Very likely it will also include a recognition that
the work we are reading reflects or "belongs to" some way
of thought labelled as a "school" or an "-ism," i.e. a
complex or "syndrome" of ideas occurring together with
sufficient prominence to warrant identification. Thus ideas
like "grace," "salvation," and "providence" cluster together
in traditional Christianity. Usually the work studied offers
us a special or even an individualized rendering or treatment
of the ideas in question, so that the student finds it necessary
to distinguish carefully between the several expressions of
an "-ism" or mode of thought. Accordingly we may speak of
the Platonism peculiar to Shelley's poems or the type of
Stoicism present in Henley's "Invictus," and we may find
that describing such Platonism or such Stoicism and contrasting each with other expressions of the same attitude or
mode of thought is a difficult and challenging enterprise.
After all, Shelley is no "orthodox" or Hellenic Platonist, and
even his "romantic" Platonism can be distinguished from
that of his contemporaries. Again, Henley's attitude of de-
fiance which colors his ideal of self-mastery is far from
characteristic of a Stoic thinker like Marcus Aurelius, whose
gentle acquiescence is almost Christian, comparable to the
patience expressed in Milton's sonnet on his own blindness.

In recent years, we have come increasingly to recognize
that ideas have a history and that not the least important
chapters of this history have to do with thematic or con-

ceptual aspects of literature and the arts, although these aspects should be studied in conjunction with the history of philosophy, of religion, and of the sciences. When these fields are surveyed together, important patterns of relationship emerge indicating a vast community of reciprocal influence, a continuity of thought and expression including many traditions, primarily literary, religious, and philosophical, but frequently including contact with the fine arts and even, to some extent, with science.

Here we may observe that at least one modern philosophy of history is built on the assumption that ideas are the primary objectives of the historian's research. Let us quote once more from R. G. Collingwood: [2]

History is properly concerned with the actions of human beings . . . Regarded from the outside, an action is an event or series of events occurring in the physical world; regarded from the inside, it is the carrying into action of a certain thought . . . The historian's business is to penetrate to the inside of the actions with which he is dealing and reconstruct or rather rethink the thoughts which constituted them. It is a characteristic of thoughts that . . . in re-thinking them we come, *ipso facto*, to understand why they were thought.

Such an understanding, although it must seek to be sympathetic, is not a matter of intuition.

History has this in common with every other science: that the historian is not allowed to claim any single piece of knowledge, except where he can justify his claim by exhibiting to himself in the first place, and secondly to any one else who is both able and willing to follow his demonstration, the grounds upon which it is based. This is what was meant, above, by describing history as inferential. The knowledge in virtue of which a man is an historian is a knowledge of what the evidence at his disposal proves about certain events.

It is obvious that the historian who seeks to recapture the ideas that have motivated human behavior throughout a given period will find the art and literature of that age one of his central and major concerns, by no means a mere supplement or adjunct of significant historical research.

The student of ideas and their place in history will always be concerned with the patterns of transition, which are at the same time patterns of transformation, whereby ideas pass from one area of activity to another. Let us survey for a moment the development of modern thought—turning our attention from the Reformation toward the revolutionary and romantic movements that follow and dwelling finally on more recent decades. We may thus trace the notion of individual autonomy from its manifestation in religious practice and theological reflection through practical politics and political theory into literature and the arts. Finally we may note that the idea appears in educational theory where its influence is at present widespread. No one will deny that such broad developments and transitions are of great intrinsic interest and the study of ideas in literature would be woefully incomplete without frequent reference to them. Still, we must remember that we cannot construct and justify generalizations of this sort unless we are ready to consider many special instances of influence moving between such areas as theology, philosophy, political thought, and literature. The actual moments of contact are vitally important. These moments are historical events in the lives of individual authors with which the student of comparative literature must be frequently concerned.

Perhaps the most powerful and most frequently recurring literary influence on the Western world has been that of the Old and New Testament. Certainly one of the most important comments that can be made upon the spiritual and cultural life of any period of Western civilization during the past sixteen or seventeen centuries has to do with the way in which its leaders have read and interpreted the Bible. This reading and the comments that it evoked constitute the influence. A contrast of the scripture reading of, let us say, St. Augustine, John Bunyan, and Thomas Jefferson, all three of whom found in such study a real source of enlightenment, can tell us a great deal about these three men and the age that each represented and helped bring to conscious expression. In much the same way, we recognize the importance of Shakespeare's familarity with Plutarch and Montaigne, of Shelley's study of Plato's dialogues, and of Coleridge's enthusiastic plundering of the writings of many philosophers and theologians from Plato to Schelling and William Godwin, through which so many abstract ideas were brought to the attention of English men of letters.

We may also recognize cases in which the poets have influenced the philosophers and even indirectly the scientists. English philosopher Samuel Alexander's debt to Wordsworth and Meredith is a recent interesting example, as also A. N. Whitehead's understanding of the English romantics, chiefly Shelley and Wordsworth. Hegel's profound admiration for the insights of the Greek tragedians indicates a broad channel of classical influence upon nineteenth-century philosophy. Again the student of evolutionary biology will find a fascinating, if to our minds grotesque, anticipation of the theory of chance variations and the natural elimination of the unfit in Lucretius, who in turn seems to have borrowed the concept from the philosopher Empedocles.

Here an important caveat is in order. We must avoid the notion, suggested to some people by examples such as those just mentioned, that ideas are "units" [3] in some way comparable to coins or counters that can be passed intact from one group of people to another or even, for that matter, from one individual to another. Our description of an idea's influence must not be oversimplified. It is always a delicate and complicated business. Ideas have usually to be expressed in words and must be so expressed in literature as opposed to music and the fine arts. Words must not only be heard or read, they must be interpreted in contextual groupings, and it is only through such acts of interpretation that ideas become available to our attention. Ideas exist not as ready-made commodities but primarily—and here we must step beyond the definition already offered—as the "meaning" latent in human efforts to communicate. Their status is neither "subjective" nor "objective" in the usual sense, but *intersubjective,* communicative, or conversational. Once removed from the give and take of actual communication, ideas lose their vitality. Their genuine existence is transitive. They pass continually from one context to another and, even within the mind of a single individual, ideas must be frequently restated, in fact continually paraphrased, if they are to retain any vitality or even genuine significance. A set formula has little more than mnemonic value and is out of place except in the most elementary textbook.

Thus the term "unit-idea" can hardly be described as referring to any recognizable entity, to say nothing of its being usefully employed by the student of literature. We can, to be sure, redefine it with A. O. Lovejoy as a tendency on the part of certain people to enjoy hearing certain propositions such as "the real is One" or "the world is full of a number of things," thus recognizing philosophical *monism* and *pluralism* as unit-ideas. However, on this level of generality, we would probably do better not to use the term "unit-idea" even as a figure of speech since its connotations are, as already pointed out, often unfortunate, but to content ourselves with the more direct expressions "tendencies," "inclinations," or "dispositions" of "thought and feeling." These tendencies may express themselves in various ways that differ greatly from one period to another. But the notion of a unit-idea interpreted as reappearing or as being transferred from one author to another or from period to period is usually an oversimplification.

In passing from author to author and from age to age, these dispositions of thought and feeling undergo continual restatement, reinterpretation, and transformation. The history of ideas is essentially a commentary upon this process, which is after all the very life of the human spirit that fashions and refashions the ideas through which it becomes conscious of itself and of its environment. As Hegel tried to show in his first great work, *The Phenomenology of the Spirit,* the history of ideas may be considered as an index of the growth of self-consciousness whereby human individuals interpret and reinterpret their position in society and in the world. It goes without saying that the emergence of this self-consciousness transforms the life of the individual, influences his social relations, and profoundly alters his attitude toward nature. Such reorientation as it appears in documentary form is a primary subject-matter of history. Thus the historian must consider all the turns of thought whereby one period of human life is distinguished from its forerunners and from its successors. He may also find himself recognizing parallels and analogies where no notion of historical continuity, involving an actual influence or contact, is likely to develop. An interesting relation of this sort may be discerned as we compare the writings of the Chinese Taoists, especially those of Lao-Tsu himself, with the utterances of European romantics, as for example, Wordsworth's "Lines Written in Early Spring." Both of these may be compared with certain passages of the Neo-Platonic philosopher, Plotinus. Some scholars find great importance in such analogies and try by means of them to outline parallel cycles of development in distant cultures. These speculations, such as those of Oswald Spengler, who "identified" ancient Stoicism with modern socialism, and saw Pythagoras, Mahomet, and Cromwell as "contemporaries," or historical analogues, are nearly always interesting and suggestive and sometimes open important paths of investigation. But like all reasoning that rests on intuited analogies, such argument must be evaluated very cautiously and never recognized as conclusive without detailed study of a more pedestrian character.

We have argued that the student of the great "-isms" of literary and philosophical history, must proceed with discretion, always recognizing that as ideas pass from one mind to another, change, and often a radical change, is bound to take place in their structure, orientation, and mode of reception. There are many instances of such contrast. Prominent among these stand the mutations that ideas most usually undergo as they pass from thinker to artist. The poet and the philosopher may be said to entertain the "same" idea, but it is most important to remember that the poetic or literary development of an idea is often imaginative, figurative, or metaphorical in nature and that this contrasts sharply with an intellectual or scientific treatment that emphasizes definition and precision even at the risk of pedantry. The thinker is concerned with implications and seeks to preserve a more or less rigorous consistency, while the imaginative writer is usually more eager to make clear how an idea affects the life and colors the emotion of the person who entertains it. He need not be greatly concerned to convince his readers that his notion is a true one or that it excludes every alternative. In any case, he is not likely to construct an argument.

In this respect the polemical and controversial energy of a Bernard Shaw, manifest in his prefaces and elsewhere, is unusual. The literary artist does not usually draw distinctions. He does not aim at definitions or at conclusions. Nonetheless his mind may be as completely possessed by an idea as is the rigorous thinking of a geometer.

Thus Shelley's sonnet "Ozymandias" is an intense exemplification of an idea although, since the poet cites but a single instance, one would hardly call the poem an argument or a proof. His "Adonais" brings vividly to mind the Platonic notions of time, eternity, and immortality without retracing Plato's often intricate dialectic. On the other hand, there are passages in the *Divine Comedy,* in *Paradise Lost,* and in Wordsworth's *Excursion* where philosophical and theological ideas are presented within a discursive pattern that approaches a logical argument. Lucretius often goes even further in his exposition of the atomic and Epicurean philosophies and works his way toward something comparable to a *Quod erat demonstrandum,* although to be sure, following an argument borrowed from the philosophers. But such an approach to formal reasoning is unusual in literature. The man of letters is generally more concerned to call our attention to ideas than he is to demonstrate or analyze them. In philosophy, however, reflection upon ideas generally takes the form of knowledge, opinion, or belief, i.e. there is usually some sort of positive assertion involved. But it is often the case in literature that the presence of an idea before our attention does not call for any logical evaluation. In such a case sheer *enjoyment* takes the place of acceptance or rejection. The idea in its embodiment is admired rather than defended. Poets, it would seem, have a way of enjoying an idea without feeling any obligation to demonstrate or verify. Thus they may readily share the experience of the myth-maker who does not pass beyond imagination into argument. The attitude of the philosopher is always less congenial.

For this reason we may argue that mythology lends itself more readily to literary treatment than does science or even philosophy, and that in the conflict which often arises between myth and science, the literary man will sometimes fall into mythological modes of thought and experience almost despite himself, as Lucretius did in his glowing invocation to Venus, that introduces a poem devoted to a materialist account of man and the world, or as Wordsworth in "The Recluse" fragment, where, despite his dislike of "gaudy verse," he invokes Urania and calls upon a prophetic "spirit" to support him in defending a philosophy of humanism. In many instances, the poet tries to retain or regain something of the imaginative appeal of a mythology even though he is intellectually committed to a scientific, or humanist, or even a materialist, view of things. After all, mythology has been at times the living motivation of a literature that has found itself quite at home within its purview. We may argue that at no time in the history of Western literature—if we are willing to omit the so-called "science" fiction of recent years—has scientific thought ever exercised so subtle and pervasive an influence as that of mythology— not even in the naturalistic novels of the nineteenth century.[4]

The student of literature will, however, gradually come to recognize that contrasts such as that mentioned above between science and mythology, while readily discernible in the thought of many writers, yield only a comparatively superficial insight into the great movements of ideas. Such contrasts hardly reveal the polarities that gradually become obvious as we set in opposition the dominant themes that characterize the great periods of thought and literature. These themes often constitute horizons within which ideas inherited from earlier periods take on a local aspect that they wholly lacked in former times. Thus we may recognize two dimensions in the study of ideas: the "vertical," as when we speak of *Platonism* in Shelley, and the "horizontal," as when we speak of *romantic* Platonism. When emphasizing the vertical axis, we recognize recurring ideas and recurring "-isms." There is always danger that we will go too far toward identifying an idea as it appears in the context of one period with its manifestation in that of another. The result is a false sense of intellectual or spiritual community with historical figures who should not be treated as our "contemporaries." Platonism, we must admit, suffers sea-change as it passes from the Athens that had survived the Peloponnesian war to the England of the industrial revolution. This transformation is a challenge to the historian who must ask not "Did the romantics understand Plato?" but rather "How did they read or 'translate' him?" Consider the Platonism of Shelley, who was quite familiar with the text of his ancient master. Here it is the difference of treatment and of emphasis that most attracts our interest. To be sure, many isolated passages may be quoted to strengthen the impression that a genuine or Hellenic Platonism resides in Shelley's poems.

> *The One remains, the many change and pass;*
> *Heaven's light forever shines, Earth's shadows fly;*
> *Life, like a dome of many-colored glass,*
> *Stains the white radiance of Eternity*

This would seem to be a fairly orthodox Platonism derived from the central image of the sun in *The Republic*. But let us recall the wider context of Shelley's thought and our comment must be considerably qualified. After all, Shelley loved movement, transformation, and the flux of sensuous qualities. This world of change has also a reality and a beauty all its own. It is no mere appearance.

> *The everlasting universe of things*
> *Flows through the mind, and rolls its rapid waves,*
> *Now dark, now glittering, now reflecting gloom,*
> *Now lending splendor, where from secret springs*
> *The source of human thought its tribute brings*
> *Of waters,—with a sound but half its own*

This stanza from "Mont Blanc" is too modern to be genuine Platonism. So also is the "myth" of the "West Wind" far removed from that of the *Phaedrus.* Furthermore, a Platonism at home with a revolutionary liberalism, based on a belief in human perfectibility and progress, a Platonism colored by romantic notions of "free" (heterosexual) love and set into verse by a poet who had once been an enthusiastic amateur of modern chemistry is a Platonism almost sui generis.

We may mention in passing that Wordsworth's Platonism is quite as unorthodox as Shelley's. For example, Wordsworth's reinterpretation of the notion of Platonic reminiscence, so vividly presented in the "Intimations" Ode, is virtually an inversion of the ancient doctrine. Plato held that in certain privileged moments we may recall or reconstitute a vision of eternal truth, lost at birth, including the first principles or foundations of mathematical order, social justice, and of sensuous and intellectual beauty. These insights become more frequent and more comprehensive as our education progresses. For Wordsworth, we "recall" less and less frequently as we grow older the glorious wealth of the world of becoming, the "mighty waters" that support our existence and are so obvious to our childhood vision. This world, like Goethe's "golden tree of life," appears as a gray shadow of its true self to the practical man of affairs and to the scientific theorist. It can be wholly present only to that "wise passiveness" which the "noisy years" of maturity make harder and harder to enjoy. Although Wordsworth's Ode is usually recognized as Platonic in spirit, it might seem to some that only the most general notion of "reminiscence" or recollection stands in common to both poet and philosopher. The details are almost wholly transformed.

These considerations call to our attention the profound contrasts existing between ancient and modern ways of looking at the world. If the reader desires another example, let him consider the ancient maxim "Know thyself," asking what it may have meant originally to the petitioners who called upon the Delphic oracle, what it meant to Socrates, and what, let us add, to Montaigne who found the Socratic use of the phrase so congenial. On the latter point Auerbach's fascinating chapter on Montaigne in *Mimesis* may be read with profit. Shelley, Wordsworth, and Montaigne recast Platonic themes but hardly because of any conscious intention to reconstruct his philosophy. We had better say that they transfer Platonism from one medium of thought and feeling to another and reshape its major concepts in doing so.

These discrepancies between ancient Platonism and its modern romantic counterpart call our attention to related ideas that are of especial signifiance for the historian. For the modern mind the immediate, the sensuous, the changing are more attractive and philosophically more significant than they ever were for Greek idealism. In the first place, the alignment of concepts that this contrast suggests constitutes an important area of historical study. But we may go further and insist that this contrast is highly pertinent to the historian's own attitude toward his subject matter. Before one can become a true historian of ideas one must learn to "take time seriously" and to recognize that time leaves its mark on ideas, as on things. Ideas can survive as cultural realities only by changing and readjusting themselves.

A sense of history and of the gradual transformation of human customs and ideas was hardly characteristic of ancient thinkers, for whom the ideal science was geometry and for whom the apparent cycles of the sun, moon, and the constellations and the somewhat more complicated motions of the planets constituted the obvious framework of a geometric universe. From this standpoint, change is subordinate to form and to law and is essentially a matter of repetition within a permanent frame. Profound change or transformation toward essential novelty is unlikely. Time, including human life, tends constantly to exemplify and reexemplify the same eternal principles. It is only within the last two centuries that we have become profoundly conscious of an historical mode of existence, and have recognized that we ourselves are "in" history or that in a sense we *are* a history that assumes new forms from age to age. There gradually emerges a sense of continuity with a past that is, quantitatively speaking, very distant from us and qualitatively very different. To be sure, we may "move about" in history by cultivating, as Collingwood among others would recommend, a sympathetic imagination that in some measure transcends the vast reaches of change. The past is still in a sense *our* past and as Hegel put it in his famous pun: "Wesen ist was gewesen ist." (Our essence is what we have been.)

This turn of thought is essentially a romantic one. Thus Wordsworth, who could speak with genuine pathos of the "unimaginable touch of time" and of "things silently gone out of mind," nonetheless in *The Prelude* described his enjoyment of the city of London and its historical monuments:

> *With strong Sensations, teeming as it did*
> *Of past and present, such a place must needs*
> *Have pleas'd me, in those times; I sought not then*
> *Knowledge; but craved for power, and power I found*

In all things; nothing had a circumscribed
And narrow influence; but all objects, being
Themselves capacious, also found in me
Capaciousness and amplitude of mind;
Such is the strength and glory of our Youth.
The Human nature unto which I felt
That I belong'd, and which I lov'd and reverenc'd,
Was not a punctual Presence, but a Spirit
Living in time and space, and far diffus'd.
In this my joy, in this my dignity
Consisted.

The love of the "far away and long ago," the pathos of "old, forgotten far off things" so characteristic of the romantics only reveals another aspect of this sense of history. We have often to admit that the past, although our own, is out of reach.

It is interesting to notice that this sense of time is first celebrated by the poets and men of letters before it exercises any profound or far reaching influence upon the work of the professional historian. The scholarly historian of the nineteenth century, especially in Germany, is clearly an offspring of romanticism, as are also the notions borrowed from Collingwood in the quotation introducing this chapter. Once this sense of history has been awakened in us, we often come to emphasize the distance between past and present even more than their continuity and their common life. There is even some danger that the modern student will, as his learning and his historical sensibility increase, despair of ever closing the gap between past and present and of offering, say, an adequate picture of the Athenian Plato or, for that matter, of the Elizabethan *Hamlet.* While such defeatism is extreme, a sober realization of historical distance should be encouraged. Certainly, it is indispensable to the scholar who must avoid reducing an idea to a recurring stereotype.

Let us briefly examine two or three examples of what we have for lack of a better term been describing as "historical distance." As Macaulay's learned school boy knows, Lord Nelson died at the battle of Trafalgar, shot down by marksmen perched in the rigging of enemy vessels. The admiral made a splendid target, for he stood his quarter-deck in brilliant full dress, wearing his many decorations despite the remonstrances of his officers. During the Napoleonic period and in the years that followed, Nelson's attitude was accepted as quite consistent with the character of a true hero, chivalrous and intrepid. It would not be generally so considered today, when soldiers are no longer paraded into battle in polychrome uniforms and when the ideal of personal combat has nearly faded from the scene. The modern civilian must make a real effort of imaginative reorientation to capture the sense of values that once presided over military life. Even the "citizen-soldier" of modern warfare is not readily equipped to do so. It is the task of the historian of ideas to illuminate these widely differing modes of thought.

The difference may be copiously illustrated by reference to literary texts. Consider, in passing, Douglas' ironical comment, in Shakespeare's *Henry IV*, on the ample wardrobe of the English king, who sent into battle a number of impersonators clad in royal armor and, on the other hand, the white plume of Henry of Navarre that was celebrated by Macaulay. Our present attitude as reflected in twentieth-century war poetry and war fiction is quite another thing. It is, however, more interesting to set it in contrast with the notions expressed by Shakespeare's Falstaff and Cervantes' Sancho Panza. Here the differences are harder to determine and are more significant although less spectacular. The twentieth-century poet, such as Pound, Owen, or Sassoon, who questions the dignity or glory of war casts a new light on Falstaff's reservations concerning military honor and on Sancho Panza's estimate of his master. In recent times such an attitude does not have to be presented as low comedy but can be taken quite seriously as a dignified and humane evaluation.

Some further illustrations of historical distance may be helpful. Let us choose a topic that illustrates the interrelationship of religion and the arts. In medieval and modern thought one finds it altogether fitting and proper to describe God as infinite or unlimited even though this may be taken to imply that finite man can never wholly comprehend the nature of deity. In earlier times, however, especially under the auspices of the Pythagorean philosophers, the notion of infinity carried a distinctly pejorative connotation. *Infinite* meant *indefinite, formless, unfinished,* as opposed to the self-contained and clearly defined structure of the finite, whose perfection lay in harmony, symmetry, and proportion. From this Pythagorean point of view, which is, in large measure, the point of view of classical art and literature, it would be little short of blasphemous nonsense to speak of an infinite God or even of an infinite good. To say that all things spring from the infinite and to introduce no supplementary principle of order such as justice or intelligence would bring one perilously close to Glycon's

> *All is laughter, all is dust,*
> *all is nothing.*
> *For all things are born*
> *of unreason.*

Here, we have what we may call the classical ideal of an organic unity, a one in many, wherein beginning, middle, and end [5] are manifest and wherein every part derives its vitality from the whole that is itself an organization of parts. This ideal is at once moral, religious, and aesthetic. And

some students have boldly argued that it is reflected in the
very structure of ancient, as opposed to modern, mathe-
matics. This ideal may be described in the words that Quin-
tillian used of the style of Pericles, *instans sibi* or *compact.*
It is, in short, an apotheosis of finitude or "closure." Classical
art and poetry of any period echo this ideal, if only faintly.
To sense this, one has only to think of the facade of a Greek
temple, as opposed to the interior of St. Sophia, or to study
the periods of classical prose or the closed symmetry of a
poem like William Browne's

> *Underneath this sable hearse*
> *Lies the subject of all verse.*
> *Sidney's sister, Pembroke's mother,*
> *Death, 'ere thou hast slain another,*
> *Fair and learn'd and good as she,*
> *Time shall throw a dart at thee!*

Cosmos, meaning world-order, has, we may remember, the
same root as the Greek verb *kosmeo,* meaning *I adorn.* Structure, especially symmetrical or periodic structure, stands for
the true classicist at the heart of nature and is also the key
to aesthetic value. The image of the sphere, that delighted
ancient philosophers from Parmenides to Boethius, symbol-
izes the notion of finite symmetry and summarizes the ideas
of order and of value. But the God of medieval and modern
thought is not so to be presented. He is infinite and his being
is unfathomable. Hence the cautious concern with which
theologians and even philosophers of our own century consider the notion of a "finite God," so possessed have we become by the feeling that such a God would lack the awful
majesty inseparable from deity. Indeed, in modern times
many of us have quite lost the classical sense of finitude or
closure. We are at home in vastness and enjoy open immensi-

ties both spatial and temporal. If we are disturbed by Pascal's "silence of infinite spaces," the sense of awe is not without a hint of exaltation; and further we rejoice in the notion of an indefinite future, a theater of progress and perfectibility. We still share Wordsworth's romantic sense that

> *Our destiny; our being's heart and home,*
> *Is with infinitude, and only there;*
> *With hope it is, hope that can never die,*
> *Effort, and expectation, and desire*
> *And something evermore about to be.*

To be sure, among the ancients, the materialist Lucretius stands in awe of a boundless universe of which our little world is but a passing feature. But this enormous and self-sufficient "happenstance" of nature is, for all its fertility, indifferent to value, and human wisdom is founded on recognition of this truth which is incompatible with religion.

The medieval mind stands between the extreme positions that we have indicated. The medieval Christian rejoices in the infinite and mysterious majesty of God, whose fulness of being can only be adumbrated in human terms, thus inviting recourse to symbol and allegory. But he lacks our modern sense of the sublimity of the physical world and of endless time. His world is finite and the future that confronts him is fixed by providential disposition. *Non in tempore sed cum tempore finxit deus mundum.* There is, for the medieval thinker, something terrifying about an infinite world or system of nature. It is not until the dawn of modern thought that we find people arguing that the production of a finite world would be somehow beneath the dignity of an infinite God. Just so in later thought we hear that it would be beneath the dignity of an infinite creator not to produce *creative* creatures. And herein lies a theme that sets modern thought in sharp contrast with ancient and medieval.

According to the Biblical story, God created heaven and earth and all that they contain, and God created man in his own image. This distinguishes man from lesser creatures and secures him a privileged place in the universe. One might suppose that man, created in the image of God the Creator, would within the limits imposed by his finite or creaturely status, be himself a creator and that through exercise of his creative agency he would fulfill his destiny as a privileged creature, and further that through failure to exploit his special talents he would forfeit something of his divine birthright. A man from Mars considering the apparent implications of the Biblical story might well anticipate some such conclusion. Nonetheless the "doctrine" that we have sketched describing man's unique status as a creative creature in God's world was very slow to take shape. In general, it is a modern view of things and it is only in a romantic consciousness that it first appears wholly reasonable. In earlier times, including the whole range of Christian thought, philosophers and theologians did not see in God's created image any suggestion of creative power. God was the only creator; indeed, for many, the only *maker* in any radical sense of the word. The divine image resident in man was recognized as human reason and the human capacity to love God and our fellow men, but it possessed no counterpart of divine power.

Against such a background, the poet and the artist will appear primarily as imitators and, although imitation involves a measure of making or fashioning, they will look for their archetypes toward an order of things already firmly established by divine fiat or supported by the more permanent features of natural process. The romantic notion of the creative power of the artist, as expressed among others by William Blake, and popularized by Browning in "Abt Vogler," as well as the notion today entertained by existentialist philosophers, playwrights, and novelists, that man can somehow "make himself," would seem ridiculous and presumptuous, if not indeed sacrilegious, before comparatively recent times. We may summarize by pointing out that in the classical and medieval periods, by far the most widely accepted representations of human nature displayed a subordinate being obliged to accept his cosmic station and its duties, obeying imperatives or accepting values ultimately not of his own making. The few exceptions, such as the Greek Sophists, are interesting primarily because they stand in protest against dominant philosophies that can be at times embarrassed but not overcome.

The romantic notion is anticipated in the Renaissance by Scaliger who calls the poet "another God," and by Tasso, whom Shelley quotes to the effect that the poet is the only true creator other than God himself, and again by certain of the mystics, among them the protestant Jacob Boehme (died 1624), who insist that man participates with God in the everlasting process of creation. But the modern movement away from the traditional mode of thought has been a very slow one continually looking backward toward more conservative beliefs. Thus even Wordsworth's creative individualism, so enthusiastically expressed in *The Prelude*, is qualified in the "Ode to Duty" and retracted in later poems. Nonetheless the idea of man as creator is not lost and tends to accompany the development of modern humanism so that today we find a widespread popular respect for "creative thinking" and for "creative activity" in general.

This tendency reaches its extreme fruition in certain phases of recent existentialism, where human self-creation is described as subject to no norms or ideal archetypes. Here human nature, as opposed to its physical and biological substructures, is identified with creative freedom, whereby we project our own pattern of human nature and create a mode

of life of our own choosing. This philosophy constitutes a
bold denial of the notion that human freedom is ever subject
to pre-established authority, historical conditions, or metaphysical limitations, although it may at times caricature itself by attributing to such nonentities a sort of pseudo reality.
For the existentialist such imaginings constitute an effort to
conceal our freedom from ourselves and to escape the responsibility that it entails. Thus Jean-Paul Sartre can hardly
endorse Antigone's great speech in which she justifies her
rebellion by appealing to an eternal law of justice that transcends her own situation.

> *I did not think your edicts strong enough*
> *To overrule the unwritten unalterable laws*
> *Of God and heaven, you being only a man.*
> *They are not of yesterday or to-day, but everlasting,*
> *Though where they came from, none of us can tell.*
> *Guilty of their transgression before God*
> *I cannot be.*

In contrast, we may cite the following from an existentialist
novel: [6]

Hélène leaned her chin on the palm of her hand. "Tell me, why
do we live?"

"I'm not one of the Evangelists," I said with slight embar-
rassment.

"And yet you know why you live." She spread her fingers fan-
wise and studied them attentively. "I don't know why I do."

"Surely there are things you like, things you want. . . ."

She smiled. "I like chocolate and beautiful bicycles."

"That's better than nothing."

She looked at her fingers once again; of a sudden she seemed
sad. "When I was small, I believed in God, and it was wonderful;
at every moment of the day something was required of me; then
it seemed to me that I *must* exist. It was an absolute necessity."

I smiled sympathetically at her. "I think that where you go wrong is that you imagine that your reasons for living ought to fall on you ready-made from heaven, whereas we have to create them for ourselves."

"But when we know that we've created them ourselves, we can't believe in them. It's only a way of deceiving ourselves."

"We do not arbitrarily create these things out of nothing; we create them through the strength of our own love and our own longing; and thus our creatures stand before us, solid and real."

The gap that separates the proto-Platonism of Sophocles from the creative humanism of the existentialist sets many problems for the student of the history of ideas. Again, the student when he distinguishes the existentialist position from that of the ancient Sophists, who declared the human individual the "measure of all things," faces a delicate and important task. The existentialist stands closer to Antigone than to the Sophist, as we usually picture him. The values and standards that the existentialist calls into being are not, as for the Sophist, evaluations imposed upon modes of conduct according to the interests of the individual who is at once agent and observer. It is something wholly different. The existentialist is not seeking to protect his interests or justify conduct already projected. He hopes rather through interpretation of his own situation to commit or engage himself in projects that will awaken and sustain interests powerful enough and enduring enough significantly to characterize his own existence. He seeks not to justify or to promote but to realize, even to create, his own existence.[7]

If the existentialism of today is of any lasting value, it is because its exponents have so clearly emphasized the central importance of the individual's consciousness of himself and of his situation. Despite the air of abrupt originality that surrounds existentialist thought, its contribution takes its place in a long tradition that has accompanied the development of art, literature, and philosophy in the West. The individual as a center of self-conscious decision has emerged slowly from a matrix of subpersonal group behavior such as that described by Lévy-Bruhl and by Bergson in his picture of a closed society.[8] Here conscience may be described as a sense of membership in a group from which the individual derives his human existence. Thus "we" and "our" precede "I" and "my." The singular pronouns only gradually acquire their full significance as we pass through ancient and medieval toward modern consciousness. Such development is often moral and religious in motivation and is manifest in the increasing prominence attached to the attitudes of conscience and of faith. Both of these include growing recognition of a selfhood whose very life springs from a sense of responsibility. The heroic figures of Prometheus and Antigone in the great tragedies and of Socrates as Plato presents him in the *Apology* and the *Crito* are assertions of a moral autonomy, essentially religious in significance, that is to be honored by both Stoics and Christians. Thereafter Christian emphasis upon the moral importance of an inner motivation, in our conduct, and Christian insistence upon the necessity of an absolute sincerity in matters of belief move gradually, despite institutional authoritarianism, toward the dominion of self-consciousness in the life of the individual, or perhaps one might say toward the emergence of self-conscious individuality. We might argue that the art and literature of many centuries reflect in one way or another a gradual and often vacillating progress toward the self-realization of the conscious and autonomous individual.

Many students have characterized the Renaissance as, par excellence, the period of individualism, suggesting a profound difference in kind between Renaissance and Middle

Ages. Thus D. A. Traversi opens his study of Shakespeare [9] declaring that

Medieval man was aware of a definite place in an established society, was firmly grounded in a universe whose nature and end were defined by Christian philosophy; the signs of breakdown which can be found in both Chaucer and Langland are still overshadowed in them by the effects of the mediaeval synthesis. *Piers Plowman,* like the *Divine Comedy,* is not the expression of an isolated individual, but of a man whose individuality speaks within a determined social, philosophic, and religious context. The dominating facts of Shakespeare's age, seen from this point of view, were the destruction of this context and the discovery of the autonomous self which we associate with the Renaissance. The inevitable result was a vast extension of interests, and a corresponding lack of any spiritual or intellectual conception by which these interests might be disciplined. The literature of the Renaissance, being concerned with exploring this new conception of the self and its possibilities, could not hope for any adequate synthesis of its experience which should transcend the personal. Shakespeare's idiom and outlook are still largely mediaeval, but the harmony or pattern which we see gradually evolving out of his work is a purely *personal* pattern, the richest and greatest of its kind that has ever existed. Mr. Eliot once remarked that "Dante and Shakespeare divide the modern world equally between them: there is not a third." It is equally true that they divide what Mr. Eliot chose, for his own purposes, to call "the modern world" into two parts: the mediaeval part, dominated by the synthesis of faith and reason, and the strictly modern part, in which the enormous possibilities of the new discovery of the individual have been explored at the expense of that synthesis.

Nonetheless, we may argue in opposition to Traversi that the Renaissance "discovery" of the individual is but one of a series of such insights that extends from primitive stages of culture through the works of the Greek tragedians and the philosophers that followed them into the history of Christian Europe. Both scholars and creative writers are still concerned, as in all probability they will be for generations to come, with these "enormous possibilities," even when with Eliot, they challenge a notion like that of romantic self-expression and emphasize an older form of individualism— that of self-fulfillment through sacrifice. The contrast, readily discernible between Sartre and Eliot, which is apparent through all their work, may be summarized in terms of their divergent interpretations of individuality.

Let us conclude our discussion of the relation of literature to ideas by completing the ancient triad composed of the notions of God, man, and nature, the first two of which we have already considered. The idea of nature has undergone several transformations throughout its long and intricate development from the days of the early Greek cosmogonists. The ancient words *physis* and *natura* both indicate an original reference to procreation. Nature was seen to be a process not only of growth but of begetting and bearing. Thus in primitive modes of thought sexual imagery is employed freely to describe the origins of things that spring from the union of sky and earth. Here a primitive philosophy of opposites is apparent arising from the wealth of mythology concerning the beginning of all things: Chaos and Cosmos, Heaven and Earth, Day and Night, Hot and Cold, Moist and Dry, and later, Odd and Even. Justice or Fate, presiding over the boundless fertility of nature, holds the competing opposites in check so that there results a world of ordered, periodic process. This is manifest in the periodic motions of the heavenly bodies and in the regularity of the seasons where hot and cold, moist and dry are held within bounds, thus yielding a moderate climate that will support life. So conceived or imagined, the orderliness of nature on the one hand and the moral values of human self-discipline or self-imposed moderation on the other are seen as springing somehow from a common origin. Nature and man respond, both somewhat imperfectly and rather reluctantly, to the same cosmic influence.

This notion lingers on for centuries. Consider Milton's lines in "Arcades":

> *. . . then listen I*
> *To the celestial* Sirens *harmony,*
> *That sit upon the nine enfolded Sphears,*
> *And sing to those that hold the vital shears,*
> *And turn the Adamantine spindle round,*
> *On which the fate of gods and men is wound.*
> *Such sweet compulsion doth in musick ly,*
> *To lull the daughters of* Necessity,
> *And keep unsteddy Nature to her law,*
> *And the low world in measur'd motion draw*
> *After the heavenly tune*

and compare Wordsworth's personification of Duty who "preserve[s] the stars from wrong." In such a world, art may be said at once to imitate and perfect or complete nature. The artist may be thought to catch the tendency or direction latent in natural growth, to free it of accidental shortcomings, and so to reveal an ideal not to be envisaged otherwise. So is the human form transfigured in Greek sculpture but still presented in its natural perfection.

According to a variant interpretation, nature may appear as autonomous or as embodying in herself the harmony sometimes said to be imposed upon her. Nature then displays a wisdom or an efficiency surpassing the human. The universal fact of growth, the fitness of the organism for sustaining life in its proper environment, the healing power of nature, the accuracy of instinct, the "geometry of the spider's web," and the intricate beauty of many living forms are all recognized as revealing the wisdom and spirit or "plastic" power of living nature, celebrated by many writers including Shaftesbury and Wordsworth. Even human consciousness itself in its spontaneous and less deliberate moments may be thought to belong to nature so that for the romanticist and the Chinese Taoist the song of the poet and the song of the bird need not be contrasted too sharply, although the poet, unlike the bird, must "return" to nature, discarding the artificiality of his civilization.

For certain of the Stoic philosophers even human reason is recognized as "natural" so that nature absorbs human nature and includes the entire life of man in her purposes. Nature "intends" man to be a rational and reasonable animal. Of course, the word "unnatural" still refers to the human error whereby we sometimes, to our misfortune, try to separate ourselves from the course that nature has assigned us, as in the case of an "unnatural" parent or child who smothers the affection that springs "naturally" in his breast or wilfully ignores the "natural" order of things that includes family life. There is, however, a further step that may sometimes be taken as we interpret nature in this way. Montaigne in his essay "Of the Useful and the Honorable" writes as follows:

Our structure, both public and private, is full of imperfection. But there is nothing useless in Nature, not even uselessness itself. Nothing has made its way into this universe that does not have a proper place in it. Our being is cemented with sickly qualities; ambition, jealousy, envy, revenge, superstition, and despair dwell in us with so natural a possession that their image is discerned also in beasts. And even cruelty, too, so unnatural a vice; for in the midst of compassion we feel within I know not what bittersweet sting of malicious pleasure in seeing others suffer; and children feel it . . .

Whoever should remove from man the seeds of these qualities would destroy the fundamental conditions of our life. Likewise in all governments there are necessary offices which are not only abject but vicious too; there vices find their place and are useful to the seaming together of our union, as poisons are useful for the preservation of our health.

Here the moral rigor implicit in the Stoic precepts is tempered by Montaigne to yield an ethic of tolerance based on a recognition of the infinite subtlety of nature's strategy.

Nonetheless, a distinction is generally maintained between nature and human nature or, most especially, between nature and the human consciousness that surveys nature and even judges her. Accordingly in ancient thought that has cleared itself of its mythological origins, we find *physis*, nature, set sharply in contrast with *nomos,* custom, and both with the aims and aspirations of the human individual. Human customs, considered by the Greek Sophists as matters of convention or agreement and included even the meanings attached to words, differ from the "natural" life of plants and animals. Thus the human individual faces two types of environment, the natural and the social, and two types of law. The Sophist delights in pointing out that the "laws" of nature are much firmer than those of human custom or convention. The latter may, indeed, be evaded with impunity by a clever and persuasive opportunist. But, as the farmer, mariner or physician will attest, the laws of nature are not to be thus scorned. Nature exacts her penalties relentlessly and commands a far greater respect on the part of the individual than the community or state, for all its pomp and air of authority, can succeed in doing. After all, man made the notions of right and wrong which are meaningless unless there is power to support them. As this line of thought continues, we find justice being defined as the interest of the stronger, that is, of the individual or party actually in power.

Here nature appears as a system of *fact* as opposed to *value* or even to purpose. The word "nature" stands for the things that are and the way they behave. As such, nature tacitly rebukes the sentimentalism of those who would ignore causes in the name of ideals or purposes. The Sophists and the "realists," the advocates of power politics, often exploit these ideas for their own interests. But for a certain type of mind, this recognition of natural necessity takes on genuine dignity, an acquiescence almost comparable to Christian resignation. We may be reminded of the philosophy of Spinoza and of Keats' lines in *Hyperion* that equate personal freedom or sovereignty with our ability calmly to envisage circumstance.

Essentially different, however, is the Christian interpretation of nature. Here nature yields her authority and her finality to God who subordinates her to man. God has created nature as a suitable environment for human life and the features of the natural order of things may be described as God's gifts to man for whom he prepares a rich domain. Nature thus appears as an abundant pool of raw materials or even as a storehouse of useful objects awaiting human disposition. The danger lies only in that man may, being too fascinated by these gifts, forget their source and in thoughtless prosperity and ingratitude ignore his creaturely and dependent status. Thus the medieval thinker is often fearful of too great a concern with nature unless she may be interpreted as manifesting the glory of her maker. Otherwise, it is insisted, man will find no lasting satisfaction in such an interest. This attitude is by no means limited to the Middle Ages. Consider for instance Herbert's "The Pulley":

When God at first made man,
Having a glasse of blessings standing by;
Let us (said he) poure on him all we can:
Let the worlds riches, which dispersed lie,
   Contract into a span.

So strength first made a way;
Then beautie flow'd, then wisdome, honour, pleasure:
Then almost all was out, God made a stay,
Perceiving that alone of all his treasure
   Rest in the bottom lay.

For if I should (said he)
Bestow this jewell also on my creature,
He would adore my gifts instead of me,
And rest in Nature, not the God of Nature.
   So both should losers be.

Yet let him keep the rest,
But keep them with repining restlessnesse:
Let him be rich and wearie, that at least,
If goodnesse leade him not, yet wearinesse
   May tosse him to my breast.

In modern times, interest in nature takes on a new aspect.
We are no longer content to enjoy the fruits of nature as we
find them. We grow eager to subject nature to our will. Thus,
with Bacon and Descartes, Europeans seek scientifically to
direct natural process according to the maxim that we may
control or transform nature by obeying her. Prediction of
natural phenomena and control of causal sequences thus become the main business of the scientist who sees in the
regularity of natural process the possibility of transforming
our environment. Nor need he stop at this point. Human nature need no longer be treated as an exception. The systems
of cause and effect that become apparent to the research stu-

dent are finally interpreted as including not only nature in the older sense but human behavior as well, and man finds himself engulfed in the determinism that Descartes had recognized as characterizing only the physical world. Here we encounter a paradoxical turn of thought. The causal determinism, that has at its first appearance encouraged man to think of himself as the master of nature, shortly thereafter persuades him that he is himself but a part of nature and, as such, subject in thought and action to the law-abiding routine of causal sequences that he has not initiated.

There is something sublime about this all-encompassing system of causation before which the modern mind stood for generations in mingled fascination and dismay. Nature so conceived combines the orderliness of the ancient cosmos with the infinite expanse of a modern universe. The result carries a certain moral significance in that it inspires humility. Thus, for Meredith even Satan will stand abashed before the majesty of astronomical determinism, "the armies of unalterable law." Here necessity appears as mathematical or Newtonian in pattern. Nature displays the precision of an ideal chronometer. No longer the "homely nurse," no longer the unruly or awkward apprentice, nature appears as something much more impersonal: a system of law abiding phenomena. All events of whatever sort "obey" the laws of nature.

At this point a singular crisis emerges that transforms once more the idea of nature. "Obedience" loses its original meaning since its opposite has been ruled out. No events ever "disobey" natural law. Thus the analogy is completely outworn. Nature is no more than a system of phenomena whose regularity, statistical or mechanical, exhausts its meaning. As such, nature becomes wholly inhuman, distant, and indifferent to our concerns. In Darwinian biology,

"Mother Nature" yields to "natural selection," a metaphor to make clear the brute fact that in the struggle for survival weaker organisms and species are inevitably eliminated. The cold neutrality of natural process, even when "red in tooth and claw," is a stupefying rather than shocking revelation, from which many nineteenth-century writers like Tennyson tried desperately to escape.

Some of the efforts to escape this notion of nature's indifference land us in further difficulty. It may be suggested that natural selection is not a wholly mechanical matter. Perhaps in some way nature actually "favors" the strong, or, at any rate, justifies the notion that power is an end in itself. Here may be heard an echo of the Sophistic ethics. The survival of the strong sets a standard of value and *nomos* is once more absorbed by *physis,* albeit a *physis* in nineteenth-century dress. Here the Christian ethic of humility and brotherly love appears as "unnatural." The kingdom of heaven is surely not of this world, where life is first and foremost a matter of competition. At this juncture, one may adopt the strategy of a Nietzsche and celebrate the *Umwertung aller Werte*—the inversion of all values. Or one may take the attitude of the "naturalistic" novelist whose intention is to describe, perhaps to explain, but never to evaluate. Here the ideal of the naturalist is primarily an intellectual one. Nature challenges the artist along with the scientist to describe and explain. Evaluation is out of place. To undertake it is a mark of presumption.

There is still another possibility. Having repudiated the idea of nature as an exemplar of value, we may insist that values and evaluation reside not in nature but in human consciousness. Thus we come upon various efforts to establish some kind of humanism that will clearly distinguish human nature from its "natural" origin, environment, or substructure. We may recall the humanism of Irving Babbitt with its doctrine of conscience or "inner check" that seems to have exercised a real influence on modern letters, especially through Babbitt's student, T. S. Eliot. Or we may consider once more the philosophy of the existentialists, for whom human *subjectivity* is wholly distinct from the order of nature. In this view the individual's way of thinking of himself actually alters, even creates, his own mode of existence. Put very briefly, our subjectivity is not a part of nature in the sense just considered. To quote Sartre, a man is not a "piece of moss, a cabbage, or a paper knife." He is not, strictly speaking, a member of a species or a type. He is not cut to pattern. He is free, like the Adam of Pico della Mirandola to choose his own status, to classify himself, to accept a future and assume obligations. The individual *exists* in his decisions and commitments. Such existence is not a matter of habit or routine; it is not a matter of accepting ready-made alternatives; it is not a matter of obedience to law, human, natural, or divine. It cannot be observed from without and it follows no predetermined pattern and yet it fashions a pattern of its own. It is human subjectivity and as such it is like nothing else in the world.

It is much too soon to evaluate the importance of existentialist thought except to point out the significant contrasts that it affords when considered along with earlier attitudes. The student interested in the immediate future of modern literature may well be concerned with the exploration of this still largely undeveloped philosophy that stands as the absolute repudiation of the naturalism of the past century.

Perhaps the above examples, chosen almost at random, will suffice to indicate to the student a possible approach to literature, an approach from which he may discern a wealth of ideas present in every period and a certain complex or contrast of ideas characterizing each period. The student will find ideas of one kind or another relevant to every author that he studies. It should, of course, go without saying that the presence of an important idea in the work of an author does not, in itself, enhance the value of his contribution. On the other hand, without some reference to the ideas expressed in a poem or a novel we may hardly speak intelligently of its value. If we follow the Kantian tradition by describing aesthetic value as residing in a harmony of understanding and sensibility, we may consistently argue that familiarity with ideas embodied in or clearly relevant to a work of art is an important auxiliary of critical appreciation. Certainly many students have found this to be the case and no scholar or critic can afford wholly to ignore the ideas that have fascinated the imagination of the author that he studies. After all, such a study can hardly fail to expand our human sympathies and ultimately to support Walter Pater in his earnest belief that "nothing which has ever interested living men and women can wholly lose its vitality."

7

Literature and the Arts

Mary Gaither

C OMPARATIVE studies of literature and the arts offer a touchy field of exploration. Not all those concerned are in agreement on the proper scope of such studies even if they are agreed that such studies are worthwhile. Terms of description which must be used as one moves from one art to another are frequently inadequate. Terms of identification, names of styles and movements, which are often common to two or more modes of artistic creation, do not always convey the same meaning. When we speak of the rhythm of a Shakespearean sonnet or of a Beethoven sonata are we speaking of the same thing? Can balance in a Van Gogh painting be described in the same terms as that in a drama of Lorca? When we speak of Expressionism in drama and painting are we speaking of the same mode? When we describe Impressionism in painting can we apply the same description of style and idea to Impressionism in music and literature? The obvious answer to all these questions is "no."

For the student of literature and the arts the problem of making oneself understood while using the terms at his disposal is a difficult one. Many critics, especially in literature, have attempted to find precise terms appropriate for elucidat-

An Associate Professor of English at Indiana University, a member of the Comparative Literature Committee of the National Council of Teachers of English, and a consultant on foreign literature for the *New Standard Encyclopaedia*, MARY GAITHER has written on children's literature and American drama.

ing a particular form. For example, John Crowe Ransom in poetry and Francis Fergusson in drama have sought to provide definitive terms when they analyze and interpret these forms of literature.[1]

Assuming that studies of literature and its relation to the other arts are desirable, and being forewarned of the complications of communication, the investigation of certain problems of comparison can be both stimulating and satisfying. The student must keep always in mind his immediate goal and not be diverted by charming but unproductive will-o-the-wisps; he must not create comparisons where they are not valid or force them just for the sake of the comparison.

The area of investigation offers countless subjects, limited indeed only by man's knowledge and time itself. However, the approaches to comparative studies of the arts and literature seem to be of three primary kinds: relationship of form and content, influence, and synthesis.[2] There may, of course, be overlapping, but the emphasis will identify the approach. In the following I should like to illustrate some of these approaches by examining some outstanding studies.

Of the three major kinds of study, only the first need be defined. Form and content is at best an inadequate description of problems which embrace the wide range of style, technique, narrative, and idea. Undoubtedly the majority of studies fall within the vast range of form and all that compounds it. Even relationships between two forms of art existing generations apart and seen only as a way of sharpening our appreciation of either may justifiably be considered in this category. I am thinking here of Stephen Spender's provocative preface to *The Novices of Sais* [3] by Novalis, published together with sixty of Paul Klee's nature drawings, not as illustrations but as parallels. Juxtaposed as they are, we are made to feel more about both Novalis and Klee than we

might have otherwise. Spender describes the work of both
the eighteenth-century poet and the twentieth-century artist
as "a curiously interior world; a world of pure art and pure
contemplation, of imagist poems, and an intense, glowing yet
humorous and meticulous imagination. The drawings here
are meant as . . . a kind of reflection of the world of Novalis within the world of Paul Klee." Another illustration of
how the juxtaposition of a poem with a painting may illuminate meaning can be seen in W. H. Auden's poem "Musée
des Beaux Arts" in which he spans human suffering by calling attention to the composition of Breughel's "Icarus." Both
these illustrations of a relationship between poetry and painting are highly subjective but no less effective for their subjectivity. They demonstrate the facile relationships between
the arts which lie close to the surface needing only a percep-
tive mind to bring them into full view. But there are other,
more formal and systematic approaches with which the student should be acquainted.

A classic study of the relationship between literature and
the arts is an essay by the eighteenth-century German critic,
Lessing. When Lessing sought to define the respective limits
of poetry and the plastic arts in *Laocoön*, he contended that
certain subjects were more suitable for painting, others
more suitable for poetry. His point of departure is the group
sculpture, the Laocoön, unearthed at Rome in 1506. In comparing the sculptor's presentation of Laocoön and his sons
in the coils of the two sea monsters with Vergil's account of
the same incident in *The Aeneid*, Lessing was concerned with
the question of whether it was aesthetically desirable only to
suggest the pain as the sculptor had done or to depict it
fully as Vergil had done. Few will deny the vividness of
Vergil's account: "He strains his hands to tear their knots
apart, his fillets spattered with foul black venom; at once to

heaven raises awful cries; as when, bellowing, a bull shakes the wavering axe from his neck and rushes wounded from the altar." [4]

Lessing accepts what each artist in his interpretation of the subject has done as being within the limits of his respective art. While the sculptor has done well in not allowing Laocoön to shriek, the poet has done equally well in allowing him to do so. Lessing's basis for this conclusion is that the natural limitations of the plastic arts (of which, for the ancients, beauty was the highest law) [5] and the natural flexibility of poetry supported such interpretations. The poet is not compelled to compress his "picture" into the space of a single moment, nor to observe any of the other limits of plastic imitation. Once he has succeeded in conveying to the reader all his hero's nobler qualities (which obviously the sculptor cannot do), the reader will give little thought to bodily form or physical action. On the other hand, the Greek sculptors have in portraying the torture felt by Laocoön reduced it to such a degree that it is compatible with beauty. Contorting the face or throwing the body into a forced position would have robbed the statue of the "beautiful lines which cover its surface in a quiet attitude" (p. 15). Had either the artist or the poet failed to recognize the laws by which his respective art governs itself, he would have failed to create an aesthetically pleasing art form.

Lessing's effort to separate the mode of poetry from that of the plastic arts is based upon two considerations: the art forms and our own modes of perception. Lessing observes that time is the element of poetry and space the element of the plastic arts (p. 91). When we look at a canvas we apprehend the whole by seeing the relation of its objects in space. When we read a poem our grasp of it depends upon a sequence of effects in time. A greater responsibility for the right choice of subject devolves upon the painter than on the poet if his end result is to convey a meaningful whole. He should therefore choose the "most pregnant moment" of action to portray. He will be able to suggest a subsequent action, but that is all he can do—suggest. The spatial form within which he must work limits him to portraying "material beauty." Material beauty is that which results from the harmony of several parts, "all of which sight is capable of comprehending at the same time." (p. 116)

While the artist is limited in what he may depict by the spatial relationship, the poet is freer in his choice of material but is limited in his means. That which the painter expresses with color and line in space is more difficult to render with words in time. The poet, rather than describing a thing or person, often depends upon describing the effect which they make (e.g. Homer describes the effects of Helen's beauty rather than the beauty itself). This the poet can do quite easily, since he does not have to restrain himself within the limits of the painter. He can move from moment to moment, idea to idea, depicting motion and action in time, all of which is beyond the limit of the painter. For Lessing, the realm of the plastic arts is limited to objects in space, while that of poetry includes movement in time.

In most modern writing and painting the principles of aesthetic perception which Lessing notes are still operative, but some modern writers, who use the stream-of-consciousness technique, have recognized the principle of spatial perception in creating a new narrative form. Spatial form is as common in literature today as it is in the plastic arts. Joseph Frank in a study of spatial form in modern literature states: "Modern literature exemplified by such writers as T. S. Eliot, Ezra Pound, Marcel Proust, and James Joyce is moving in the direction of the spatial form. This means the reader is intended to apprehend their work spatially in a moment of time, rather than as a sequence." [6] The method of perception is the same as that described by Lessing in the plastic arts, but the object of the perception is different.

Mr. Frank points out that the reader receives the whole impression of the complete works of writers such as he has mentioned, not page by page, nor action by action, but by means of "reflexive reference" whereby the reader fits together reference after reference and gains at the conclusion of his reading a complete picture of what the poet or novelist has accomplished through spatial form. Modern poetry in particular "is based upon a space-logic which demands a complete reorientation in the reader's attitude towards language." The reader must relate and organize apparently isolated fragments and word clusters to an implied and focused situation within the poem itself. The principle of reflexive reference is a basic conception of modern poetry and establishes the link between modern poetry and similar experiments in the modern novel. From Flaubert to Joyce and Proust, Mr. Frank demonstrates this principle which produces spatial form and reaches its culmination in a relatively unknown novel, *Nightwood* by Djuna Barnes.[7]

Mr. Frank feels that "just as modern artists have abandoned any attempt at naturalistic representation" so has Miss Barnes abandoned "any pretensions to . . . verisimilitude," and the result in the latter case is "a world as strange to the reader at first sight, as the world of abstract art was to its first spectators." In his detailed analysis of this novel Mr. Frank sees that what holds the chapters together is not progressive action of any kind, either physical action or thinking, but rather the use of images and symbols which have to be constantly referred and cross-referred to one another "throughout the time-act of reading." He concludes that since the unit of meaning in *Nightwood* is usually a phrase or sequence of phrases "it carries the evolution of spatial form in the novel forward to a point where it is practically undistinguishable from modern poetry."

Applied to a novel less obscure and esoteric in idea but equally spatial in form, Virginia Woolf's *Mrs. Dalloway*, Mr. Frank's theory can be given further proof of validity. The time covered in *Mrs. Dalloway* is one day in June, 1923. In this day we move through certain sections of London taking in the sights; smelling the odors of a big city; hearing the noises of buses, an aeroplane, the voices of beggars; meeting shoppers, saunterers in the park, the crowds that move to and fro in the streets. We also move in and out of a few selected homes, a doctor's office, stores and shops. Within these two physical bounds of particular time and place, Virginia Woolf presents Clarissa Dalloway and the handful of other characters who are necessary to an understanding of the main figure and the complexity of themes expressed. As the doctor in Miss Barnes's *Nightwood* serves as the unifying factor for what seem to be unrelated parts, a unifying factor, but not progressive action or thinking, holds together Mrs. Woolf's novel: the use of certain symbols and images which occur and recur throughout the space of the novel — the party which Mrs. Dalloway is giving and which provides the culminating point of the piece, the striking of Big Ben and other motifs of time and sound, the sun images, the seemingly disconnected lines from *Cymbeline* and *The Winter's Tale*, the flower symbols, unidentified personages — all add up to the total effect. We must make note of them, relate them to the major characters, else the intended identity of the two figures of Clarissa and Septimus remains lost and the whole work meaningless. We must almost literally stand still in space and move back and forth in time, not only with the characters but by ourselves, in order to fit together by "reflexive reference" the parts of the whole and apprehend the work "spatially in a moment of time rather than as a sequence."

The interrelation of the arts may often help the critic toward a deeper understanding of the work that he studies. But we may go further: the artist himself may profit by recognizing such an analogy. T. S. Eliot in his essay on "The Music of Poetry" [8] states explicitly what the study of music may contribute to poetry:

I think that a poet may gain much from the study of music. . . . I believe that the properties in which music concerns the poet most nearly, are the sense of rhythm and the sense of structure. . . . The use of recurrent themes is as natural to poetry as to music. There are possibilities for verse which bear some analogy to the development of a theme by different groups of instruments; there are possibilities of transitions in a poem comparable to the different movements of a symphony or a quartet; there are possibilities of a contrapuntal arrangement of subject-matter.

Upon reading this we think of Eliot's *Four Quartets* and try to find a comparison between the form of the poems and the analogous musical form. Miss Helen Gardner [9] has carried out this comparison and found it fruitful. Her careful analysis deepens our appreciation of the poems themselves; it also verifies the poet's own theory as stated above.

Four Quartets is composed of four poems, each named for a place related to a time in the total experience of men. Burnt Norton, East Coker and Little Gidding are English villages, .the Dry Salvages a group of rocks off the New England coast. Each poem is divided into five parts which Miss Gardner sees as "five movements each with its own inner structure." The first movement "contains statement and counter-statement" similar to the "first and second subject of a movement in a strict sonata form." The second movement treats a single subject in two different ways, the effect of which Miss Gardner says is "like hearing the same melody played on a different group of instruments, or differently harmonized, or hearing it syncopated, or elaborated in variations." The third movement presents less of a musical analogy; the fourth is seen as a "brief lyrical movement" after which the fifth "recapitulates the themes of the poem with personal and topical applications and makes a resolution of the contradictions of the first."

Besides calling our attention to the apparent composition of the poems along principles of musical form, Miss Gardner indicates the recurrence of images, symbols, and certain words which thus take on a deepened and expanded meaning. Eliot himself describes this "music of meaning" but without specific reference to *Four Quartets.* He writes:

The music of a word is, so to speak, at a point of intersection: it arises from its relation first to the words immediately preceding and following it, and indefinitely to the rest of its content; and from another relation, that of its immediate meaning in that context to all the other meanings which it has had in other contexts, to its greater or less wealth of association. . . . My purpose here is to insist that a "musical poem" is a poem which has a musical pattern of sound and a musical pattern of the secondary meaning of the words which compose it, and that these two patterns are indissoluble and one.[10]

Miss Gardner in going beyond the musical composition and treatment of thematic materials in *Four Quartets* finds another musical reminder in Eliot's treatment of images "which recur with constant modifications, from their context, or from their combination with other recurring images, as a phrase recurs with modifications in music." The images and symbols are common, obvious and familiar when we first meet them but "as they recur they alter as a phrase does when we hear it on a different instrument, or in another key, or when it is blended and combined with another phrase, or in some way turned round, or inverted." By the method hinted at by Eliot himself Miss Gardner's analysis does much to enhance the poet's work by showing us ways of "listening" to it that might not have occurred to us.[11] Such an effort, satisfying as it is, suggests a way to approach the work of other poets who have also become aware of this "music of meaning." It goes without saying that such studies as Miss Gardner's can be done only by those with knowledge of musical forms sufficient to point the way.

In passing we may point to another illustration of what light the knowledge of another art, in this case a particular mode of painting, can shed on the understanding of a poem. This may be seen in Sir Herbert Read's tracing the parallel between dream-formation and poem-formation in one of his own poems.[12] In doing so, Read makes quite clear the relation between surrealism in art and surrealism in literature and the source of both in the psychology which gave surrealism its impetus. The consideration of the rhyme employed and the examination of the images lead him to describe such a poem, i.e., a surrealist poem, "as the manifest content of a dream whose latent thoughts have been turned into sensory images or visual scenes; the abstract, that is to say, is merged again in the concrete form from which it sprang."

Up to this point we have been concerned with relationships without reference to a common denominator of time or cultural influence. It has been pointed out that the knowledge of principles of one medium may suggest new approaches to a totally different medium of artistic expression. We turn now to parallels that are found to exist between art and literature as a result of their contemporaneity. It is difficult here to steer clear of the problem of influence. It is also difficult to avoid the implication that different art forms of the same period developed under the same influences.

An enterprising study that tries to allow for the possibilities of such influence is Helmut Hatzfeld's *Literature Through Art* which the author subtitles "a new approach to French literature." The restriction of the study to the literature and art of one nation has obvious advantages not the least of which is the consideration of two art forms conditioned by the same factors and thus more likely to reveal a community of reflection. The theory underlying Hatzfeld's examination of literature and art is simply that a consideration, side by side, of different art forms within the same cultural epoch must increase the possibilities for interpretation. Placing a poem or novel beside a painting or piece of sculpture may very well reveal a new meaning of the literary text, may illustrate the different expression of the same motif or theme "according to the separate domain and medium of poet and painter," may prove mutual influences and inspirations. The emphasis of this comparative study, however, is the "cultural pattern of the epoch."

The author, in considering texts and art works from the same periods, has brought to bear on his comparisons "the common spiritual root behind the related examples." The conclusion drawn from this extensive study of the interrelations of culture and artistic expression is that the literature and art of any given historical epoch may be approached from seven categories: 1] details of a literary text elucidated by a picture, 2] details of a picture clarified by a literary text, 3] concepts and motifs of literature clarified by the arts of design, 4] motifs of pictures elucidated through literature, 5] and 6] literary-linguistic forms and literary-stylistic expressions in literature and art, and 7] borderlines between literature and art.[13]

Hatzfeld's method does provide illuminations of both literature and art and deepens our insights into the character of the artistic expression. Comparison of the landscapes of Claude Lorrain and the dialogue of Racine's dramas underscores the concept of formal beauty and idealized arrangement of nature held by the seventeenth-century poets and painters. The full description, poetic language, the melancholy air to be found in the writing of Chateaubriand are exemplified in paintings of Girodet-Tricson, Delaroche, David, and Gérard, all contributing to certain aspects of the romantic spirit that dwelt on the exotic and foreign, the "soulless physical beauty." The key to the "dark, cryptic, and the ununderstandable" in Rimbaud's "Mystique," from *Les Illuminations,* may be found in Gauguin's painting "Jacob Wrestling With the Angel," and the psychic conflict in Van Gogh is paralleled in the poems of Émile Verhaeren. An equally convincing parallel both in form and content is to be seen in the comparison of Courbet's "Funeral at Ornans" and Flaubert's description of Emma's burial in *Madame Bovary.* In both, exactness of detail conveys an objective picture of a given moment in life. Hatzfeld's study may be criticized for its definitions and choice of illustration, perhaps even for the theory upon which it is based, forcing at times comparisons which are artificial. But it does give insights into the meaning of the literature and art of a given period and it does suggest the potential of the philological approach.

A different approach to a study of the relationship of literature to the arts is Calvin Brown's *Music and Literature.*[14] Instead of being concerned with parallelisms from a cultural and philological point of view, Brown considers the relationship of literature and music based upon the elements

they have in common, upon the instances of collaboration between the two (from the folk epic to opera), and upon the
cases of influence of a writer upon a musician, a musician
upon a writer. Brown provides so many specific examples of
relationships between literature and music that it is hard to
demonstrate his method. However, the chapters on Whitman
and Aiken serve to show two different kinds of analysis of
the same literary form. Whitman's "When Lilacs Last in the
Dooryard Bloom'd" is analyzed for its musical development
of symbols, an unconscious and inspired musical treatment
by a "musical illiterate." Brown sees the poem not as one
"about" the death of Lincoln but as "the complex and beautiful interrelationship in the poet's mind by which a number
of hitherto insignificant things have come to symbolize a
complex experience" (p. 194). The chapter on Aiken offers
a contrast in subject, for the poet here is consciously and deliberately creating poetry based upon musical principles.
Using his knowledge of Aiken's intention Brown illustrates
copiously from Aiken's poetry the formal musical arrangement which the poet uses, concluding that Aiken, more than
any one else who has tried, has succeeded by means of musical symbols and techniques to "let us hear whole concerts of
this fleeting, elusive music of the mind" (p. 207). Brown is
not concerned with historical development or the reflection
of any common cultural background—he takes all music and
all literature as his province in this study. Although not so
interesting as Hatzfeld's *Music and Literature*, Brown's work
offers less to argue with and undoubtedly gives the student
more concrete suggestions for problems of comparison and
methods of research.

One of the areas to exert an influence upon comparative
studies of literature and art has been that of art history.
Heinrich Wölfflin's *Principles of Art History* (1915) formu-

lated the theory of artistic creation on the basis of the way things are seen and felt. Occupied with the contrast of Renaissance and Baroque, Wölfflin described their respective features as they reflected different levels of perception and contended that Baroque is a natural development from Renaissance and not a decline, that the change can be demonstrated by looking at the art work in five different aspects: the image itself (linear-painterly), the arrangement in space (flat-deep), the way the parts of the whole are combined (distinct parts-unified whole), the structure (closed-open), and the view of the whole (clear-blurred). The importance here of Wölfflin's principles is the effect they have had upon literary historians in providing them with similar means of interpreting literary styles. Oskar Walzel [15] in Germany and Fritz Strich [16] in Switzerland applied Wölfflin's method to English (Shakespeare) and German literature with partial success.

The significance of these attempts to apply the principles of art history to literary history lies in the discovery that one cannot simply borrow the basic concepts of one art medium and apply them to another even of the same period, though one may find both art forms containing common elements. Since there is not a parallel development in form and style, the principles for interpreting a given art form must derive from the nature of the work itself. Attention to one art of the same period will undoubtedly suggest concepts for interpreting another, but they cannot merely be transferred. Hatzfeld's study does not attempt to establish basic concepts for interpreting both literature and art of the same period, but rather gives seven ways by which a study of literature through art may increase our understanding of both without insisting upon a parallel development.

A more recent attempt to describe and interpret literature through art styles and art criticism is Wylie Sypher's *Four*

Stages of Renaissance Style.[17] The author is prompted by
what others after Wölfflin and Walzel discovered—that working with contrasts like Renaissance and Baroque tends to
oversimplify the matter, improperly makes art fit a pattern,
and does not take into account all the varieties and movements that cannot fit into either of the two opposites. Sypher's approach is based entirely upon style. Rather than talk
about parallels in styles between the arts, he prefers to use
the term "analogy" between styles to describe the various
ways in which the arts reflect social changes, each style with
"its own evolution, transformation and eventual disappear-
ance" (p. 7). In the emergence of these styles there are frequently "exchanges" of techniques between arts when the
technique of one penetrates another as sculpture in painting, narrative in music, water color in oil painting. When
there are combinations or interpenetrations of several techniques there are what Sypher calls "transformations" of
style: "the tone poem in music uses techniques that are pictorial and narrative, generating at the intersection of three
opposing techniques an equivocal order of art with inher-
ently nonmusical values of color and anecdote" (p. 9). And
as there are analogies of style so may there be analogies of
form—the way in which the artist arranges his material—
and Sypher contends that "if we can find analogies of form
within the various arts of the renaissance, we possibly can
define for literature as well as for painting, sculpture, and
architecture the mechanisms of a changing renaissance
style that emerges, transforms itself, re-emerges, and at last
plays itself out in a severe equation" (p. 10).

It is thus that Sypher examines the literature, painting,
sculpture, architecture of three centuries and shows how
their corresponding changes in style reflect various factors
that give identity to the styles—sometimes pure, sometimes

transitions—and how these styles form a sequence of four stages: renaissance, mannerist, baroque, and late-baroque. These styles, however, do not arise and develop simultaneously in each country. There are "lags" from one country to the next, from one art to the next. And the work of one artist may even reflect at different times different styles.

At present one may distinguish different trends in this field of studies. Extreme skepticism against past accomplishments and present endeavors is authoritatively represented by Wellek and Warren's *Theory of Literature*.[18] Mr. Wellek's chapter eleven, "Literature and the Other Arts," forms the end and, in a way, the climax of "the extrinsic" (and therefore the undesirable) approach to the study of literature. After an excellent and swift survey of both practice and theory from Horace to Walzel the chapter concludes with a grave warning not to attempt a synthesis too soon. "Only when we have evolved a successful system of terms for the analysis of literary works of art can we delimit literary periods, not as metaphysical entities dominated by a 'time spirit.' Having established such outlines of strictly literary evolution, we then can ask the question whether this evolution is, in some way, similar to the similarly established evolution of the other arts. The answer will be, as we can see, not a flat 'yes' or 'no.' It will take the form of an intricate pattern of coincidences and divergences rather than parallel lines." (p. 124)

However, the wary attitude of the pure theorist is not shared by the majority of researchers in the field. The center of their activity is to be found in the *Journal of Aesthetics and Art Criticism,* founded in 1941. The journal is full of lively controversies, but the group represented by it, the American Society for Aesthetics, is constantly striving for synthesis, no matter how tentative and how temporary. In a presidential address (1956) before the society, H. Hungerland pointed to both conflict and compromise: "The scientific investigation of aesthetic phenomena has been hampered by a pseudo-conflict between 'relativistic' and 'universalistic.' . . . I should like to suggest that probably 'the aesthetic response' in general can best be defined in terms of the core of a number of overlapping areas. The areas seen as overlapping would be the aesthetic-response-to-literature, the aesthetic-response-to-music, etc., and one should not expect the general definition to be applicable in all respects to all the areas." [19] Again and again one finds in the pages of the journal calls to carry on the work in spite of conflicting theories: "I do not share the view of many aestheticians . . . that the adequacy of evaluation depends primarily on a satisfactory critical theory." Or, "we should cease to expect to supplant emotionalist theories by formalist theories or vice versa. There is no choice to be made between these, and if it is offered, something of value is in danger of being ignored." [20] But the most substantial documentation of the widespread activity in the theory of the arts and their relations is found in the journal's annual "Selective Current Bibliography for Aesthetics and Related Fields" compiled by H. Hungerland.

Still less concerned with theory and dedicated to the literary point of view is a discussion group of the Modern Language Association, "Literature and the Other Arts." The papers before this discussion group frequently treat the relation of a particular author to the sister arts. Here, too, an important by-product has been an annual bibliography, a digest of which was published in 1959.[21]

With all art for its province, the subject offers countless possibilities for study, from chance associations between single works of art to highly complex patterns of interpenetration of the literary and art work of entire cultural epochs. Nor is this approach to the study of the arts an artificial one.

The serious artist and critic are ever-conscious of the "natural affinities" that exist between art and literature, and almost without exception allow these affinities themselves to suggest the parallels, the influences, the borrowings that become the basis for comparative analysis. At times the artist himself is consciously aware of themes, techniques of composition, formal arrangement, and development of ideas belonging to work of another art. This awareness may provide only an inspiration or it may be more obvious in an actual expression. Lessing, Baudelaire, T. S. Eliot, for example, provide convincing illustration of this consciousness and its fruits. For the comparatist, the point has this significance: the relevance of literature to the arts is not an invention of the critics; it is an actual fact acknowledged by the artists themselves.

8

Literature for the Unlettered

Stith Thompson

T HOUGH the title of this chapter may seem paradoxical, it was not made so deliberately to pique curiosity. It is actually about as accurate a statement of the topic as possible. Of course, a narrow definition of literature would always imply writing and reading and would utterly exclude those old tales, songs, myths, legends, rituals and orations which are directed toward those who do not habitually read. Though it may take some indulgence on the part of the reader, the term literature is here applied to such manifestations of the human spirit as those, since they serve the same purpose for the unlettered as written literature does for readers and writers.

Unlettered has been chosen rather than illiterate to describe the beneficiaries of such literature. For "illiterate" has in these days taken on a bad odor. We are apt to think of a person surrounded by public schools but failing to take advantage of opportunities—in a word, shiftless, unambitious, perhaps low in intellectual powers. But we must remember that the lack of ability to read and write has not always had this connotation even in our own culture. Few of our seventeenth- and eighteenth-century grandmothers went far

STITH THOMPSON, Distinguished Service Professor of English and Folklore, Emeritus, at Indiana University and past president of the American Folklore Society, edited the *Motif-Index of Folklore* and wrote *The Folktale*. Professor Thompson has long been recognized in this country and abroad as an outstanding authority in folkloristic studies.

beyond signing their names—if they did not actually content themselves with making a cross at the bottom of a deed or mortgage.

If by literate persons we mean those who are in the habit of getting their information from writing or print instead of from the spoken word, we must realize how restricted this group is. Outside of a relatively few countries of Europe and lands that they have influenced, the vast majority still remain unlettered, and as we go back across the centuries the readers become an ever smaller and more select class. Even in the great days of Egypt, of Greece and Rome, most of the writing was for a small elite, and only when the oral medium was employed, as in the orations or the dramas or the recited poems, did the great mass benefit by literature.

This general lack of the art of reading and writing among a people, whether Chinese, Melanesians or ancient Greeks, means that the attitude now commonly held toward the illiterates among us must be abandoned when we broaden and deepen our outlook. It is a fair guess that there are proportionately as many talented people in an unlettered group as among readers. These peoples have their leaders and their led. They have tale-tellers and listeners, epic poets and rhapsodes and spellbound audiences, musicians, dancers, orators, statesmen, warriors—as well as men and women sages. The high intelligence of those who went to the theater in Athens has often been remarked, but the great mass of them observed and heard and talked, but could not read. And if this was true in Athens, how much more so in Sparta or Macedonia!

The expanding of the capacities of the human spirit which has accompanied the use of writing accounts for the most remarkable difference between the gifted men of today and those of five thousand years ago or of far-flung primitive peoples. Short as the time span since the first hieroglyphics, and few as the lettered have been, it is through writing that the carefully considered thoughts of man have been handed down to become a part of the intellectual and artistic world of those who can read. Philosophy, science, law—all become permanent and are expanded by each lettered generation. And, above all, the finely wrought turn of phrase, or the exactly patterned poem, or the tale told with superb artistry is fixed for all time—no longer fluid, no longer uncertain, no longer dependent on the fluctuations of memory and forgetfulness. The world of those who read is, or at least can be, of infinitely greater richness than that of the unlettered.

But the very extent of unlettered humanity in all past ages, and even now, makes the study of its artistic and literary endeavors a challenge not only for the ethnologist but also for the student of letters. The tales told and the songs sung by the cave dwellers in Spain two hundred centuries ago, by those who tended the flocks of Abraham, by the subjects of the great Inca, by the present-day Eskimo, by the Yugoslav peasant or American backwoodsman—have these anything in common, anything which contrasts with the products of the writer's pen?

Of course, some of these people we shall never learn about, for they are beyond our reach. We can see the paintings of the cave men, but can never hear their tales. But though there are large areas which we may not explore, more than enough remain to occupy us if we would examine the literature meant for those who do not read. In the separate endeavors of all of these peoples to learn to tell tales or sing songs which others would enjoy and keep on telling and singing, did the unlettered storyteller or poet find that certain devices were successful and certain others were not successful? In other words, did he hit upon some of what we would call laws of composition? Or is this oral literature characterized merely by certain deficiencies, lacks which only writing can supply? As we look at the oral literature over the world and in all time, can we perceive any evolution, any development—for example, from simple to complex, from crude to artistic?

Perhaps it may be well to come at once to this question of evolution of oral literature. In the early years of this century, it was still the fashion to speak of the evolution of culture. Respectable ethnologists were still arranging people into strata, saying that a particular tribe belonged to the very lowest culture, and another somewhat higher, and that it was possible to arrange all the peoples of the globe according to a hierarchy, beginning at simple and going to the most complex. It was also assumed that all of the separate elements of culture would evolve within this framework, and that one tribe would certainly be like another, even though in the opposite part of the world, if they belonged on the same step of the evolutionary ladder.

But little by little ethnologists have given up such naive ideas. While the geologist may recognize his strata and always be confident that a particular formation lies above another, no matter where found, the student of culture must realize that every people has developed in its own way, that changes and movements have proceeded unevenly. It is not possible to say that because a tribe in Central Asia manifests a certain kind of oral literature, another tribe in another part of the world roughly its equal in general complexity will have the same kind of oral literature. The bold scheme of a comprehensive study of the evolution of literature based upon the tales and songs of all of the peoples of the world arranged in order, let us say from one to twenty, and filling in all the gaps in the evolutionary scheme—that we have had to give up entirely. Too many elements enter into a particular culture, some coming from local environment, some from the influence of neighboring tribes, and some from unexpected drives in particular directions. The narrative art of a tribe in the South Pacific or central Africa may have little relation to the material culture of that people.

If the evolution of literature must be abandoned as a pleasant delusion, the study of literature of the unlettered populations of the world is not thereby made less important or less valid. On the contrary, with a growing awareness of all the complexities which enter into the literary tradition of such peoples, this investigation becomes more and more challenging. What seemed to an earlier generation to be the working of a very simple law of development now appears as the result of a complex of many forces.

One will look in vain for any sharp line of demarcation between the oral literature of so-called primitive peoples and that of the unlettered who are surrounded by a civilized society. There are, however, some general differences, and we ordinarily find ourselves dealing with the literature of primitive peoples separately. This is largely a matter of convenience. For though we may be thinking only of primitive peoples on certain days of the week, even on these days some consideration of modern peasants will always be creeping in. With this understanding, we may observe something of the range of the oral literature of peoples whom we now call primitives.

In the world of the preliterates, of the natives of Australia and New Zealand, and of Oceania, of the Indians of North and South America, of the Africans south of the Sahara, and of many scattered peoples in Southeast Asia, we find much in common in spite of large individual differences. In every one there will certainly be found some types of literary expression, usually myths and legends, and songs which we can only call lyric. But there is one form which is almost entirely absent from groups like this—narrative song.

The ballad students of an earlier generation were always looking for the ballads of primitive peoples to show something of the evolution of the great epics. I recall one of my old professors whose skepticism about this theory I did not then suspect. I suggested to him a certain study which would involve looking into the narrative songs of the American Indians; and he consented—I think now with a certain dry amusement. But I had to come back to him after some weeks of search and confess failure because I could find no such songs among the American Indians. Then he suggested that I try the Africans. My luck was no better there. It simply turned out that there were no narrative songs among the American Indians or the Africans—nothing, certainly, which would foreshadow anything like the epics as Europeans know them.

Though short lyric songs of many peoples have been collected and are worthy of study, the best of all subjects for the comparative study of literature in its full range is prose narrative. Tales, legends, or myths are to be found everywhere and are known also among our peasant groups and in our own literary tradition. People with so simple a culture as the Central Australians have legends and myths, some of them dealing with the world of long ago and some with their own contemporary life. And through all the range of primitive peoples, according to their temperaments and their environment and their tribal associations, myths have developed in some places, legends in others, and in still others artistic fictional tales—all according to the vital interests of the particular people. For the literary expression of a simple group must be functional: it must play a real part in the life of the tribe. The very fact that it persists as a part of the activity of the people shows that it has served a purpose and continues to do so. But this does not mean that it is necessarily serving any utilitarian end, that it has any practical economic value. For even in the Trobriand Islands, where Bronislaw Malinowski has so well studied the process of mythmaking and where myths contribute to the magic which these folk use for their coral gardens, even there life is more than food and raiment.

Perhaps the most potent force making for the production of all literary forms among primitive peoples as well as in our own culture is the great need for relief from boredom. The long hours of the night around the tribal campfire in war as well as in peace, the tedious days or weeks of voyages or journeys by foot or caravan, and the festive hours of relaxation in taverns and bazaars or at the banquets of chiefs and kings—all of these occupy a large part in the life of simple peoples, as well as in our own. For these occasions nothing has been more satisfactory than the telling of stories—amusing or informative or edifying.

All peoples enjoy tales which make them laugh. Of these stories, when we consider them the world over, there is a great variety. Very often—and not alone among the simplest peoples—the humorous tale is merely one of discomfiture, showing a kind of sadistic delight in seeing someone, preferably a person or being of great dignity or even divinity, brought down to the level of ordinary mortals and properly cudgeled or disgraced. The great culture hero of our northern Indians appears now as the dignified Hiawatha and now as the fool taking pity on the creaking limbs of the tree and getting caught between them. Or the amusing tale may concern the cleverness which overcomes stupidity or malice. Hence the whole cycle of anecdotes the world over of the clever fox or rabbit or jackal and his tricks on the stupid bear.

And it is not civilized man who first invented the risqué tale. People everywhere have been interested in grossly exaggerated stories of bodily members and their functioning, of stupendous sexual prowess, of the breach of the tribal sexual tabus, and of clever and sometimes brutal seductions; but such stories are ubiquitous and of course have not ceased with the invention of writing.

For more serious moments, whether informally or as a part of ritual observance, men everywhere and presumably at all times have had a great interest in hearing about the past, in learning of the world about them and speculating on the mysterious powers that seem to govern the life of nature, of man, and of brutes. Stories, therefore, of spirits and demons and often, on a higher plane, of gods and demigods, both in some vast historic past or now in their relation with men, have always interested primitive man—not to speak of the kings who listened to Homer's poems or the Sunday school child of today—or at least of yesterday. The world which encompasses us, the sun, moon and stars, the animals, the trees and plants—how did all of these come to be? In response to his natural curiosity, primitive man has told tales of the creation of the universe and of the arrangement of all things as they now are. Almost all peoples have their first chapter of Genesis and their Metamorphoses, and doubtless had them thousands of years before Moses or Ovid. History, science, theology, philosophy, or at least the rudiments of these, have always interested men in their leisure time and have contributed incidentally to their education.

Stories of heroes and their incredible success in the face of monstrous adversaries—dragons, gigantic evil spirits, or overwhelming human opposition—have exercised the inventive imagination of primitive tale-tellers and held their audiences. Every group has made up its own heroes, and though the possible details of the hero's birth, his youth, and his adventures are definitely limited by the very nature of life, there is no necessary common pattern to them all. Maui, the semidivine hero of the Polynesians, is engaged in unbelievable supernatural adventures, tossing islands about over three thousand miles of ocean. The Iroquois heroes spend their time escaping from or overcoming the evil plots of malignant human beings; and other heroes before and after Hercules have journeyed through hell and brought home Cerberus. Or like Orpheus they have sought to regain some primitive Eurydice.

But the fictional tales of primitive man are not confined to the exploits of heroes. When we remember that in our present-day folktales the supernatural is taken for granted, we need not wonder that the stories of simpler peoples should be filled with magic wonders, with journeys to other worlds —above, below or across—and with transformations from man to beast, with werewolves, and witches and fairies. And there is always the absorbing interest in luck of all kinds, in the finding of buried treasure, in the unexpected reunion of separated friends or loved ones, of the help, often undeserving, which comes to those in trouble and of strange adventures that may happen from some insignificant accident— these are some of the elements out of which primitive fiction is composed, and which we still see in the fairy tales of today.

Sometimes these fictional narratives become quite as complex and well constructed as any European fairy tale. I happen, for example, to have worked for some years on a single North American Indian tale—one which seems to be purely native and which has spread over a good part of the North American continent. Certainly this tale indicates an interest in storytelling and considerable invention on the part of the man who made it up, perhaps centuries ago. I cite it because it will illustrate something of the capacities of primitive peoples in constructing tales: Two girls are sleeping out one night and see two stars. Each of them wishes that she may be married to one of the stars. The next morning they find themselves in the upper world, one of them married to a young man, and one to an old one. The girls live there for some time, but they are forbidden ever to dig in the ground. One day, merely out of disobedience or sometimes because they have been egged on to do so, they dig in the ground and see below their old home and their tribe. They are seized with a longing to return and sometimes with supernatural help or with the aid of some animal, they make a long rope and descend upon it.

From that point the story is handled in several different ways, and each of these handlings constitutes a complex and continuous tradition. Sometimes the girls are lodged in a top of a tree and various animals pass below trying to induce the girls to come down. Finally they promise one of the animals that they will marry him and so they are allowed to descend. Later they deceive this animal and reach their home. Other whole sections of the country have put a different introduction to this story, so that there is only one girl who ascends to the upper world, and in that case she has a son by the upper-world husband and this son becomes the great hero after they descend and reach their home. The adventures of this hero, then, may extend to hours of tale-telling.

For us the telling of such a tale, extending, as I have suggested, into hours, may seem tedious; but we must remember that primitive man and indeed most men everywhere have infinite leisure and patience. It is not unusual to hear of tale-telling that lasts with due interruption for many days. And just as there seemed to be a premium on length for the me-

dieval romances, there is often a feeling among the unlettered that a story is good in proportion to how long it lasts.
Some tribes consider a story successful only when it succeeds eventually in putting everyone in the audience to sleep.
The bedtime story is no modern invention.

Though the tale is a way of making primitive man's leisure more pleasant and amusing, it is often told under very
strict rules. Some peoples find their lives very much ordered
by seasons of the year and by the succession of day and
night. Sometimes among such groups stories of a certain kind
must not be told in the summer, sometimes not in the winter.
There are stories suitable for daytime and for night; stories
that only men can tell or women; finally, stories that belong
definitely to the ceremonial life of the people. These may
be told only as a part of the long rituals that accompany
religious observances.

If one wishes to see the way in which stories are worked
into rituals, he could not do better than to examine the cere-
monials of the Navaho or the rites of the Grand Medicine
Lodge of the Ojibwa. In the latter we have stories that tell
the sacred legend which is illustrated by the activities performed in the ritual. Hiawatha, or Nanibozho as his real
name is, has a brother who, while skating over the lake, is
pulled under by the evil spirits and dies. After the mourning of the hero in his tipi, there appears at the door the spirit
of his brother with a live coal. This is handed to Hiawatha
and he is told that it is a symbol of eternal life and that he
should form the Grand Medicine Lodge in order to keep
the spark alive. This tale is now a central part of the lodge
ceremonial.

One of the great moot questions among folklorists today
is: which of these came first? Was there first a ritual and
then a myth to support the ritual, or was the ritual invented

in order to illustrate the story? It seems to me that such speculations as this are useless. It may well be shown that among such historic peoples as the Greeks and the peoples of the ancient Orient stories were sometimes invented to illustrate pre-existing rituals. And yet we cannot conclude that this is a universal experience or that it is even typical of primitive man. Was the Easter celebration first or the story which that celebration illustrates? Those who worry overmuch about the mutual relations of ritual and myth also concern themselves with trying to make a sharp line between myth and tale. I am sure that no such line can be drawn, and that certainly none that we might draw would be recognized by any primitive group. For practical purposes we may well think of myth as a story of the gods and heroes and the beginnings of things; but all the tales of preliterate groups are filled with the supernatural and heroic, and it is quite impossible to say where this heroic world leaves off and the world of everyday begins.

Some of the materials and some of the functions of the tales of primitive peoples, and, in many respects, the tales of all unlettered peoples, have now been suggested. Do these oral tales possess any common characteristics as distinct from the written fiction which has overshadowed them in our own civilization?

When we begin to examine large bodies of literature meant for hearers rather than for readers, we perceive certain traits dictated by the circumstances of all oral literature. This is as true of the narrative poems which perhaps underlie our great epics as it is of the tales, because the same type of composition and preservation is present in both. It must be remembered that all of this literature is told by someone, and that the teller has learned what he is telling from someone else. He knows that faithfulness to the tradition is the most valued of all qualities in the tale-teller or the singer of the epic song. He must, if possible, transmit it as he has heard it. This sometimes requires a prodigious memory. One has only to consider the long rituals of the Navaho, extending sometimes when they are taken down to hundreds of pages of print. These rituals are delivered from memory and they are ineffective unless they are remembered exactly. It is said that the Homeric poems were thus carried on by bards for two or three centuries at least, and we know of present Yugoslav epic poems which are as long as the *Iliad* or the *Odyssey* and which are given entirely from memory. I have listened to hour-long tales in the west of Ireland and have been assured by those who have tested the recordings of these tales over long periods that they are remembered precisely as they are told.

For this kind of memory it is natural that the literature of oral peoples should have taken on a form that would assist the narrator. Thus we find in all tales and poems a large amount of repetition. Similar situations bring forth similar descriptions. Tales open and close with formulas. Huge sections are repeated verbatim. Those of us who studied Greek in school will remember the joy we used to have in coming across whole pages in Homer which repeated something we had already worked up some days before. The parts of primitive and folk narrative which are purely formulistic have never been thoroughly studied, but we know now from the efforts of Professor Lord of Harvard that, in the Yugoslav epics and in the Homeric poems at least, the formulistic and formulaic constitute much the larger part of the poems. So it is with all folk tales: always repetition and formulas. And these formulas extend beyond the merely verbal, because the characters themselves become stereotyped. Only sharp contrasts, blacks and whites, appear in such tales. Actual characterization is almost missing. Realism seldom appears in any of the stories, but rather absurd exaggerations, supernatural happenings of all kinds, often with no motivation. Even in such semisophisticated stories as those of the Arabian Nights practically all of these qualities are still present. I think it might be easy to find exceptions to some of the things I have said about the style of oral literature: one could point out the remarkable, and sometimes tedious, explanation of motives in the tales of the Kota of India. But by and large, primitive tales lack adequate motivation.

As for the songs of primitive peoples, they contain little text and are nearly all music, and are of most interest to the musician. Aside from the songs of love, war, or magic, there are some beautiful productions which we can only call chants. Such are the prayer-songs of the Papago and the long chants already mentioned in the Navaho rituals. These have much in common with such poems as those in the Egyptian Book of the Dead, with their repetition, their saying the same phrase over and over and over again, the kind of repetition which Jesus condemned in Israel and which is still a part of the ritual of the Russian Orthodox Church.

What happens to such primitive forms as the oral folk tale and the oral poem when they are in the hands of the unlettered within a civilization of readers and writers? Is there a difference, really, between the literary productions of primitive peoples and the peasantry of Asia and Europe? Many differences of course exist, but none of these are really profound. The folk tales of European peasants have the same formal characteristics as those of primitive peoples, but in general they are more tightly knit, are better motivated, and have the kind of beginning, middle, and end which Aristotle approves. On the other hand, the peasant stories of many of the sophisticated Oriental peoples are extremely hard to outline. Unless they have been borrowed directly from Europeans they are likely to ramble interminably and apparently without reason. A story told in India seems to be almost without form, but when the same one is found in Europe it is well constructed. Do we have a case of a chaotic Indian tale coming to Europe and taking on form, or do we merely see the disintegration of a good European story which has found its way to India? Perhaps the best folk tales nowadays in our Western culture are to be found in Ireland, where they are still preserved by professional folk-tale tellers who learned them years ago from a master who had learned them from a previous master. As they come into our own continent, both north and south, these European folk tales have a tendency to degenerate. The very conditions of a peasantry, illiterate but often endowed with abilities, are lacking in the United States as well as in most of the rest of America. Such tales are definitely relics, and one has to go into remote corners to find them. They are often very interesting when found, but they are interesting as relics, and not as a vital part of our culture.

In talking about literature for the unlettered, I hope I have not given the impression that there is any sharp boundary line between the unlettered and the lettered world. The differences are smoothed over by many transitions. Some literary forms act as bridges for this gap. Perhaps the most interesting of all these is the epic, the so-called folk epic— especially the *Iliad* and the *Odyssey*. The Homeric poems were first of all oral and they remained so for several centuries before they were written down in Athens. After the remarkable analytical work recently done on the Yugoslav epics which are still being sung in Serbia and Macedonia, the oral devices in the Homeric poems cannot be denied. Were there heroic poems before Homer, telling of the Trojan war or possibly of the adventures of a hero like Odysseus? In spite of the present emphasis upon the creative ability of the poet who brought these epics together, it seems to me that there is every evidence of a society in which oral heroic songs were sung and that the time and place were only waiting for the great master to appear and to compose them into enduring epics. In Finland, also, there were and are many hundreds of heroic songs. These were gathered together more than a century ago and deliberately put into an epic called the *Kalevala*. These oral songs which lie back of the *Kalevala* can be studied, but they are no longer being composed. They are written down, and the epic is written, and though it reflects much of the oral phraseology, it is no longer a poem that would be learned and transmitted from singer to hearer.

In Russia there survives a live tradition of epic songs. These are based upon events in Russian history, many of them a thousand years old. The singers, however, are usually illiterate and they compose in a purely formulistic style. Much like them, but also different in many respects, are the already mentioned epic songs of Macedonia. As these become written down, will they also become like the Finnish epic songs and the *Kalevala*, fixed and stereotyped? It seems quite likely that with the advance of literacy this will happen. There is an accelerated tendency toward writing, and as we record more and more of the oral tales and put them into our libraries, the live tradition of oral tale-telling in our own culture has a tendency to dry up.

For two thousand years now, folk literature has been affected by written literature. Tales heard from the folk may be taken over, as by Apuleius in the case of Cupid and Psyche during the second century of our era, and then they may again become oral, or the written form may be merely one of hundreds of different versions. It is certain that the great printed collections of Basile or Perrault or Grimm have affected the tradition of our tales in Europe in a way that is permanent. Today, in a great many parts of the Western world, such folk literature is merely a survival and as such is interesting to the scholar who goes to recover it before it is entirely lost. Or its preservation may become merely a matter of romanticism, merely an enthusiasm over a simple form which is different from what we meet everyday. All folklorists have at least a partly antiquarian point of view, so that they look around in holes and corners to see if they cannot rescue some remnant of a dying tradition.

But it will not do to be nostalgic about these things, for centuries of experience and association have habituated us to the written or printed page and to a different world of thought and literary style. After the Greeks had shown the fine nuances of expression which their remarkable language permitted them and had left their works fixed for all time on skins or papyri, the intellectuals of our Western world would never revert to the old, eternally changing, eternally fluid literature of their unlettered ancestors or neighbors. In spite of cultural setbacks, of stupidity and villainy, we are the inheritors of three thousand years.

If we would understand our literature well, however, we should know the soil from which it grew—the long hundreds and thousands of years when men spoke or sang and listened and kept what they had heard in memory. Person to person, generation to generation, the clever to the stupid or the stupid to the clever—so the spoken word of two thousands years before survives, is lost, or changes. Such literature never subjects itself to a final text. It produces many beautiful products, beautiful in their own way, but not in ours. For the great advance toward artistic perfection in literature came only with the written word.

Who is responsible for composing unwritten literature? In most cases we do not know at all. Outstanding men have certainly always existed. Who were the poets who preceded Homer by a thousand years? Were they priests? vagabonds? or mere local geniuses? One of these days, perhaps, we shall know more about the history of the poet, about the artist and his place in the culture of the world. And much of such history will deal with literature for the unlettered.

BIBLIOGRAPHICAL NOTE

Cf. E. B. Tyler, *Primitive Culture*, 2 vols. (London, 1871, and New York, 1958) ; A. S. Mackenzie, *The Evolution of Literature* (New York, 1911) ; Francis B. Gummere, *The Beginnings of Poetry* (New York, 1901) ; Bronislaw Malinowski, *Coral Gardens and their Magic* (New York, 1935) and *Myth in Primitive Psychology* (New York, 1926) ; Stith Thompson, *Tales of the North American Indians* (Cambridge, Massachusetts, 1929) and *Motif-Index of Folk-Literature*, 6 vols. (Copenhagen and Bloomington, 1955–58).

9

Tragedy and Moralism
Euripides and Seneca

Norman T. Pratt, Jr.

A COMPARISON of the dramas written on the theme of Phaedra and Hippolytus by the Greek Euripides and the Roman Seneca will be used here to indicate some differences of orientation between the two major types of tragic drama surviving from antiquity.[1] This essay presents a basis of differentiation, not a study of the plays in full detail. By the same process we shall try to throw some light upon a major transition in the course of European tragedy, at the point where the classical Greek dramatic tradition ends, and the trends of the "modern" period, including Shakespeare, begin to emerge.

In recent years it has become the literary fashion to emphasize the ritual origin of Greek tragedy and, often, to analyze its form and to interpret the meaning in ritualistic terms. It is, to be sure, one of the few things which we can come close to knowing about the origin of Greek tragic drama that one of its sources was ritual song performed in worship of Dionysus. Dionysus, whom we often think of as the god of wine (Roman Bacchus) was actually a fertility divinity

NORMAN T. PRATT, JR., Chairman of the Department of Classics at Indiana University, is the author of *Dramatic Suspense in Seneca and in His Greek Precursors* and has made a study of Stoicism in Senecan tragedy. He has been Visiting Professor at Columbia University and, since 1956, editor-in-chief of *The Classical Journal*.

linked with nature's reproductive power and with the cycle of
life and death among living things, and conceived of in male
terms. Most specifically, he was associated with the life cycle
of the vine: its production of harvest, the death-like pruning
of its vegetation after harvest, and its reproduction at the advent of the new season.

There is very much that we do not know about all this; the
skein of available evidence is scanty and tangled. But it
seems clear enough from data concerning such fertility rites
and from the evidence of the plays themselves that Greek
tragic drama received from ritual—like the ritual of
Dionysus—a conception of nature: nature as a complex of
forces which bring health or disease to plants and animals.
One purpose of such ritual was to effect a reconciliation between individual living things or social organisms and the
powers of nature: to avert the destructive impurities, to
achieve life-nourishing purity.

The strong tendency in recent work on Greek tragedy, to
approach these dramatic creations as founded on and conditioned by ritual, has contributed considerable illumination
—as well as much distortion when carried to extremes. For
example, Francis Fergusson's influential analysis of *Oedipus
the King* [2] is built upon the following ideas: "The Cambridge
School of Classical Anthropologists has shown in great detail
that the form of Greek tragedy follows the form of a very ancient ritual, that of the *Enniautos-Daimon,* or seasonal god."
"It is this tragic rhythm of action which is the substance or
spiritual content of the play, and the clue to its extraordi-
narily comprehensive form."

It would be unjust to be captious about this method, for it
has succeeded in revealing implications and dimensions
which are fresh discoveries, and in reminding readers that we
are dealing not only with a great literary tradition, but also

with dramatic creations which are rooted in communal ritual. However—to give a very familiar and generally discredited example—serious distortion results from viewing Oedipus as a ritual scapegoat through whom the impurities of the city are exorcised. It is one dimension of the drama that impurity and abnormality in the family of Laius have brought upon Thebes a taint which must be removed—this must be recognized if we are to understand the role of Apollo the purifier in the drama—but at the end of the tragedy we are left, not with a purified Thebes, but with a suffering tragic hero and the mystery of his experience. The point must be made that there is a great difference in level of intellectual maturity between the plays themselves and the ritualistic concepts by which the "Cambridge anthropologists" and their followers analyze the texts. The fifth-century dramatist shows himself to have been far more sophisticated than this kind of analysis represents him to be. Another major danger is that the imprint of ritual thus tends to become a kind of mechanistic factor which presses the drama into a formal mold. The creative function of the dramatist is seriously slighted.

Even so, a strong ritualistic motivation is apparent in the texts. A ritualistic concept is found in the orientation of these tragedies toward the issues involved in the relations between man and the powers controlling the universe. Further, the human situation in relation to these powers characteristically involves impurity or abnormality or injustice which calls for some kind of purification. There are many guises of purification in the texts.

A second general point is also essential for the understanding of Euripides' *Hippolytus* and, for that matter, most of the Greek plays. The Greek conception of divinity is radically different from the Hebraic-Christian idea familiar to Western readers of Greek literature, and is often a source of serious misunderstanding. For example, modern readers of Homer are often mystified by the action in the first book of the *Iliad* when Achilles is about to draw his sword in the quarrel with Agamemnon, but Athena suddenly appears to check him; or in the *Odyssey* by the repeated appearances of Athena to help Telemachus who is struggling to make decisions and to achieve maturity in a difficult personal situation. What is the significance of Athena's appearances? Does Homer expect us to believe that Athena appears physically, or is this simply a metaphorical way of saying that Achilles' better judgment prevailed, or that Telemachus is approaching adult intelligence? The answer seems to be that Homer does ask the reader to accept her appearance as a physical action *and* that a kind of metaphor is involved. Athena is a divine person, she has a personal identity which can be described and recognized; her emotional and intellectual make-up is well defined. But it is equally important to observe that Athena characteristically appears in situations which involve the application of mind to practical situations; on this basis we can understand how her functions as goddess of warfare and as mistress of handicraft could be absorbed into the fully developed conception of her nature. In these Homeric passages she exemplifies the Greek way of saying that active intelligence is more than the thinking mechanism of an individual creature; it is a significant and pervasive aspect of experience. It is bigger than human. It is "divine."

This conception of divinity has a number of important implications for the understanding of the Euripidean *Hippolytus*. For one thing, in Greek literature of the classical period generally, the gods are not pure symbols. One has to reckon with them as personalities and as symbols. For another, one has to be very careful in analyzing the relationship between divine powers and human actions. Much that has been writ-

ten about Greek tragedy as "tragedy of fate and determinism" founders on the false assumption that all aspects of
divinity in these strongly religious dramas involve forces
which are external to human affairs and directly determine
human actions. Analysis based on this assumption often produces the conclusion, or the strong tendency toward it, that
the freedom of the human being is severely restricted by
divine control. Bothersome questions arise. Why does the
dramatist devote so much attention to the delineation of human character if the role and significance of character are so
restricted? If men are close to being puppets manipulated by
external forces, does the human scene have enough status,
can it be taken seriously enough to be "tragic" at all? Or do
we have simply pessimism—or optimism?

It is true that the Greeks were intensely aware of the constant impact of outside elements upon man's experience. This
recognition is fundamental in their earliest literary document
which has survived, the *Iliad*. But the idea of absolute pre-
determinism is *not* characteristically Greek. These people
keenly felt the instability of human fortune under the impact
of bigger-than-human forces, but they were also strongly
individualistic and insistent upon human prerogatives,
whether the context be political or intellectual; this is perhaps
one reason why the role of "fate" is a matter for such intense concern. In any event, on this whole matter there is a
wide range of positions taken by individual poets, as well as
other thinkers, and these must be analyzed in terms of the
individual poem or drama. There was no orthodoxy on such
issues comparable to that found in the Christian tradition.
One of the points which matters greatly is the way in which
the individual artist uses this conception of the gods. Are his
gods more significant as active personalities? Or as symbols?
Even though exact answers may elude us, at least rough

distinctions are possible, as between the gods of Aeschylus'
Oresteia and of the *Hippolytus*. The appropriate answer will
matter greatly. When, as in the *Hippolytus*, the gods function
primarily as symbols of the phenomena which are manifested
by the human figures in their characters and actions, the
artist is not saying that human action is determined by the
gods in any absolute sense, but is universalizing the factors
present in the human situation. The notion "tragedy of fate"
is dangerous and intricate.

The prologue of the *Hippolytus* confronts us with these
issues immediately. Aphrodite (Cypris), claiming the honor
due to her as an Olympian, announces that she will punish
Hippolytus' scorn by death at his father's hands, and that the
process of revenge requires Phaedra's death also. The
goddess is heartlessly protecting her own interests. At the
end of the drama, Artemis' attitude is comparable: [3]

> *Cypris shall find the angry shafts she hurled*
> *against you for your piety and innocence*
> *shall cost her dear.*
> *I'll wait until she loves a mortal next time,*
> *and with this hand—with these unerring arrows*
> *I'll punish him.*

It is very difficult to state Euripides' religious views
clearly, probably because he did not resolve some issues himself. His views are the product of an uneasy, sophisticated,
critical mind moved by the rational tendencies of his time.
But it seems possible to approach somewhere near the center
of his position in this drama, by using the notion of symbolic
personalities sketched above. The symbolic aspect of Aphrodite and Artemis is of the utmost importance in the drama. In
this aspect the goddesses are, in fact, the whole context of the
tragedy. However, *as personal deities* they raise grave doubts

for the dramatist. Artemis describes the relationship among the gods as a matter of mechanical protocol:

> *For it was Cypris managed the thing this way*
> *to gratify her anger against Hippolytus.*
> *This is the settled custom of the Gods:*
> *No one may fly in the face of another's wish:*
> *we remain aloof and neutral.*

The human reaction to this thought is elsewhere expressed sensitively by the chorus:

> *The care of God for us is a great thing,*
> *if a man believe it at heart:*
> *it plucks the burden of sorrow from him.*
> *So I have a secret hope*
> *of someone, a God, who is wise and plans;*
> *but my hopes grow dim when I see*
> *the deeds of men and their destinies.*

Professor Kitto interprets Artemis' words this way: "She paints Olympus as a place of moral chaos—which can indicate only that what these deities represent, instinctive passions, is independent of reason and morality." [4] The whole point appears to be somewhat sharper, because Euripides seems also to mean: "If you look to these gods as personalities for comfort and rational concern, you are probably deluded; they seem to be indifferent and irresponsible."

But at any rate the main function of the goddesses is to represent sexual passion and ascetic purity as "divine" phenomena, that is, as motive forces which are pervasive and persistent. Passion is the force which moves the dramatic action, but the motive of purity is essential for the impasse which produces tragedy. In other words, the phenomena represented by the goddesses are in destructive collision. The

Greek way of saying this is found in some more words of
Artemis:

> *For that most hated Goddess,*
> *hated by all of us whose joy is virginity,*
> *drove her with love's sharp prickings to desire*
> *your son.*

Hippolytus and Phaedra are then victims of the force of
sexual love. But victims in what sense? The drama has often
been interpreted to mean that they are victims of their own
extremes. Throughout the text such notions as "moderation"
and "excess" are reiterated. But are the characters and actions of Hippolytus and Phaedra (and Theseus) extreme in
such a way that their excesses could be resolved by some
principle of control?

Essentially the two main characters express humanly the
full force of the phenomena figured by Aphrodite and Artemis. Phaedra takes her own life and causes, through Theseus'
curse, the death of Hippolytus not because she is weak or
irrational, but simply because she is overpowered by love.
Every reasonable demand that she try to achieve control is
satisfied by her own description of her strong and self-conscious struggle to conquer love "with discretion and good
sense." She makes the point herself:

> *I think that our lives are worse than the mind's quality*
> *would warrant. There are many who know virtue.*
> *We know the good, we apprehend it clearly.*
> *But we can't bring it to achievement.*

Honesty and loyalty are her natural characteristics. The evil
which comes from her: the false accusation of Hippolytus and
her vindictiveness toward him—these are the products of
shame and the desperate attempt to secure her children's
future, as the results of being overpowered.

In some respects Hippolytus is one of the most disagreeable figures found in the Greek plays. The Greeks of the fifth-century audience probably felt even more strongly than we do that he is disastrously contemptuous of a fundamental law of human experience. Very obtrusive indeed are his pride, self-love and violence. However, these faults come essentially from his extreme dedication to the purity of forest and meadow, to the chastity of uncivilized nature figured by the Maiden Goddess of Wild Things, Artemis. It is a barren and unnatural commitment, as Euripides clearly feels, but it makes a legitimate claim for attention and respect. Incidentally, these values associated with Artemis could of course be recognized immediately by Euripides' Greek audience; the modern reader has to re-create the original context in this respect.

And Hippolytus is good. This is acknowledged—not only by himself!—by the Messenger (whose statements are factual), Artemis and Theseus. His quality is also demonstrated in the final stages of the action where he is compassionate toward Theseus and frees him of guilt. His death is caused in part by refusal to break his oath of silence. It is typical of Euripides' wry-faced manner to create this disagreeable fanatic whose moral purity is nevertheless authentic.

It is impossible, then, to find in the drama, as the dramatist has shaped it, any means of control or moderation which could be realized. Phaedra has struggled for rational solution, but is overwhelmed by "Aphrodite." Any kind of adjustment by Hippolytus is unthinkable. The *Hippolytus* is not primarily a "tragedy of character" but of the conditions of human existence. Everything points in this direction: the prominent roles of Aphrodite and Artemis, and of what they stand for; the characters of Phaedra and of Hippolytus. Further, in the form of the drama, the power of "Aphrodite" and its collision with the qualities of "Artemis" are represented as a "storm from the sea" (along with related ideas) in a substantial pattern of figurative language throughout the text. For example, Aphrodite's first word in the Greek text of the prologue calls herself "mighty"; by a simple verbal repetition the Nurse later refers to her as coming to men like a "mighty wave" (line 443). Phaedra is tossed by a storm (315) and struggles to swim out (470). The traditional epithet of Aphrodite as the "sea-born queen" is used with special point (415, 522)—whereas Artemis frequents "dry land beyond the sea" (149). In the first stasimon (525–64) Eros and Aphrodite are linked with stormy elements (530, 559, 563). The sound of the conversation of the Nurse and Hippolytus overheard by Phaedra is the sound "of rushing water" (576).

The second stasimon is a brilliant development of this figurative theme. In the first half (732–51) the thought moves from the here and now to distant places around the sea where, in contrast with the flux of the sea, the human grief of the sisters mourning the death of Phaethon is fixed in beauty, and where the gods dwell in brightness and security. In the second half (752–75) the chorus, moving in thought from Phaedra's distant home in Crete to nearby Athens, identifies the ship which brought her with Phaedra herself, and anticipates the suicide of Phaedra who, metaphorically, is "foundering under bitter misfortune" (769). Theseus looks upon a sea of disaster (822–24). The final catastrophe is caused by the sea monster sent by Poseidon.

Euripides clearly communicates his conception that the tragedy of *Hippolytus* comes from evil which is organic in the natural order of the conditions in which humans live. It is essentially this "natural" evil that produces the extremes found in the characters and actions of Phaedra, Hippolytus and Theseus.

Turning to the *Phaedra* (or *Hippolytus*) of the Roman Seneca takes us over a wide gap—in time, kind and quality. His plays, of the first century A.D., are usually thought of as conscious imitations of various Greek tragedies (apparently Seneca was particularly attracted to the themes dramatized by Euripides), although we suffer from having little substantial knowledge of Latin tragic drama before Seneca. In any event we are here interested not so much in the point-to-point relationship between the Euripidean and Senecan dramas as in some explanation of the differences between them as types of drama.

Senecan drama is not directly related to communal ritual like the Greek. It is the product of the study and presumably —though this is moot—was written to be recited to literary groups rather than staged. Condemnations of Seneca the dramatist are commonplace. His works are, in comparison to the Greek, second-rate melodrama loaded with rhetoric, mythological and other lore, and violent action (sometimes, as in the *Phaedra,* horribly violent). They are excessively intense in matter and form.

However, these plays challenge analysis for several important reasons. The striking disparity between the Greek and Roman products in the same dramatic tradition calls for explanation. Also, the ubiquitous historical influence of Seneca upon English and European drama of the sixteenth and seventeenth centuries makes it essential to understand the nature of the source; and it must be remembered that Senecan influence was not merely a regrettable fact, but in a number of ways had a positive salutary effect. For example, the fully developed structure and language of the Senecan play disciplined the drama written under its influence; or again, the device of introspective monologue, which was shaped by rhetorical and Stoic elements in Seneca, became a powerful tool for later dramatists. Finally, most critics appear to take it as a personal insult that Seneca undertook to write drama, and there has been relatively little effort to understand what made the plays what they are—for good *and* bad.

The writer has suggested elsewhere that Stoicism formed Senecan drama much more fundamentally than has been realized.[5] It is obvious, of course, that Stoic themes, along with others, appear in the texts. More latently, conceptions from this source seem to have directed the very premises underlying Senecan drama. We are on sure ground in one respect, namely that Seneca was formally a Stoic and wrote a large amount of philosophical essays and epistles which can be brought into relationship with the plays.

A very brief sketch of Stoicism is necessary. It is a very comprehensive, and somewhat paradoxical, system based on the equation "virtue $=$ reason $=$ nature." Virtue is the greatest good for man and is achieved by the exercise of reason, the highest human capacity. But the force of reason is not merely human. It permeates all of nature, producing harmony, system and direction toward the good. This power in nature is also described in religious terms; it is equated with god, it is divine. (It is also, paradoxically, associated with the material fire.) Thus the potential rationality in man stems from his participation in the divine. The human being and the universe are, then, parallel organisms constructed in the best possible way for the realization of good through reason.

One familiar, but crucial, point should be stressed. Tragic drama is, of course, concerned with various forms of evil as they touch humans. A system like Stoicism which is essentially optimistic is hard put to account for imperfections in a world where reason is believed to be the dominant force. The prose writings of Seneca, like all Stoic literature, present a whole battery of arguments attempting to meet the issue: Evil only seems to be evil, and must be part of nature's rational plan; imperfection tests and develops man's mettle; what seems to be evil can be neutralized by man's understanding of "what is in his control" and what is not; evil can be converted to good by endurance, etc. For our purpose the most interesting question is: How does a dramatist with Stoic ideas—or at least this Stoic dramatist—account for catastrophe in tragic drama?

The Stoic philosopher deals with imperfection primarily in terms of the moral condition of the human being. Men's behavior is a battleground of reason vs. passion. The most frequent theme in Stoic writings is that error and evil result when passion overcomes reason. For example, rage, the most common emotion in the Senecan plays, is considered temporary insanity in the first book of Seneca's essay *On Anger:* It is "the most hideous and frenzied of all the emotions," [6] contrary to nature and principal enemy of reason. On the other hand, practice of the virtues of wisdom, courage, moderation and endurance not only eliminates weakness within man, but also negates the effect of catastrophe coming from without.

The parallel to what is found in the *Phaedra* is very close. Seneca has written a dramatization of criminal psychology, charged with extreme abnormality and irrationality; indeed, this is the main source of the intensity and horror which are Seneca's failings. A few illustrations will show that the formulation of these elements is Stoic. Phaedra recognizes in herself the curse of unnatural love received from her mother (this is only mentioned in Euripides). She introspectively states the moral conflict: "Quid ratio possit? Vicit ac regnat

furor." "What can reason do? Passion has conquered and
now rules supreme." [7] Theseus is a mad adulterer. Hippolytus can hardly be anything else than a rather colorless
victim, for destruction comes wholly from Phaedra, and
there is no significant impasse between the two as in Euripides; he speaks as a Stoic when he praises life in the
woods and identifies it with the Golden Age.[8] The Nurse both
preaches Stoic virtue to Phaedra and urges Epicurean indulgence upon Hippolytus. Perhaps most significant of all is
the thought of the Nurse that "base and sin-mad lust . . .
has made love into a god and, to enjoy more liberty, has given
passion [*furori*] the title of an unreal divinity." [9] Love and
passion are moral conditions in men, not conditions of
existence. The contrast with Euripides is radical.

Similar features can be found in all the Senecan plays.
Also, there are instances where the opposite side of Stoic
morality is seen, i.e. where reason prevails and Stoic virtues
overcome catastrophe. For example, in the *Troades*,
Astyanax and Polyxena face death with such equanimity that
they are victors. It seems apparent that Stoicism led Seneca
the dramatist to a completely moralistic view of error and
catastrophe: Evil is either externalized as the workings of
fate or fortune which can be nullified by reason, or is thought
to be caused by the deterioration of character which results
when passion destroys reason. This is a far cry from the characteristic Greek view that evil is organic in the natural order
of things and cannot be eliminated by mere rationality.

In fact, it is very doubtful that the effect of tragedy can be
achieved in drama written on these Stoic premises: Such an
explanation of human experience is too simple and shallow;
it eliminates the possibility of a significant relationship between, on the one hand, what men do and suffer and, on the

other, the sources of this experience both within and outside of man. The mystery essential to tragedy is gone.

Other important factors, of course, contributed to making Senecan drama what it is. But Seneca's Stoicism was a source of basic limitations. Composing tragic drama under these limitations and on these premises—whether consciously or unconsciously—the dramatist was restricted in what he could achieve. He chose to intensify, to portray the psychology of behavior, particularly irrational behavior, powerfully and vividly. The center of dramatic attention was turned inward. This new orientation made Senecan drama a landmark in the development of psychological drama, and was carried by Senecan influence wherever it went.

10

The Background of the Romance Epic

Agapito Rey

LITERATURE has always reflected the conditions and spirit
of the period when it was produced, although frequently
poets have tried to disguise or adorn reality or the factual
portions of their works with the addition of fictitious characters and incidents, often making it difficult to distinguish between real and imagined details. This is particularly true in
the Homeric epic in which history, legend and myth are
blended into a homogeneous whole. These characteristics of
the Greek epic were continued by the Latin classical poets until the dawn of the Middle Ages; but then the epic tradition
was lost and several centuries had to pass before it was re-
vived.

With the fall of the Roman empire in the fifth century, as
the old provinces broke away from Rome to form new nations, Latin literature declined, before the new nations could
develop literatures of their own. Most of the intellectual efforts of the Middle Ages were directed to furthering the
Christian church and its doctrine. Theology was the dominant theme of the times, expressed, of course, in Latin. But
the masses did not speak Latin, and new languages gradually
emerged in the old Roman Provinces. By the twelfth century

Professor of Spanish at Indiana University and a member of the Franciscan
Academy of History and the Centro de Estudios Hispanicos, AGAPITO REY
has published several volumes on Hispano-American relations. He spe-
cializes in medieval literature and has recently published an edition of
El Libro de los Cien Capitulos.

these languages had attained a high degree of perfection and began to replace Latin in literary expression. There was a great cultural upsurge in the twelfth century, and from this period date the first great literary monuments in the vernacular in Europe. This was also the era when influential monastic orders rose in Western Europe, and they became the cultural and literary centers of the time.

During the early Middle Ages the Teutonic peoples were going through an heroic age, an age of pride and courage full of legend and epic personages, but whose feats were not adequately written out. The heroic deeds of Teutonic heroes told in Icelandic Sagas are written in prose or in brief narrative poems of which only fragments are known; these poems are heroic but not epic. "Most of them," as W. P. Ker points out, "seem to be wanting in the breadth of treatment, in the amplitude of substance, that are proper to epic poetry." The murdering of relatives or friends, or the avenging of their deaths, lack the breadth and national dignity that characterizes the epic. Ker calls sagas "prose histories of the fortunes of the great Icelandic houses." The thirteenth-century Icelandic *Edda* of Snorre Sturluson, while in prose contains verse quotations from old heathen poems. It is a scholarly study of Northern myths, and in this process of trying to give literary expression to myths, says Ker, "is found the beginning of historical literature in an heroic or epic form."

The Nibelungenlied, a narrative poem of the thirteenth century, contains many legends and traditions mixed with historical elements of the Teutonic people. In this poem the dwarf Nibelungs help Gunther to win the hand of Brunhild; Siegfried marries the superhumanly strong Kriemhield, who avenges the death of her husband years later by killing Hagen, and she is in turn slain by Hildebrand.

The chief extant example of old English epic, *Beowulf,* can be compared, at least in extension, with the epic of other lands. Its 3,182 lines fall short of the *Roland* by 1,000 lines, but exceed by far all other known fragments of old Teutonic heroic narrative poetry. The *Beowulf* is the work of an educated man who wrote his poem to be read rather than sung. Some Teutonic epic legends are preserved in this poem ascribed to the eleventh century. It is the specimen by which Teutonic poetry must be judged. The story deals with King Hrothgar, whose palace has been ravaged by two monsters who appear at night to slay the retainers. Beowulf comes from Sweden to pit his skill against the monsters. The poem tells of Beowulf's arrival into the land of the Danes and his slaying of the monsters Grendel and its dame. Then Beowulf returns to his land where he reigns for fifty years, then he slays another ravaging dragon there but is mortally wounded in the combat and dies, and his remains are consumed in a great funeral pyre.

The Anglo-Saxon epic represented by *Beowulf* must have developed from humbler beginnings, although we do not have older examples to follow this evolution. Speaking of its merit Ker considers it too simple with nothing too much in the story, since besides killing monsters, Beowulf has nothing else to do. After he has killed Grendel and Grendel's mother in Denmark he goes home to his own Guntland, until years later when he meets his last adventure. The three parts which compose the poem, while different, blend very well to form the whole. "The great beauty, the real value, of *Beowulf*," says Ker, "is in its dignity of style. While the main story is simplicity itself, the merest commonplace of heroic legend; the poem is unmistakably heroic and weighty. The thing itself is cheap; the moral and spirit of it can only be matched among the noblest authors." What makes it great is not the action but the humanities of the interludes and conversation of Beowulf and Hrothgar.

The real epic period in Europe begins with the invasion of Spain by the Moors in 711, for it marked the beginning of the long struggle between Christians and Moslems for faith and country, which are the main themes of the epic. There was no epic poem narrating the defeat and death of Rodrigo at the hands of the Moors, but the legends woven in Spain about the end of this Gothic king survived in numerous ballads and in the chronicles.

The Romance epic had its origins in the heroic songs of the Visigoths and the Franks. The French epic, the first to develop in Europe, assimilated many of the themes that were characteristic of the Germanic and Nordic songs. The Spanish epic assimilated them also, but later, through the French epic or the recitations of Nordic minstrels who visited Spain during their pilgrimages to Saint James. The themes most commonly narrated in the early Germanic songs were treason, betrayal, and vengeance, which were then generally used in the epic intended to be sung or recited. G. Paris spoke of the French epic as: "esprit germanique dans une forme romane," but this Germanic influence was refuted by Bédier.

Militant Christianity found outlets for its vitality in crusades and pilgrimages. In the midst of these church-inspired activities the epic made its appearance in France and Spain, and there seems to be a certain relationship between the development of the epic and religious fervor. The epic was composed and sung to exalt the crusades in the Holy Land and to glorify the heroes who fought the infidels in Spain.

The Latin poets furnished the models and the technique for the new literary genre. The two best known examples of the Latin epic transmitted to modern literatures were Vergil's

Aeneid and Lucan's *Pharsalia*. These epic poems were not
intended to be sung as was the Greek epic. Vergil's poem is
based on events that happened many centuries before, in
which the historical background, the legendary and the
imaginative are harmoniously blended. On the other hand,
Lucan's work narrates contemporary events still fresh in the
minds of the readers. The *Pharsalia* is an historic epic,
about the same length as the *Aeneid,* dealing with the Roman
civil war which culminated in the defeat and death of Pom-
pey and the murder of Caesar. Lucan's poem not only chronicles contemporary events but the poet himself takes sides in
the struggle he records. The civil war was a fight against the
tyranny of Caesar, and young Lucan aligned himself with
those who fought for liberty. His was a revolutionary departure from the imperial epic based on remote Hellenic
themes. Lucan's poem ends abruptly before the death of its
antihero, Caesar. Lucan had incurred disfavor with Nero and
the young poet at twenty-six years of age had to take his life
in the same manner that his uncle, Seneca, did under similar
circumstances. Lucan gives poetic flavor to his poem through
rhetorical additions, although his characters are too garru-
lous. There was opposition to his innovation. Quintilian did
not even rank Lucan as a poet, so accustomed was he to the
Vergilian epic. Petronius did not consider the *Pharsalia* an
epic poem, because there is no intervention in it of the deities. Similar discussions over the propriety in utilizing modern or ancient themes in the epic and the tragedy were re-
vived in France in the seventeenth century, and Boileau
criticized Corneille for his enthusiasm for Lucan.

In the classical epic men and gods mingle in the battles,
and the war heroes are gods or men conceived by gods.
Achilles, Aeneas and other epic heroes, if not gods, are
pictured as their descendants and endowed with supernatural

powers. On the other hand, Roland, the Cid and other heroes of the modern epic, are real people, free from any mythical origins, who live and die like other mortals. Roland died defeated by a superior army; the Cid died a natural death in bed as most people do, with no sign whatever to indicate that a hero had passed away. No miracles intervene in their lives or deaths. Even in the *Nibelungenlied,* realism dominates the magic elements, which have only a limited intervention in the development of the poem.

Though the classical epic tradition was nigh forgotten in the Middle Ages, in the twelfth century the epic form came to life again, now written in the vernacular. Several factors contributed to this radical change. There was in this period a great cultural awakening, which was the cause and effect of the spread of Christianity. Influential monastic orders were established in Europe, and they helped to revitalize the cultural life of the times. The monasteries became the centers of learning, the fosterers and protectors of the arts. The abbeys were dedicated to individual patron saints, and often these abbeys claimed to possess relics of saints and other important personages, whose virtues the abbeys tried to extol. They encouraged the writing of many long poems narrating the lives and the miracles attributed to those saints and relics. Some of the important abbeys were located in strategic places along the routes followed by pilgrims on their way to Santiago and other holy places, and these abbeys courted favor and prestige through their pious cultural works.

Roland's purported tomb was shown to travelers at Saint-Roman de Blaye, and his oliphant (horn) at Saint Seurin in Bordeaux. These ecclesiastical foundations must have been responsible for the writing of the *Song of Roland,* just as the monks of Saint-Denis, to attract attention to the relics housed in their abbey, motivated the composition of the

Pelerinage of Charlemagne. This poem deals with relics supposed to have been brought back by Charlemagne from his
journeys to Constantinople and Jerusalem, although there is
no evidence to show that Charlemagne ever made such a
pilgrimage. Another epic dealing with the rescue of relics
was the *Fierabras.* The Crusades had given rise to extensive
traffic in relics, in which there was considerable fakery and
fraud. But as such relics were venerated by the faithful,
poems were written to narrate miracles attributed to them
and thus to attract more visitors. In such a manner was built
the reputation of Saint James of Compostela and other
shrines. This pious rivalry blended perfectly with the
preaching of the Crusades to wrest Jerusalem from the Moslems, and to help the Christians who were finding it difficult
to contain the Saracens in Spain. The newly-founded monastic orders were a strong motivating force in literary creation in the eleventh and twelfth centuries. They sought to
channel the aggressive enthusiasm of the Christians into the
struggle against the Moslems. Poems were written to sing the
heroic exploits of the crusaders and to arouse religious fervor; and at times to build up the prestige of some leaders.
The twelfth century is the greatest period of epic production. The epic is the product of the genius of a poet who
was able to give artistic expression to a culminating historical period. Patriotism and love of country and religion are
the basis of epic poetry. In the *Song of Roland* the poet often
speaks of his "douce France," and the composer of the *Poem
of the Cid* evokes his "Castilla la gentil." An epic poem is the
glorification of a national hero who gives his all for his faith
and country. It is a poetic biography, usually anonymous.

These medieval epics, written to be sung before people
who no longer spoke or understood Latin, had to be composed in the vernacular. The oldest and best example of the

new epic is the French *Chanson de Roland.* This poem, as we know it today, dates from the beginning of the twelfth century. It contains 4,002 ten-syllable lines, with a caesura after the fourth syllable, the characteristic line of French epic poetry. The colophon reads: "Here ends the chronicle which Toroldus narrates." We do not know whether this Toroldus was a minstrel, the poet who composed the *Song,* or the copyist of the manuscript. Whoever the author was, he must have been well acquainted with the Latin epic and with Latin chronicles.

The historical basis for the poem are contained in Eginhard's *Vita Karoli,* which narrates how, on the return of Charlemagne from an expedition to Spain in 778, the rearguard of his army was attacked by the Basques at a mountain pass in the Pyrenees and a Roland, prefect of Brittany, was killed. Out of this meager historical information and numerous current legends the poet produced a masterpiece. He made the Saracens the attackers of the rearguard, and the obscure Roland becomes a nephew of the King and the central figure in the poem. Roland refuses to blow his horn and seek help when attacked; he does so finally before he dies. Charlemagne comes to the aid of his men to find them slaughtered, he routs the Saracens and avenges the death of Roland and his companions. The French had been betrayed by Ganelon, stepfather of Roland; he was tried and executed. Slain with Roland at Roncesvalles were Archbishop Turpin, Olivier and the Peers of France.

The real aim of the poem was the glorification of Charlemagne as defender of Christianity and crusader against the infidel, and the title must have conformed to this aim. The manuscripts bear no title; the editors of the text named it the *Song of Roland,* although Roland is killed early in the story, and Charlemagne is the one who defeats the Moors at Zara-

goza and returns triumphant to France. The battle of Roncesvalles, in which Roland was killed, was the subject of extensive popular legends, and in the thirteenth century the theme
of epic poems in France and Spain. The French *Roncevaux*
is older than the Spanish *Roncesvalles*, of which only a fragment survived. Both are re-elaborations of the *Song of Roland*. Early Spanish legend, widely used in the ballads, created a national hero, Bernardo del Carpio, to oppose and
defeat Roland at Roncesvalles. The subject is treated at
length by Bernardo de Balbuena in his poem *Bernardo o
victoria de Roncesvalles* (1624).

Charlemagne was a German in language and nationality,
but as a ruler of the Christian empire pious legends rose
around him and he became the central figure around whom
were woven the early epic poems of the Carolingian cycle
exalting the struggle against the Moslems. No direct model
has been established for the *Roland*. The poet takes his materials from legendary tradition. The historical events were
contaminated by the popular fancy and the creative genius of
the poet. The background of the Carolingian epic is more
legendary than historical. While it is true that French expe-
ditions crossed into Spain to fight the Moors, the characters,
the geography and other details in the *Song of Roland* seem
to be the product of popular legends and the poet's imagination. More than three hundred years had passed since the
events sung had taken place and neither the narrators nor
the listeners troubled themselves much about accuracy. The
King Charles named in the song could have been any of the
three kings by that name who ruled in the late eighth century
(Charles Martel, Charlemagne, Charles the Bald). Roland,
Olivier, Turpin and other personages mentioned in the
poem are fictitious, as is much of the geography. But, who
cared? Spain was a remote country for the French listener

and accuracy was of no consequence; what mattered was to glorify the King of France as the champion of Christianity.

Some critics believed that epic poetry was a late creation, based on chronicles and other documents and objects. Thus, according to Bédier, the twelfth-century epic would be a creation of that period and not rest on a poetic tradition. Menéndez Pidal and his school hold a different view; they maintain that the epic springs from the enthusiasm over contemporary events elaborated by minstrels and poets. The fact that there are no poetic examples before the twelfth century does not preclude the thought that some existed before. There may have existed an epic legend transmitted orally that formed the basis for the *Song of Roland* and other early epic poems.

Some years after the *Roland* the *Poema de Mío Cid* was composed in Spain. The poet did not seem to follow any particular verse pattern, although fourteen-syllable lines predominate. In contrast with the fantasy prevailing in the *Song of Roland,* the Spanish epic conforms to reality in most details. The characters are taken from history, as are the events narrated, and the geography is extremely accurate, as is attested by the *Historia Roderici* and other early chronicles of the Cid. The time element is the important factor in both poems. The *Song of Roland* narrates events that took place almost four hundred years before, in a remote country, among strange people; while the *Poem of the Cid* was composed only some forty years after the death of the Cid in 1099, and there were people still living who remembered him and his exploits and who could have pointed out any gross inaccuracies in the poem. Furthermore, the Spanish poet knew intimately the territory traveled by the Cid; the Moors were not fantastic monsters, but quite normal people who had been living in Spain for more than three centuries, with long periods of peace and friendly intercourse despite religious differences and rivalries.

The crusading spirit of the French epic is missing in the *Cid*. There is no forced conversion of Moslems or slaughter in the name of Christianity as is the case in the *Roland*. On the contrary, often the Moslems become friends and allies of the Cid and pray for his success. Both sides fight for land and power, not for religion. The only bellicose and crusading priest we meet in the poem was a Frenchman who joined the Cid at Valencia. He was a brave soldier, more interested in killing Moors than in converting them. The Cid appointed him bishop of the newly conquered city. The Cid did not start out on any altruistic or patriotic mission, but was driven to heroic deeds by necessity. He had been banished from his land by a jealous king and he had to make his way as a soldier like many an oriental war lord. There is no bragging on his part; he fights bravely in order to survive and to protect his men, his wife and daughters. On one occasion he asks his wife to watch from a tower and see how he and his men fight to defend Valencia, and also that she may know how men earn their bread. Men join the Cid attracted by his personality or by hope of spoils, not by unselfish, lofty motives. The Spanish king is not moved by any high motives either; he is no champion of Christianity as Charlemagne is made to be in the French epic. The Spanish epic is realistic, historically accurate, in the Lucanian model. The French epic is closer to Vergil, but the latter's influence on the *Roland* is only general and not in details.

Treason and vengeance are the main forces that motivate the epic. In the Homeric epic it was the desire to avenge the abduction of Helen that started the Trojan wars. The carnage that ends the Nibelungs is the result of the treacherous murder of Siegfried by Hagen and the avenging of this death. In

the *Roland* Ganelon betrays his stepson, an act that results in
the defeat and slaughter of the French at Roncesvalles. The
traitor is quartered for his crime. Similar punishment is
meted out to Bellido Dolfos for having treacherously killed
King Sancho in the epic, the *Siege of Zamora*, of which only
fragments have survived. Sometimes these vengeances spring
from personal feuds, as in the *Infantes de Lara*. In the *Cid*,
too, in the last part of the poem, the hero seeks redress from
his sons-in-law, and the case is settled on the field of honor
with their defeat, without bloodshed, one of the few episodes
in the poem not supported by history. Personal offenses often
lead to national wars. The rape of count Julian's daughter by
King Rodrigo induced the count to open the gates of Spain
to the Moors and furnished the basis for the fight between
Christians and the Saracens and the origin of the epic in
Western Europe.

There is no need to catalog here the epic poems of the
twelfth and thirteenth centuries. In France they were quite
numerous, and they fall into the categories we have discussed above. In the thirteenth century the genre began to decline. In France the epic was turned into metrical romances,
"chevaleries," tales of adventure or chivalry in verse, such
as the *Mainet*, which narrates the childhood and youth of
Charles Martel, entirely legendary. The sojourn of young
Charles in Toledo and his escape to France with a Moorish
girl do not rest on historical tradition, but on the imagination
of the poet.

By the fourteenth century the epic was a thing of the past.
The *Song of Rodrigo*, written in Spain during this period, is
at best a rhymed chronicle of the youthful exploits of the Cid,
entirely the product of fantasy. In Italy the themes of the
French epic were reworked into imaginative narrative
poems. Italy never had a national epic, but the influence of

the *Song of Roland* was felt there as in Spain and elsewhere. The fantastic character of the thirteenth-century French epic appealed to the Italians who were not interested in historical deeds. Some of the fantastic elements found in the *Roland* were exploited by Jehan Bodel in his *Chanson des Saisnes* (1200) as he narrates the love intrigues of Baudouin, Roland's younger brother. The cycle of the Roland legends was utilized in the fourteenth century by Andrea da Barberino in *Il Reali di Francia,* a reworking of the Roland theme, in which the knights of the Round Table are put through all sorts of fantastic exploits devoid of any pretense of historicity.

France was richer in epic production than her neighbors, but the epic spirit soon died there. In Spain, on the other hand, while few epic poems survived, the epic tradition was preserved for centuries in the chronicles and ballads, some of which descended directly from the epic and narrative poems. The compilers of medieval chronicles accepted both epic poems and ballads as historical documents and prosified them in their compilations, and from the old Spanish chronicles we have been able to fill in the missing portions of the incomplete *Poem of the Cid,* preserved in a lone truncated manuscript. We have more than one hundred ballads detailing every phase of the Cid's life. The historical ballads, which were fragments of epic poems, or elaborations of episodes of them, were sung to the people by the minstrels and in this manner the epic legends were preserved in the oral tradition and transmitted by word of mouth through the centuries.

The ballad exploited both lyrical and heroic elements, both of Spanish and of foreign character. Many French epic legends which died out in France were preserved and popularized in Spanish ballads. The popularity of the ballads of the Carolingian cycle is equaled only by the ballads narrating the relations between Christians and Moors previous to the conquest of Granada in 1492. With the introduction of the printing press, the old traditional ballads began to appear in print, first in broadsides, then collected in books called "Romanceros" or "Cancioneros." From the fifteenth century onward, the ballad became a literary genre extensively cultivated; and poets often wrote ballads in the style of the old ones, making it difficult at times to distinguish between the traditional ballads and those newly composed. The function of the ballad was to inform and to entertain, and this function the ballad retains to this day. In Mexico, under the name *corrido*, it is used to inform the humble people about important events, and there is no major national disaster, uprising, or horrid crime that is not sung in the market place soon after its occurrence, and the narrative circulated in broadsides. The historical ballad flourished also in Scotland and elsewhere, but nowhere did it show such strong vitality as in Spain. "The Castilian romances," says Entwistle "are unsurpassed in Europe for their number, vigour, influence, dramatic intensity, and veracity."

During the Renaissance there was a reawakening of interest in the Greek and Latin epic. New editions and translations of the classics were brought out during this period, and there was a revival of the epic in Italy and Spain. Vergil was then widely followed by the poets, both in his epic and lyrical poetry. But the Italian epic can hardly be classed as such; it belongs rather to the novels-of-chivalry type into which the early French epic had degenerated, completely fabulous, though on an historical theme. The best example is found in Ariosto's *Orlando Furioso*, in which the legends of the French epic, already fantastic in the original, become absolutely imaginary and incredible. In this work, which is a

sequel to Boiardo's *Orlando innamorato,* Ariosto introduces
magic rings, flying horses, enchanted castles and other fantastic trappings to narrate the doings of Roland and his peers,
in forty-six cantos of some one hundred octaves each.
Ariosto's vogue was widespread for a long time.

Torquato Tasso's *Gerusalemme Liberata* is likewise a mixture of fable and history. He adds so many imaginative episodes that the biographical character of the *Jerusalem* is
completely lost, and we can class his poem as a rhymed
novel with an historical background. It was first published in
1581, comprising twenty cantos of some hundred octaves
each. Tasso does not tell the story of the Crusades, but limits
his narrative to the siege and conquest of Jerusalem in 1099
under the leadership of Godfrey of Bouillon, the main character and central figure in the poem. Being a biography of
the hero, as in other epics, his name should have given title to
the poem. Originally Tasso had planned to entitle it *Gotti-
fredo,* and it appeared in some printings under such title.
The poem is based on William of Tyre's Latin chronicle of
the Crusades, *Historia Belli Sacri* . . . Perhaps in imitation
of the "pious Aeneas" theme then in vogue, Tasso exploits
the halo of saintliness that had been created around Godfrey
of Bouillon already in the twelfth century. During the long,
protracted siege of Jerusalem, Godfrey and his Christian
armies are tempted and ensnared by evil spirits in various
forms and shapes, but angels, saints and the Lord always
come to their rescue in the nick of time. In the end the Moslems are defeated, Jerusalem is taken, and Godfrey is elected
king. History and legend are intimately mixed. Some of the
characters are fictitious, but most of them are to be found in
the chronicles. The opening lines tell of the purpose of the
poem: *Canto l'arme pietose e'l capitano/Che'l gran sepulcro*

liberó di Christo (I sing the exploits of the pious army and the captain that liberated Christ's great sepulcher).

The period of the Renaissance in Spain coincides with the discovery and conquest of America, rich in heroic exploits. The Spanish poets did not have to search in mythology and ancient legend for inspiration and epic characters. The struggles of the conquistadors with men and nature in the New World furnished abundant epic elements. These heroic deeds were sung in epic poems and rhymed chronicles. The most noteworthy was Alonso de Ercilla's *Araucana,* which narrates the struggle between the Spaniards and the Araucanian Indians in Chile. The Spaniards fought bravely for the conquest of the land, but they found their match in the heroic resistance of the Araucanians in the defense of their country against the invader. Ercilla was a Spanish captain in the invading forces, but his treatment of the Indians was so forceful and sympathetic that modern Chile considers the *Araucana* as her national epic. It is an epic in true Lucanian fashion which narrates not only contemporary events, but even some in which the poet took direct part himself. But Ercilla was a man of his times, and like other poets of the period, he swelled his poem with stories extraneous to the Chilean war. He uses hundreds of octaves to narrate the story of Dido and Aeneas as told by Vergil, the defeat of the French by the Spaniards at the battle of St. Quentin, and even some incidents in Ercilla's own life. All of this increased the *Araucana* to enormous proportions. A common characteristic of the Renaissance epic is its inordinate length; the *Araucana* contains around 22,000 lines, the *Orlando Furioso* some 36,000 lines and the *Gerusalemme Liberata* about 16,000, against the 4,000 of the *Roland* and the *Cid.*

Another good example of the Renaissance epic is to be

found in Luis Camoens' *Os Lusiadas*, published in 1572. It is a poem in 10 cantos containing 1,102 octaves, which narrates the heroic deeds of Portuguese navigators, particularly Vasco da Gama and his voyages to India early in the sixteenth century. Camoens follows closely the narratives of Gama's explorations, but he adds a great deal of fantasy. Saints and pagan gods are invoked quite frequently to help the Portuguese against the heathens. In the style of his day, Camoens studs his poem with stories and episodes extraneous to his main theme. While he belongs to the Spanish type of epic poets faithful to the Lucanian tradition, in his use of miracles and the like Camoens is closer to Tasso than to Ercilla.

The variations in historical approach we have noted in the epic apply also to other literary genres. In his historical plays Shakespeare utilizes the chronicles as sources of the events he dramatizes. His main characters and historical background are faithfully drawn from the chronicles, but the details and some of the secondary characters are imaginary creations of the poet. Similar methods were followed by Lope de Vega and other contemporary Spanish playwrights who found their subjects in chronicles, ballads and legends from different ages and countries. In France the concepts of dramatic art were more rigid. The French Academy ruled that only kings from ancient Greece and Rome were worthy characters for the tragedy. The exploits of the Cid were considered too recent to merit dramatization, and Corneille was criticised for his play *Le Cid*, adapted from a Spanish play, which was itself based on ballads. There are no plays in France portraying the exploits of her medieval heroes.

The blending of history and fiction is general also in the historical novel, in which the plot usually develops in an historical background enriched with intrigue and detail. This type of novel bears the same relationship to the chronicles as does the epic; both tend to exploit historical characters and situations embellished with fantasy. A good example of the early historical novel is found in the *Guerras Civiles de Granada* (1595), by Ginés Pérez de Hita, which, while based on an historical background and authentic characters, is mostly fictitious in its details. It preserves many elements characteristic of the epic: quarrels between the Zegrís and Abencerrages, rival noble families of Granada in the years preceding its conquest by Ferdinand and Isabella, with numerous murders, treacheries and cruel vengeances reminiscent of the *Nibelungenlied*. Parallel with this brutality the author presents the jovial aspects of Moorish life in their elaborate feasts, jousts, sports and love making. Many of the incidents portrayed had been sung in ballads, more than eighty of which Hita included in his work. The love story of Abindarráez and Jarifa, inserted separately as a short story, was utilized later by Chateaubriand in his *Le dernier Abéncerage,* in which he also included some of the numerous ballads collected by Pérez de Hita. More recent examples of historical novels could be cited, such as Victor Hugo's *Quatre-vingt-treize* and Charles Dickens' *A Tale of Two Cities,* both dealing with the French Revolution, both based on historical background but whose details are entirely fictitious. While preserving the same relation to the chronicles as the epic, the historical novel is less biographical, and individual heroes do not dominate the action of the story as they do in the epic.

BIBLIOGRAPHICAL NOTE

For general reference, cf. J. Bédier, *Les Légendes épiques,* 4 vols. (Paris, 1908–13) ; John Clark, *A History of Epic Poetry* (Edinburgh, 1900) ; Jessie Crosland, *The Old French Epic* (Oxford, 1951); J. Evans, *Life in Medieval France* (Oxford, 1925); W. P. Ker, *Epic and Romance: Essays in Medieval Literature* (New York, 1957) and *The Dark Ages* (New York, 1904); R. Menéndez Pidal, *La Chanson de Roland y el Neotradicionalismo: Origen de la epica románica* (Madrid, 1959); E. von Richthofen, *Estudios épicos medievales* (Madrid, 1954); Martin Riquer, *Cantares de gesta franceses* (Madrid, 1952); I. Siciliano, *Les Origines des Chansons de Geste* (Paris, 1951), and H. O. Taylor, *The Medieval Mind*, 4th ed. (London, 1930).

11

West European Romanticism
Definition and Scope

Henry H. H. Remak

T HE student of literature cannot, like his colleague in the
sciences, rely on the availability of basic terms with clear-
cut and universally accepted meanings. Even within the
realms of scholarship restricted to one national literature, connotations like Baroque, Enlightenment, Realism, Impressionism, etc. give rise to extremely variegated if not contradictory evaluations. Further difficulties arise when scholars
blithely use a term arrived at by their interpretation of a national development without qualifying it as to national origin
and applicability. Van Tieghem's *Le Romantisme dans la littérature européenne*, for example, places Romanticism [1] in
sharp contrast to Classicism. This may be true for *French*
Romanticism and *French* Classicism, but certainly not for the
attitude of *German* Romanticism toward *German* Classicism,
or of English, Italian and Spanish Romanticism toward their
national brands of Classicism, for that matter. Morse Peckham's sprightly "Toward a theory of Romanticism" should
have been entitled "Toward a theory of *English* Romanticism," since the reader will look in vain for a consideration
of Romanticism outside England.[2] Examples of this kind can
be multiplied at will.

In the following pages, we shall pass in review some definitions and reasons for nondefinition of Romanticism, and

pick out and compare a number of strands held to be romantic in an attempt to find out whether or not and to what, if
any, extent we may legitimately speak of Romanticism as a
European phenomenon. The conclusions reached must be
regarded as distinctly approximate. Romanticism has been
chosen because it combines the elements of momentousness
and controversy more than any other period connotation. For
our present purposes, it does no more than to serve as an illustration of the kinds of difficulties and painful decisions
encountered by the student of comparative literature when
examining the usefulness and essential composition of literary labels employed in more than one country. The same could
and should be done for such coinages as Renaissance,
Baroque, Classicism, Realism, Symbolism, Expressionism,
etc.

The first quandary facing us is that of limitation. Ideally,
our analysis should include literatures anywhere in the
world. Our knowledge, time and space do not permit us to do
that. We shall restrict ourselves to the five important West
European literatures (English, French, German, Italian and
Spanish). For the same reasons, we shall have to forego,
largely, consideration of the other arts. It stands to reason
that a full-fledged examination of European Romanticism—
as of other literary currents or movements—would gain im-
measurably if we admitted as evidence insights gained from
the fine arts and the music of the respective periods (as well
as from philosophy, politics, sociology and economics, in
appropriate cases). In both these neglected categories, off-
the-beaten-path literatures and spheres related to literature,
comparative studies have barely made a beginning.

Another decision has to be reached: Should a difference
be made—and if so, how strict a difference—between Romanticism as an alleged historical movement and romanti-

cism as a forever recurring emotional condition? Peckham (somewhat rashly, we think) doubts any connections between both; Baldensperger affirms them. Connections or not, Barrère, Berr, and Van Tieghem favor a separation; Kluckhohn and Praz propose to reserve the term exclusively for historical Romanticism. Babbitt, Croce, Grierson, Lucas, de Meeüs, and Peyre, however, seem to consider the two as one. Recent Italian scholarship appears to seek to combine both views. Siciliano calls Romanticism a unique spiritual phenomenon manifesting itself in all activities of art and thought from the early 1700's to our own days. Marcazzan wonders whether contemporary Decadentism is still part of the Romantic movement or whether it represents a new stage of development. Mittner connects German Romanticism as a historic movement with German romanticism as an eternal tendency of the German spirit.[3]

While there are, in our own judgment, undoubtedly affinities between both categories of "romanticism," we must, for our purposes, focus on the alleged historical phenomenon, or else any attempt to delineate "romanticism" as a period movement collapses a priori.[4]

A large and respectable body of critics [5] maintains that Romanticism cannot be compressed into a formula at all. Individualism and fluctuation, as primordial constituents of Romanticism, do not admit, they say, of a generally definable doctrine. There are as many definitions of Romanticism as there are authors chosen to represent it.[6] At any rate, the divergences between the Romanticism of a particular country and that of another overshadow whatever resemblances may exist. There are, to be sure, romantic writers and features; there may be a romantic period; perhaps there are Romanticisms, but there is no Romanticism. These critics are apt to remind us that the romantic writers themselves seldom used the controversial term and cast doubt on its usefulness. The effect of the skeptical attitude taken by these scholars can be measured by the increasing abandonment of "Romantic *school*" in favor of less definite terms ("movement," "current," "temper," or even "foci of friendship"). But these "nominalists" have been challenged by such articulate and incisive observers as Praz, Wellek and Peckham, who assert that the task of defining Romanticism as an international movement is far from hopeless. Wellek and Peckham have actually come forward with specific solutions and definitions. We shall very briefly list a few of the skeptical as well as of the affirmative views.

Perhaps the most formidable exponent of the "negative" camp is the eminent historian of ideas, Arthur Lovejoy. His thesis that we should think of Romanticism*s*, not of Romanticis*m*, was first stated in a 1924 *PMLA* article (reprinted in the *Essays in the History of Ideas*, 1948), and amplified or modified in the last chapters of the *Great Chain of Being* (1936) as well as in his 1941 article in the *Journal of the History of Ideas*.[7] It must be remembered that Lovejoy's negative attitude toward *one* type of Romanticism prevailing in Western Europe is only part of the intended proof of his general conviction that scholarship has laid too much stress on the systematic and consistent elements in writers, and has tended to ignore, belittle or explain away divergences, inconsistencies, contradictions and struggles which are the trade-mark of outstanding authors (uniformity being more characteristic of smaller minds).[8]

Henri Peyre has undertaken to weaken the chronological unity of West European Romanticism by pulling France from under it. The great French Romantic poets, Peyre holds,[9] are Baudelaire, Rimbaud and Lautréamont, whose works appeared decades and up to a half century after those composed by authors hitherto taken for granted as representing the Romantic generation: Hugo, Lamartine, Vigny and Musset. If, Peyre says, we insist on locating genuine French Romantics in the first decades of the nineteenth century, we must either resort to lesser celebrities like Gérard de Nerval, or to such figures as Balzac (commonly classed as a realist), Michelet (a historian), Delacroix (a painter) and Berlioz (a composer)! [10] This apparently paradoxical view is much less so when it is seen that, like Lovejoy's position, Peyre's attitude is a spoke strengthening a wheel, part of a more general theory. In Peyre's case, his attack on Western European Romanticism as a fairly homogeneous movement fits into his overall belief that the notion of literary generations should be substituted for that of movements and schools. It is not surprising to find that Wellek, the champion of the concept of a pan-European Romanticism, happens to be a notable proponent of the belief that literary movements are reliable tools in the literary carpenter shop. Again and again, we find upon closer scrutiny that the arguments for or against the existence of a West European literary movement called "Romanticism" are only a skirmish or, at best, a battle in a crucial war of literary history.

This observation applies with equal or greater strength to Benedetto Croce, whose spirit seems to hover over the battlefield as the patron saint of the "negative" contingents. Croce has attacked the idea and the practice of literary history, claiming that it may be history, but has little to do with literature. Much, indeed most that has gone on by the name of literary history belongs, according to him, to other realms of knowledge: biography, sociology, ideology, philosophy, politics, religion, etc. To Croce, the study of literature ought to mean the analysis of rare, isolated masterpieces of rare, isolated great men and women of letters. Each work must be viewed as a separate entity, as something unique, without reference to other phenomena, authors or even other works by the same author.[11] Croce's aesthetics have undoubtedly proved to be a boon to contemporary literary criticism; at the same time, his theories, if fully accepted, would wreak havoc with the realm of literary history and with it spell the end of such period concepts as "Romanticism." In its place, there would be lone masterpieces dotting an otherwise blank map, without lifelines between them: literary anarchy, in short.[12]

The authors of the two papers on English Romanticism in the *PMLA* symposium (1940), Elizabeth Nitchie and Hoxie Fairchild, also align themselves with the skeptics. Miss Nitchie does not even believe that there is *an* English Romanticism.[13] Fairchild, by stressing the insularity of English Romanticism, saps the argument for a European Romanticism. His accentuation of the evolutionary (rather than revolutionary) aspects of Romanticism, which he relates, as does Van Tieghem, to eighteenth-century literature, points in the same direction; the advocates of a coherent European Romantic movement are bound to underline the original contributions of Romanticism (Wellek, Peckham). More recently, Friederich remarks that "the use of any one [common denominator for Romanticism] usually requires a twisting of the interpretation of a considerable portion of romantic literature in order to make it a product of the common denominator." [14]

It is clear that the advocates of an essentially identical European Romanticism are under much greater pressure than their adversaries to come through with definitions of Romanticism. Attempts at such definitions are legion.[15] Very generally speaking, there seem to be two main types of definition, with a transitional area in between.

In the first kind of definition, one or two alleged traits of Romanticism are singled out and made to stand for Romanticism as a whole. Madame de Staël tells us that Romanticism refers to chivalry. For Hugo, Romanticism is Liberalism in literature. Hedge sees in it mystery and aspiration, Lanson a lyrical expansion of individualism, Lucas an intoxicating dream, Immerwahr an imaginative literary process. Ker and Geoffrey Scott underscore its cult of the past, Picon its dedication to originality, Deutschbein its concern with synthesis, Milch its nationalism.

Frequently, a sharper definition of Romanticism is sought by contrasting it with other movements, especially Classicism. Romanticism is essentially a reaction against the excesses of intellectualism (Jasinski), change following upon fixity (Barzun), urge rather than restraint (Guérard), strangeness added to beauty (Pater), or cancellation of the classical equilibrium by a process of irrationalistic intensification (Petersen). Despite his strictures on genre and movement definitions, Croce says that romantic literature is a spontaneous and violent effusion of feelings which indulges in vaporous and indeterminate images, half-sentences and powerful, dim outlines, while classicism portrays pacified hearts, sage designs, precise personalities, equilibrium and clarity (representation being to classicism what sentiment is to romanticism).[16] Gundolf, while similarly protesting that Romanticism is no unified "Weltanschauung," let alone a system, but represents a new "Weltgefühl" which has arisen as a primary "Erlebnis" in a few men of genius, nevertheless ventures to compare the contest between "Klassik" and "Romantik" to a struggle between male and female lovers, between the generative and the birth-giving, the plastic and the musical, day and night, dream and intoxication, shape and motion, centripetality and centrifugality, Apollo and Dionysus. By others, Romanticism is said to incarnate the will to love, self-abandonment, individualism, subjectivity, symbolism, exoticism, bizarreness, mystery, suggestiveness, movement, extremeness, uniqueness, incompleteness, infiniteness, etc., etc., whereas Classicism is said to stand for the will to power, self-control, social organization, objectivity, stability, finiteness, the typical, etc., etc. Differences in presentation are in the foreground of Saintsbury's statement that Classicism introduces an idea directly, whereas Romanticism leaves it to the imagination of the reader, and of Barrère's remark that the Romantic *élan* of feeling and imagination carries words along and away with it, whereas Classicism imposes the measure of words on the emotions.

These contrasting definitions tend to be aphoristic and subjective. We are not left in the dark about the preferences, on the one side, of Goethe (the classical is the sane, the romantic the in-sane) and of Irving Babbitt or Frank Lucas whose somewhat more cautious characterizations echo Goethe's, or, on the other side, of A. W. Schlegel (the romantic is organic and picturesque, the classical is mechanical and plastic), of Stendhal (Romanticism is the literature which pleases people today, Classicism is the literature which pleased their great-grandfathers) or Berchet (the contrast between classical and romantic poetry amounts to the difference between the poetry of the dead and of the living).[17]

More recently, the attempt has been made to clarify the meaning of Romanticism by comparing it to the Renaissance or to the Baroque. Granting certain instructive parallelisms, not much, as Barrère suggests, seems gained by shouldering the additional burden of defining terms which are just about as controversial as Romanticism.

A transitional kind of definition attempts to dwell on, more or less, one central denominator broad enough to support the claim that it covers the entire movement. We think of Friedrich Schlegel's description of Romanticism as "progressive universal poetry," of Guérard who calls it a reaffirmation of life, of Poulet to whom it means a more acute consciousness of the enigma of the self and of the world, of Herford and Barrère who see in it an extraordinary development of imaginative sensibility, or of Hankiss who after despairing of ever reconciling the apparently disparate phenomena of the Romantic movement finally arrived at its "key": intensity.

Sometimes this common denominator appears as a fusion or polarity of two forces. Bowra (one of many critics who follow their insistence that Romanticism defies formulation by still another definition), speaking of English Romantic poets, calls the Romantic movement a prodigious attempt to discover the world of spirit through the unaided efforts of the solitary soul, and Fairchild, also with English Romanticism in mind, refers to the illusioned view of the universe and of human life, produced by an imaginative fusion of the finite and the infinite. Legouis and Cazamian stress the Romantic interplay of emotion and imagination. For Jansen, Romanticism is marked by the cleavage between dream and reality, past and present, the far-away and the near-by.

We are now well on the way toward a second type of definition which honestly tries to be all-inclusive and arrives at what its deviser considers an irreducible minimum of about three Romantic features. These may be considered essentially heterogeneous or coexistent (Lovejoy),[18] or viewed as successive steps on a Romantic ladder (Peckham). Some of them may be listed as follows:

FAIRCHILD: *1*] Naturalism,[19] *2*] Medievalism, *3*] Transcendentalism.

GUNDOLF (interpreting F. Schlegel and Schleiermacher):
1] Infiniteness ("Unendlichkeit"), 2] Individuality
("Individualität"), 3] Companionship ("Geselligkeit").

CARLYLE: 1] Dynamism, 2] Unconscious Mind.

LOVEJOY: 1] Organicism, 2] Dynamism, 3] Diversitarianism.

WELLEK: [20] 1] Creative Imagination (for the view of
poetry as knowledge of the deepest reality), 2] Organic
Nature (for the view of the world), 3] Symbol and
Myth (as primary determinants of poetic style).

PECKHAM: 1] Dynamic Organicism (reaction against
eighteenth-century static mechanism—"the watch"),
2] Negative Romanticism (rejection of static mechanism
but no—or not yet—acquiescence in dynamic-organic
universe), 3] Positive Romanticism (acceptance of
dynamic-organic universe—the "tree").

Among these ultracompressed statements there still are
differences in catholicity. Fairchild's definition seems to
contain more specific and limited elements (medievalism,
transcendentalism), probably due to his preoccupation with
England and personal inclinations. On the other hand, Peckham is trying to force Carlyle's, Lovejoy's and Wellek's
interpretations into a super-general, all-embracing formula
—a definition to end definitions. But we must keep in mind
that this ultrarefinement may be, at least in part, of a linguistic
nature, for "dynamic organicism," e.g., is not too meaningful
until it is spelled out by Peckham: change, imperfection,
growth, diversity, the creative imagination, the unconscious.

Despite Peckham's matchmaking optimism that he may
have presided over an effective marriage of hitherto recalci-

trant molecules, the prognosis for a lasting union is unfavorable.[21] It is more than likely that we are facing a
permanent dilemma in the production of definitions: they are
either too narrow or too general. General definitions will
be attacked as lacking in precision and being surcharged
with subjectiveness, as being so elastic that they are no
longer very expressive. Reservations, exceptions and specifi-
cations will be tagged on. The resulting definition will then
become so complicated and cumbersome that demands for
greater simplification and generalization will be heard. Definitions are subject to a constant process of inflation and
deflation, of expansion and contraction. Such tugs of war,
let us add, are not only inevitable but healthy in the field of
literary history.

Joining the battle of grand definitions is, however, not
necessarily the only way of contributing to a solution of
the problem we face. As a matter of fact, it is difficult not
to become somewhat suspicious about the genesis of these
"keys" to Romanticism. We have a feeling that they came
about in the following manner: The scholar in question, in
reading several Romantic works or authors, develops a hunch
that past definitions are not satisfactory; he pounces on one
or two or three elements, or combinations of elements,
which, to his mind, have been overlooked or improperly
evaluated; he goes through the Romantic literature of (we
trust) more than one country hoping, of course, to "discover"
that his hunch is justified, that the elements he is looking for
are really "there," that his theory is "right." Even the most
detached student and scholar engaged in such an adventure
will find it hard to resist the temptation—of which he may
not be conscious, or only semiconscious—to "adjust" or
minimize evidence pointing in a direction opposite to his
pet theory. The impression persists that the evidence did not

contrafuerte

come first and the conclusion second, but that the evidence is selected to buttress conclusions.[22] This subtle lure is particularly potent in discussions about Romanticism, a subject capable of involving scholars emotionally as well as mentally, and all the more so since, as we have seen, theories about Romanticism are apt to be keystones of even wider controversial systems.[23]

Another approach more likely to avoid these pitfalls (to the extent that it is humanly possible to escape them) offers itself to the student of comparative literature, an avenue more tedious but, perhaps, more reliable in the long run. Shutting out any fixed preconceived notions about the unity or lack of such of West European Romanticism, we should set about to make a list of alleged representative Romantic characteristics and try to ascertain, for each single one, whether and to what extent it exists in five key literatures of Western Europe. From the tabulated results, conclusions can be drawn as to the national or international character of Romanticism. This is precisely the procedure repeatedly urged by scholars who have written on Romanticism as a supranational phenomenon and are aware of the conjectural tentativeness of their efforts.[24]

We have attempted to draw up such a table, with the distinct understanding that it cannot expect to be more than a rudimentary model, an illustration of a method of procedure. A completely authentic coverage of this vast problem would almost have to be a co-operative undertaking. Again a codification seems, offhand, like a far too mechanical and certainly most unromantic procedure to be applied to Romanticism. But the appearance of complete objectivity is deceptive. The very selection of the items in the table must, in the last analysis, be subjective, and every single entry under every single country is a generalization and there-

fore open to doubt and debate.[25] This is unavoidable and requires no apology.

The key words had to be extensive enough to be significant for more than one country, but sufficiently distinct to
satisfy us that the extent of the occurrence of the mood or
attitude covered by it could actually be measured in each
country. No claim is made that these key terms have equal
qualitative values; there is not and never will be agreement
on that score. It can only be hoped that the final balance will
be so lopsided as to eliminate inevitable disagreements
about the respective weighing of each item as a determinative
factor. There is nothing sacrosanct about the arrangement,
but a different one could not alter the final outcome much.

For the sake of more reliable results it has seemed pref-
erable to be conservative and to eliminate consideration
of pre-Romanticism (with very few exceptions) in the "Elements" table. In the influence table we could afford to be
more generous and included not only pre-Romantic influences
on the Romantic generations but also a few "semi-" or "post-
Romantics" like Landor and the Brownings.

In order to arrive at an affirmative decision on the existence of a Romantic feature in Western European literature,
it had to be located in at least three out of the five literatures
examined. Germany, France and England counted, however,
somewhat more heavily than Italy and Spain. For a "yes"
answer to the question whether a Romantic trait existed in a
given literature, a great density or preponderance of this
characteristic in the literature within a limited period was
not required; what mattered was a significant increase or
change as compared to the preceding period(s). The fact
that a feature may appear in two or more countries within
the chronological boundaries we have set does not, of course,
imply that the concepts in question were identical for each

country concerned. "Medievalism," e.g., did not mean the same to Hugo as it did to Novalis. Nevertheless there is a minimum basis of medievalism shared by both which is significant. Nor do we take it for granted that in such cases an influence has been operating. It does seem to us, however, that in borderline cases the burden of the proof should be on those *denying* a common causal bond; during the Romantic period, isolation was less normal than kinship.[26]

Although the question whether these common factors are due to direct influence, similar *ambiance,* or coincidence may give rise to interesting explorations, it is not of primary importance to the argument. The fact that within approximately the same period certain tendencies or, to use Wellek's coinage, "sets of norms" different from preceding and following ones, either as such or in their evolutions, combinations and accentuations, manage to assert themselves in several countries, points to a supranational literary condition regardless of the causes involved. It needs perhaps to be said that the labeling of certain authors, works or tendencies as "romantic," or the absence of such designations, by contemporaries of Romanticism or later observers cannot be primary determinants in our own conclusions about the existence or nonexistence of Romantic trends in the countries concerned.

Granting that some decisions in the "Elements" table could seem too close for comfort to other observers and may be subject to reversal, still the evidence pointing to the existence in Western Europe of a widespread, distinct and fairly simultaneous pattern of thoughts, attitudes and beliefs associated with the connotation "Romanticism" is overwhelming. We believe that an extension of the investigation to Scandinavia and Slavic countries would support this conclusion.[27]

The tally contains some surprises. If it is at all reliable, certain clichés may have to be abandoned: that Romanticism as a whole is "vague" and "unrealistic," that it is opposed to classicism and to the eighteenth century, that it has a set body of metaphysics, and that it is politically liberal (or, for that matter, "reactionary").[28] We see that West European Romanticism possesses a reasonable cohesiveness and shares in certain attitudes toward the past, but with notable qualifications; and that there is sweeping agreement in general attitudes and in specific artistic tendencies.[29]

A number of general observations may now be made with regard to supranational influences during the Romantic period: *1*] Contemporary Romantic authors exerted relatively little influence abroad during the Romantic period. Among those that did—very moderately, in some cases—are A. W. Schlegel, Jean Paul, the Grimm brothers, Schelling and E. T. A. Hoffmann; Chateaubriand, Madame de Staël, Hugo, Lamartine and Dumas Père; Scott (the most influential of all) and Byron; Manzoni and Leopardi. (None from Spain.) *2*] Far stronger was the influence of older (sometimes considerably older) authors on the Romantic movements in other countries: Böhme, Herder, Bürger, Goethe, Schiller, Kant; Rousseau; Shakespeare, Milton and eighteenth-century pre-Romantics in England (Richardson, "Ossian," Percy, Young, Gray, etc.); Dante, Vico; Cervantes and Calderón. *3*] The strongest influences on West European Romanticism were German, English, and those of Rousseau. *4*] Germany's tendencies are more extreme than those of any other country. *5*] England's literature appears to be best balanced during the Romantic period; undoubtedly her vigorous eighteenth-century pre-Romanticism (or sentimentalism) and her political steadiness acted as stabilizing factors. *6*] France is the intermediary par excellence between

Elements of West

Element	Germany	France
		COHESIVENESS
Chronology (approximate)	1790's–1830	[1800 Chateaubriand] 1813 (Staël)-1843 (*Burgraves*)
Self-consciousness as a movement or group	Yes	Yes
Coherent body of similar metaphysics, theory, criticism	Primary in beginning, secondary later	Criticism, definitions: yes; metaphysics: little
Pervasiveness of the Romantic movement	Strongest influence on German culture in last 150 years	Yes, but not as strong as in Germany (Berlioz, Delacroix, Michelet, Cousin)
	ATTITUDE TOWARD THE PAST	
Interest in non-classical mythology (esp. Nordic)	Yes	Yes, but less than Germany
Interest in folklore, primitivism	Very strong	In primitivism, but little in folklore
Medievalism	Very strong	Yes, but not widely stressed
Anti-neoclassicism	Yes (aspects of French classicism), no (German classicism)	Yes, though classicism remains strong in France

European Romanticism

England	Italy	Spain	Western Europe
COHESIVENESS [1780's] 1798–1830	1816–1850's	1830–1845	**Yes**
Relatively little	Yes	Yes	Yes
Less than Germany and France, despite Coleridge, Shelley	No	Little	No *
Much more limited (but Carlyle)	Romanticism restricted to literature and politics (but greater picturesqueness of language)		Ques.
ATTITUDE TOWARD THE PAST Yes, but less than Germany	No	No	Yes
18th-century interest sustained and intensified	Little	Much interest in ballads and folklore	Yes
Yes	Yes	Yes	Yes
Little	No	No	No

Element	Germany	France
Against pre-scribed unities of time and place	Yes	Yes
Anti-18th century	Strong rational strain.	Only to extent it was dominated by classicism

GENERAL ATTITUDES

Element	Germany	France
Imaginativeness	Yes	Yes
Cult of strong emotions, sen-sualism	Stressed emotions but very intellec-tual at first; sen-sual current	Fairly restrained
Restlessness, boundlessness	Strong	Less strong, but DeStaël, Musset
Individualism, subjectivism, in-troversion, cult of originality	Yes, but loneliness and politics led to collectivism	Yes
Interest in nature beyond "belle na-ture"	Great surge	Increased under-standing
Greater positive emphasis on Reli-gion	Yes, Catholic trends	Yes, within limits
"Mysticism" †	Interest in all phases.	A marked fashion, but did not last
Weltschmerz, Mal de siècle, etc.	Yes, but not pri-mary	Yes, but notable ex-ceptions (Hugo)

England	Italy	Spain	Western Europe
Yes	Yes, except at beginning	Yes	Yes
Derived much from 18th c.	No	Yes, for political reasons	No

GENERAL ATTITUDES

England	Italy	Spain	Western Europe
Yes	Yes, relatively	Yes, relatively	Yes
Wordsworth vs. Byron, Shelley	Emotionalism accentuated but rarely overflowing, forms set, themes not very passionate or sensual, desire for clarity		Yes (?)
Less strong, but Shelley, Byron	Less strong	Less strong, but Espronceda, Larra, others	Yes
More restrained than in Germany, but Byron.	More restrained	Relatively little	Yes (?)
Increased understanding	Little	Little	Yes
Restrained, no Catholic trends	Traditional place of religion not affected either way		Yes (?)
Limited interest	Not much interest	Little	Yes (?)
Yes, but not primary	Yes, but not primary	Relatively little	Yes

Element	Germany	France
Liberalism	Sporadic, generally weak	Constantly increasing after conservative start
Cosmopolitanism	Yes, but seeking "Volksseele" abroad	Yes, but seeking "couleur locale" abroad
Nationalism	Strong	Restrained

		WORKS
Supremacy of lyrical moods and forms	Yes	Yes
Reawakening of national epic	Yes, within limits	No
Historical drama and novel	Yes	Yes
Greater flexibility of form	Yes	Yes, but less than Germany
"Vagueness"	Pronounced, but seldom extreme	Not strong because of persistent classical influence
Symbolism	Yes, especially in early R.	Yes
Rhetoric	Yes, but moderate	Yes
"Romantic Irony" ǁ	Yes	Relatively little (Musset)

England	Italy	Spain	Western Europe
Contradictory picture ‡	Yes, but with strong patriotic connotations		Ques.
Yes, but well in hand; Characteristic of later Romantics	Moderate	Little	Yes
Self-assured but restrained, regionalism; Characteristic of earlier Romantics	Very strong	Very strong	Yes (?)
WORKS			
Yes	Ques.	Ques.	Yes
Yes	Yes	Yes, within limits	Yes
Yes	Yes	Yes, mostly drama	Yes
Yes, but controlled §	Little	No	Yes
Generally, no	No	No	No
Yes	No	No	Yes
Yes	Yes	Yes	Yes
Little (except Byron)	Little (Leopardi ?)	Very little	No

Element	Germany	France
Exoticism	Yes, but not central	Yes
Realism (incl. regionalism, local color), more precise differentiation	Yes, increasingly	Yes

Note: A "yes" entry indicates that the element was present. A "yes (?)" entry indicates that the element was present but not overwhelmingly so. "No" indicates that the element was not present, and "Ques." (questionable) that its presence has not been conclusively settled. The number of "no" entries could, of course, have been increased at will if we had included in our chart a greater number of supposedly Romantic features known or strongly suspected to be restricted to one country or at most two, or highly controversial "romantic" traits. We can only plead that we acted in good faith in considering only those concepts which have been regarded as unifying factors of European Romanticism. It is the quantity and intensity of affirmative rather than negative items which is significant.

* Professor Orsini has called my attention to the possibility that the "no" verdict in this column might be interpreted as doing less than justice to the tremendous interest and advance in literary criticism shown in German, French, English, and Italian Romanticism. This is not my intention; rather my present scepticism is, perhaps wrongly, directed at the

England	Italy	Spain	Western Europe
Yes, but far from universal	No	Yes (Mahometan influence)	Yes
Yes	Yes	Yes	Yes

---

assumption of a *coherent body of reasonably similar* criticism.

† Includes interest in the un-, semi-, or subconscious, dreams, divinations, hallucinations, phantasmagory, hypnosis, the occult, cult of death, the "marvelous," etc.

‡ Early liberalism gives way to conservatism—Wordsworth, Coleridge, Southey—but on the other hand we have Byron, Shelley, and Hazlitt.

§ It must be remembered that the classic tradition was weaker in England and Spain than in France and Italy; hence in the first two countries there was no violent reaction against classic rigidity of form. In Germany, the first Romantic wave followed immediately (or accompanied) the climax of neoclassicism.

‖ For a concise description see Blankenagel in "Romanticism: A Symposium," p. 7; for a full and long overdue treatment see Morton L. Gurewitch's subtle "European Romantic Irony," PhD diss., Columbia University, 1957.

Romantic

INFLUENCE *of* → on ↓	GERMANY (*also as locale*)	FRANCE
ENGLAND	*By* Böhme, Goethe, Herder, Schiller, Kant, Fichte, A. W. Schlegel, J. Paul, Schelling. *On* Blake, Wordsworth, Coleridge, Crabb Robinson, Carlyle, De Quincey. Bürger, Goethe, A. W. Schlegel→ Scott. Goethe→ Byron, Shelley. Tieck, Novalis→ Carlyle.	Limited influence of Rousseau
ITALY	Not much. *By* Goethe (→ Manzoni), A. W. Schlegel. Bürger→ Berchet, Schiller→ Manzoni. (de Staël!)	Rousseau, Chateaubriand (→Leopardi) & de Staël had certain impact.
SPAIN	*By* Herder, A. W. Schlegel, Grimm bros.→ Böhl de Faber. Goethe (*Faust*)→ Espronceda (*El diablo mundo*)? Schiller discussed in *El Europeo*.	Limited by Rousseau (political & social ideas), Chateaubriand, de Staël, Béranger, Delavigne, Hugo, Lamartine, Dumas père. Spaniards in Fr. incl. Larra, Rivas, Espronceda, Martínez de la Rosa.

Influences

ENGLAND (*also as locale*)	ITALY (*chiefly as locale*)	SPAIN (*chiefly as locale*)
	On Byron, Shelley (S. Rogers, Hazlitt, Hunt). Dante→ Byron, Shelley, Hunt. Eng. travelers in It. include Coleridge, Keats, Beckford, Landor, R. & E. Browning	*On* Southey, Byron, Beckford. Calderón→ Shelley. Intermediaries: Blanco-White, translations by Lockhart.
Limited *by* Shakespeare, Milton & Eng. pre-R (Richardson, Young, Sterne, Gray, "Ossian") & by Scott, Byron, Shelley. *On* It. pre-R (Baretti, Foscolo). Scott→ Manzoni.		*On* Berchet, Monti.
Limited *by* Shakespeare, Young, "Ossian," Scott, Byron.	*On* Martínez de la Rosa. Theses of *Il Conciliatore* briefly known (*El Europeo*). Monteggia in Spain.	

INFLUENCE *of* → *on* ↓	GERMANY (*also as locale*)	FRANCE
GERMANY		Pervasive *by* Rousseau, restricted by Diderot. *On* German pre-R (Sturm & Drang).
FRANCE	*By* Goethe (*Werther*→ *René, Faust, W. Meister,* lyrics), Klopstock (→ Vigny), Bürger, Schiller's dramas, A. W. Schlegel, Novalis (→Senancour), J. Paul (→ Vigny, Hugo), E. T. A. Hoffmann, national character (idyllic, medieval, etc.). *On* de Staël, Constant, Stendhal, esp. 2nd Fr. R wave: Hugo, Quinet (←Herder), Nodier, Nerval, Cousin, Ampère, Michelet, etc.	

ENGLAND (*also as locale*)	ITALY (*chiefly as locale*)	SPAIN (*chiefly as locale*)
By Milton and very strong *by* Shakespeare and 18th-c. pre-R (Richardson, Young, "Ossian," Percy, etc.). *On* German pre-R & R. Richardson, Sterne, Fielding, Smollett→ J. Paul. Scott→ Hauff. Byron.	*On* Goethe (←Manzoni), Heinse, Tieck, F. Schlegel, Chamisso (←Corsica), Eichendorff, Werner, Waiblinger, Heine. Dante→ A. W. Schlegel.	*By* Cervantes, Calderón, ballads, esp. *On* (Herder), Tieck, A. W. Schlegel, Schelling, Eichendorff, Heine. (Lope→ Grillparzer.) Locale→ F. Schlegel.
By Milton, Shakespeare, "Ossian," Young, Gray, Byron (→Lamartine, Musset), Scott. *On* Chateaubriand, Stendhal, Hugo, Vigny, etc. Wordsworth→ Sainte-Beuve. Th. Moore in Paris.	*On* de Staël, Stendhal, Musset, Deschamps, Barbier, Quinet, Hugo, Mérimée, Delavigne. *By* Sismondi. Dante (little). Some by Vico (→Quinet, Michelet) and Manzoni. Leopardi→ Musset, Vigny. Fr. travelers in It. incl. Chateaubriand, Lamartine, G. Sand.	*By* Sp. drama. *On* Sismondi, V. Hugo, A. Hugo (←ballads), Mérimée, Musset, Gautier, Dumas père. G. Sand in Mallorca. Maury's & Ochoa's anthologies of Sp. lit. published in Fr.

Germanic and Romanic countries, in all directions. The Romantic movement came to the Romance countries after it had gained a strong foothold in Germany and England. French Romanticism is more pronounced and prolonged than that of any other Romance country. 7] Italy and Spain form a Romantic "bloc" apart, exhibiting many similarities despite the dearth of interplay between them: a patriotic, political, practical romanticism; powers of tradition and of a set way of life acting as buffers against striking changes; a long tradition of coexistence between classical and romantic elements in their national character and literature makes for restraint and precludes spectacular developments; this explains probably the considerable vogue in Italy and Spain of the well-balanced Scott. 8] Italy and Spain (and, to a lesser extent, Germany) influenced other countries chiefly as romantic locales. 9] The same author may have exerted a very different type of influence in different countries. Rousseau's influence in Germany was primarily of a literary and pedagogical nature, whereas his influence in Italy and Spain was mainly political and social.

Although we hold, with Wellek, that the concept of movements (or at least currents) is vital to literary history as a discipline, let us not forget that it *is* a relativistic concept. Recent research is moving away from the idea that the succession of literary periods corresponds to a predestined, violent swing of the pendulum; it is shying away from brilliant theories of dialectic historical contrasts championed not long ago by German scholarship (Strich, Korff). Instead, it has emphasized the gradual transition between periods, the overlapping and the simultaneousness of contrasting literary phenomena (e.g. Naturalism, Impressionism and Symbolism in the 1890's). As linguistics has followed philology, so the descriptive method has succeeded (though not supplanted) the causal-historical approach in literary scholarship. With regard to Romanticism, we are more keenly aware now that there was a strong "pre-Romantic" element in what we like to call the Age of Reason, but we also know that there is a pervasive rationalistic element in, or running concurrent with Romanticism; that there are vigorous Realistic elements in Romanticism as well as Romantic ingredients in Realism; we even admit that Classicism may have romantic connotations, and that the survival of the classical tradition in Romanticism is greater than we had suspected previously.

The way from Rationalism and Sentimentalism via Romanticism to Realism, Naturalism and Symbolism can perhaps best be described by Miss Nitchie's image of a zigzagging road along which the view on either side differs from that on the other, but only by degrees. We might add, however, that these gradual differences accumulate as the journey proceeds, and that the landscape at the end of the trip is bound to vary considerably from the scenery at the beginning of the literary expedition.

SELECTED CRITICAL BIBLIOGRAPHY

1   INTRODUCTORY ARTICLES

BORGESE, G. A. "Romanticism," in *Encyclopedia of the Social Sciences*, XIII (1942), 426–34. Remarkable, packed international survey of the historical roots and (especially ideological) aspects of the Romantic movement. Bibliography.

MARCH, HAROLD M. "Romanticism," in Joseph T. Shipley (ed.), *Dictionary of World Literature* (New York, 1943), pp. 492–95. Informative, sensible introduction to the word, the movement and its implications from a comparative point of view, with good selective bibliography.

Samuel, R. H. "Romanticism," in S. H. Steinberg (ed.), Cassell's *Encyclopedia of World Literature* (New York, 1954), pp. 478–80. Brief sketch of European Romanticism followed by a number of bibliographical references (General, National, Theory).

2 GENERAL SURVEYS

Van Tieghem, Paul. *Le Mouvement Romantique.* Paris, 1923. Collection of basic comments on Romanticism by its outstanding representatives in England, Germany, Italy and France, carefully excerpted, translated, introduced, annotated and connected. Summary bibliographies. Thoroughgoing revision of first edition (1912).

Farinelli, Arturo. *Il Romanticismo nel Mondo Latino.* *3 vols.* Turin, 1927. Traces chief features of Romanticism (individualism, primitivism, medievalism, etc., etc.), to which author devotes separate chapters, through Italy, Spain and France (primarily) and Catalonia, Portugal, Romania and Latin America (secondarily). Incidental consideration also given to Germany and England. Forceful, alternately lyrical and dramatic, highly personal but richly informative treatment hostile to theoretical attempts of compressing Romanticism into formulas. Volume III entirely devoted to bibliographical notes, organized by countries, and to an extremely detailed table of contents amounting to a summary of each chapter (almost sixty pages). No index.

Strich, Fritz. "Europa und die deutsche Klassik and Romantik," in *Deutsche Klassik und Romantik* (Bern, 1949), pp. 339–63. Sweeping survey of the European antecedents and effects of German Romanticism. Strich's dialectic generalizations on the basis of national characteristics are in need of much pruning. This essay was first published in 1928.

"Romanticism: A symposium," *PMLA*, lv (March 1940), 1–60. Objective but interesting surveys of Romanticism in England (Fairchild, Nitchie), France (Havens), Germany (Blankenagel), Italy (McKenzie) and Spain (Tarr), with ample documentation and selected, annotated bibliographies. Represents excellent introduction to Romanticism as a European phenomenon for the nonspecialized student of comparative literature.

BARZUN, JACQUES. *Romanticism and the Modern Ego.* Boston, 1943. Revised, expanded version entitled *Classic, Romantic and Modern* available in Anchor paperback edition, 1961. Self-assured, animated, highly readable lectures, amazing in their breadth but already somewhat dated, in defense and explanation of Romanticism (and romanticism) as pan-European phenomena. Note particularly "Romanticism—Dead or Alive" (pp. 3–26), "The Classic Objection" (pp. 52–80), "Romantic Art" ("romanticism is realism," pp. 81–108), "The Four Phases of Romanticism" (i.e. Romanticism, Realism, Symbolism, and Naturalism, pp. 134–60), and " 'Romantic'—a Sampling of Modern Usage" (pp. 213–30). Notes, references, and index.

VAN TIEGHEM, PAUL. *Le Romantisme dans la littérature européenne.* Paris, 1948. Best factual survey of European Romanticism, including Pre-romanticism and the transition to Realism. Describes and compares various national Romanticisms as units, then traces certain ideas, sentiments and forms through the major as well as less well-known (Dutch, Scandinavian, Slavic, Hungarian, Portuguese, Brazilian, etc.) literatures. Written without exceptional finesse, but with integrity. Clearly organized and readable. Suggestive of many topics for papers and theses. International bibliography (books and periodical articles) and index of names.

BERNBAUM, ERNEST. "The Romantic Movement," in *The English Romantic Poets: A Review of Research* (New York, 1950), pp. 1–37. Despite the apparent limitation to England, Bernbaum's pithy and cutting survey of critical literature on Romanticism is relevant to the entire European movement. No index. Reprinted unchanged in second edition, 1956.

ABRAMS, M. H. *The Mirror and the Lamp: Romantic Theory and the Critical Tradition.* New York, 1953. Also available in W. W. Norton paperback edition, 1958. While primarily concerned with the English theory of poetry during the first four decades of the nineteenth century, considers also relations of English critical theory to foreign, especially German thought. Its thesis (that Romanticism brought about a basic shift of stress from the audience to the poet himself, from the mirror to the lamp) is relevant to European Romanticism as a whole. Copious notes, detailed index.

FRIEDERICH, WERNER P., and MALONE, DAVID H. "Pre-Romanticism" and "Romanticism," in *Outline of Comparative Literature* (Chapel Hill, 1954), pp. 199–331. General observations, followed by a wealth of references to supranational influences in European and American literature. Suggestive of many topics for papers and theses. Index, but no bibliography.

WELLEK, RENÉ. *A History of Modern Criticism: 1750–1950*. New Haven, 1955. *Volume* II, *The Romantic Age*. Sees the rejection of neoclassicism and the establishment of a dialectical and symbolistic view of poetry as the unifying factors in Romantic criticism. Thorough treatment of German, English, French and Italian criticism, and of relevant aspects of German philosophy. Complete scholarly apparatus (bibliographies, notes, chronological tables, index of names, topics and terms). Written in a clipped, incisive and admirably lucid style. Promises to be standard work on criticism in the Romantic age for decades to come.

MARCAZZAN, MARIO. *"Romanticismo Italiano e Romanticismo Europeo," Humanitas* (Brescia) XI (1956), 33–50. Upholds the basic cultural unity exemplified by European Romanticism which admits, of course, of many ethnic, political, historic etc. variations in countries (such as Italy) and groups of countries.

OPPEL, HORST. "Englische und deutsche Romantik," *Die Neueren Sprachen*, no. 10 (1956), pp. 457–75. Without minimizing national differences (as those between English and German Romanticism), Oppel defends the usefulness of the concept of a European Romanticism provided it is interpreted historically and sociologically.

PICON, GAËTAN. "Le Romantisme," in *Encyclopédie de la Pléiade, Histoire des Littératures, II, Littératures Occidentales* (Paris, 1956), pp. 140–61. Superb introduction to the main features of European Romanticism. Brief bibliography.

FOGLE, RICHARD H. "The Romantic Movement," in *Contemporary Literary Scholarship*, ed. L. Leary (New York, 1958), pp. 109–38. Although concerned with trends of contemporary scholarship on English Romanticism only in the last thirty years, this rich and sprightly "bibliographie raisonnée" provides a valuable frame of reference for students of European Romanticism, particularly on pp. 109–18.

MASON, EUDO C. *Deutsche und englische Romantik.* Göttingen, 1959. Lively, readable, and critical confrontation of English and German Romanticism.

3 DEFINITIONS

CROCE, BENEDETTO. *"Le Definizioni del romanticismo,"* *La Critica,* IV (1906), 241–45. (Reprinted in *Problemi di Estetica* [Bari, 1910], pp. 287–94). Croce distinguishes between three types of romanticism: moral, artistic and philosophical. Political romanticism, being a consequence of philosophical romanticism, is rejected as a fourth category. Writers and works should be studied as to which of these types—singly, in combination with each other or with nonromantic elements—they exhibit.

BABBITT, IRVING. "The terms Classic and Romantic," in *Rousseau and Romanticism* (Boston, 1919), pp. 1–31. Also available in a Meridian paperback edition, 1957. Biased but not unreasonable confrontation of these terms, without distinguishing between Romanticism as a period and an ever-recurrent romantic attitude, temper or mood, by a scholar frankly concerned about state of the world and, in particular, about the naturalistic fallacy. Favors a classicism based on experience vivified by imagination, as against a romantic indiscriminate apotheosis of imagination. See also the introduction and the last chapter, "The present Outlook." Extensive bibliography and index.

GRIERSON, HERBERT J. C. "Classical and Romantic: A point of view," in *The Background of English Literature and Other Collected Essays and Addresses* (London, 1925), pp. 256–90. Example for an urbane discussion of the classical and romantic systoles and diastoles in ancient, medieval and modern literature. First published in 1923.

LOVEJOY, ARTHUR O. "On the Discrimination of Romanticisms," in *Essays in the History of Ideas* (Baltimore, 1948), pp. 228–53. Spirited plea for the abandonment of the categories used in classifying "movements" and substitution of simpler, more distinguishable, diversely combinable components. First published in *PMLA*, xxxix (1924), 229–53. The reprint contains a few additional characterizations of Romanticism proposed subsequent to 1923.

ROBERTSON, JOHN G. *The Reconciliation of Classic and Romantic*. Cambridge, England, 1925. Dissatisfied with the obscurities and contradictions in current definitions of Romanticism, Robertson finds that initial contrasts between the Classical and the Romantic diminish progressively until the advent of their common adversary, Realism, reveals that their differences were far less important than had been thought previously.

AYNARD, JOSEPH. "Comment définir le Romantisme?" *Revue de Littérature Comparée*, v (1925), 614–58. Sees in European Romanticism a revolution marked by sensibility, anxiety and nostalgia, but without a common program or common principles. Interesting pages on the far-reaching differences between Romantic literature and (first-class) art in France, the latter being more realistic and sincere.

KAUFMAN, PAUL. "Defining Romanticism: A Survey and a Program," *Modern Language Notes*, xl (1925), 193–204. Urges co-operative effort in compiling definitions, assembling a critical bibliography, analyzing the existing chaos of definitions with particular attention to the relationship between "romance" and "romanticism," to the distinctions between romanticism as form, content or temper, and as an aesthetic, psychological, philosophical, political or merely human phenomenon. Also advocates finer discrimination of diverse elements in writers labeled "romantic."

PRAZ, MARIO. "*Romantic;* An approximate term," in *The Romantic Agony* (New York, 1951), pp. 1–16 (notes: 17–21). Also available in a Meridian paperback edition, 1956. Defense of "romantic" as an approximate but necessary definition of a peculiar kind of sensibility in a fixed historical period, from which it should not be detached. Sensible argument, impaired by restlessness and lack of firmness in its organization. First published in 1933. Translated from the Italian.

LUCAS, FRANK L. *The Decline and Fall of the Romantic Ideal.* New York, 1936. Spirited, intensely personal essays on the nature, past and future of romanticism with many illustrations from European literatures. Second edition (1948) unchanged except for omission of an essay on Iceland.

LOVEJOY, ARTHUR O. "Romanticism and the Principle of Plenitude," in *The Great Chain of Being* (Cambridge, Massachusetts, 1936), pp. 228–314. Shift from uniformitarianism to diversitarianism, prepared (especially in theory) during the Enlightenment, as the most distinctive single feature of the Romantic revolution. See especially pp. 292–99.

LOVEJOY, ARTHUR O. "The Meaning of Romanticism for the Historian of Ideas," *Journal of the History of Ideas,* II (June 1941), 257–78. While asserting that the proffered interpretations of Romanticism have been so incongruous and opposed as to make it useless as a verbal symbol, Lovejoy admits the existence of a "Romantic period" and singles out three important "Romantic" ideas which were destined to gain far-reaching political significance: holism or organicism (*Das Ganze*), voluntarism or dynamism (*Streben*), and diversitarianism (*Eigentümlichkeit*).

WELLEK, RENÉ, and WARREN, AUSTIN. "Literary History," in *Theory of Literature* (New York, 1948), pp. 262–82, in particular 274–82, 343–45 (notes, in particular 345) and 380–83 (bibliography, in particular 381–82). A moderately revised second edition appeared in 1956; also available in Harvest paperback edition, 1956. "Romanticism" used as one of the illustrations of the crucial periodization problem faced by literary history. Succinct bibliographies on other period terms: Renaissance, Classicism, Baroque, Realism and Symbolism.

WELLEK, RENÉ. "The Concept of 'Romanticism' in Literary History," *Comparative Literature,* I (1949), 1–23, 147–72. Impressive defense of the essential unity of the Romantic movement in Europe, based on numerous, specific examples taken primarily from English, French, and German, incidentally from Italian, Spanish, Scandinavian and Slavic literatures and criticism. Valuable references. Some questionable evaluation of detail does not affect general soundness of thesis.

PECKHAM, MORSE. "Toward a Theory of Romanticism," *PMLA*, LXVI (March, 1951), 5–23. By adding his concepts of negative and positive Romanticism to the notion of dynamic organicism derived from Lovejoy, Peckham hopes to have found the keys to a valid theory of Romanticism. While his argument is limited to English literature, it is potentially applicable to other European literatures. Written with an unabashed, refreshing gusto. Bibliographical equipment is uneven.

LEVAILLANT, MAURICE. "Problèmes ou Problème du Romantisme?" *Revue des Sciences Humaines*, LXII-LXIII (Apr.– Sept. 1951), 89–92. Witty account of the attempts to streamline French Romanticism so as to squeeze it into neat jackets of periodization. Proposes to substitute the notion "current" for those of "movement" and "school."

BARRÈRE, JEAN-BERTRAND. "Sur quelques définitions du Romantisme," *Revue des Sciences Humaines*, LXII-LXIII (Apr.– Sept. 1951), 93–110. Although chiefly concerned with French Romanticism, this article presents a vivid picture of the innumerable combinations, reservations, exclusions and additions involved in the maddening process of arriving at a definition of Romanticism. Attributes many difficulties to confusion arising from viewing Romanticism as a historical phenomenon ("fait de guerre") and/or an artistic-aesthetic term ("fait d'âme").

PECKHAM, MORSE. "Toward a Theory of Romanticism: II. A Reconsideration," to be published in *Studies in Romanticism*, I (1961). Amends his earlier theory by acknowledging that organicism and the values derived from it are products of the Enlightenment, but these values are constitutive to late Enlightenment, instrumental to Romanticism.

4   BIBLIOGRAPHIES

BALDENSPERGER, FERNAND, and FRIEDERICH, WERNER P. *Bibliography of Comparative Literature.* Chapel Hill, 1950. "Romanticism": pp. 353–56. Supplementary bibliographies in *Yearbook of Comparative and General Literature*, II (1953), 123–24; III (1954), 1959–60; and VI (1957), 146–47; III and VI contain a few descriptive and/or critical comments on bibliographical items.

DERBY, J. RAYMOND, and NURMI, MARTIN K. "The Romantic Movement: A Selective and Critical Bibliography." This immensely valuable bibliography which appeared in *English Literary History* beginning in 1937 (for 1936), has been published annually in the April issue of *Philological Quarterly* from 1950 (for 1949) on. Covers "movement" rather than period. The English section is limited to 1800–37, but the other sections are not. While, unfortunately, it does not have a comparative section, its subdivisions by languages—English, French, German, Danish (1953–58), Spanish, Portuguese, Italian (since 1954) —list comparative studies along with many others. Inclusion of Slavic and Scandinavian sections would be highly desirable. Some entries are followed by (sometimes extensive) descriptive and/or critical remarks. Lists many reviews.

12

Modes of Criticism: Studies in HAMLET

Ulrich Weisstein

I N THE fourth chapter of their *Theory of Literature*,[1] René Wellek and Austin Warren broach the distinction between literary theory, "the study of the principles of literature, its categories, criteria and the like," on one hand and literary history and criticism on the other. Among literary theorists one may distinguish between two basic types: those who, like Aristotle in his *Poetics*, proceed inductively from a body of familiar works to generalizations about them and those who, like Kant in his *Kritik der Urteilskraft*, insist on applying preconceived general laws to specific aesthetic phenomena. Literary history and criticism, on their part, involve the study of concrete works of art, be it by themselves, in relation to each other or in their historical context. The historical approach to literature and art cannot, and should not, be separated from the critical, since the facts on which the critical act is based must first be assembled, catalogued and organized by the historian. It is in this sense that Wellek and Warren can speak of art objects as being both eternal (i.e. preserving a certain *Gestalt* or identity) and historical (i.e. passing through a process of traceable development).

ULRICH WEISSTEIN, Assistant Professor of English and Comparative Literature at Indiana University, has published on modern German literature, German-American literary relations, and the relationship of literature and the arts. He has made a number of translations from contemporary German poets and is now completing a critical study of the novels of Heinrich Mann.

The act of criticism proper, which concerns us in the present paper, is subject to an infinite number of refinements and variations, no handy prescription governing the use of which is available. The selection of appropriate methods in each individual case must be guided by logic and common-sense in conjunction with an awareness of the historical circumstances that will increase with the growing experience of the critic. In every instance one should defend before one-self the reasons underlying the use of a particular method by anticipating possible objections to it. To illustrate this point, we might briefly touch upon two examples of false method-ology. A recently undertaken existentialistic interpretation of Joseph von Eichendorff's novella *Aus dem Leben eines Taugenichts* is both incompatible with historical scholarship (since Existentialism was unknown to Eichendorff) and with the spirit in which the work was conceived and written. It fails, for instance, to take account of its humorous aspects. Similarly, there appears to be no basis for treating the *Divine Comedy* as a *drama* of the mind, since Dante aimed at emulating the Vergilian epic, and no internal evidence suggests a kinship of the poem with ancient tragedy.

In summing up the problem it can be stated that it is as wrong to fall back on a single approach to a given work or body of literature—the kind of critical monism which has been so very much apparent in recent years—as it is foolish to believe that all approaches are equally valid or legitimate. Since the purpose of this paper is primarily a pedagogical one—to encourage prospective literary critics to be more resourceful, and to keep them from being overly eccentric— Shakespeare's *Hamlet* has been selected as a suitable object of demonstration. The case of *Hamlet* is symptomatic in so far as the vast literature on the subject,[2] which even the specialist cannot possibly hope to digest in a lifetime, offers striking illustrations of nearly all the prominent types of literary criticism. Lest my intentions be misunderstood, however, I should like to stress that I have chosen examples solely for their suitability to shed light on the critical modes under discussion, and this often without regard to their intrinsic merit. Accordingly, some of the most able pieces of *Hamlet* criticism have been ignored.

It would be foolish critically to approach a literary text before agreement has been reached on its authenticity and its exact *Gestalt.* Handwritten manuscripts, where they are available, will have to be consulted and compared with the earliest printed editions. In the case of *Hamlet,* as with all Shakespearean plays, the difficulties are multiplied by the fact that no autograph manuscripts have come down to posterity, and the *Urtext* has to be reconstructed with the help of inferences drawn from the collocation of the Quartos and the first Folio.[3] What, for instance, are we to make of the considerable difference in length between the Quarto and Folio editions of the play? A knowledge of Elizabethan stage practices and conventions is also required in this phase of the investigation. Even legal questions may enter into the discussion, for the absence of copyright laws helps to explain why prompters' copies and pirated versions could circulate among the publishers of the day. In extreme cases recourse may even be had to techniques like Edward Sievers' *Schallanalyse* (which proved too subjective to be transmissible to subsequent generations of scholars) or G. U. Yule's statistical method.[4]

In many instances the results of textual criticism substantially aid in the interpretation of a passage, a scene or an entire work, just as misunderstandings on this level (such as Hamlet's supposed fatness) may give rise to vain specula-

tion on the part of certain critics.[5] Difficulties of this kind—
not all of them capable of being satisfactorily resolved—
abound in *Hamlet*. Nor can the richness of this play be fully
savored without an understanding of Elizabethan English in
general and Shakespeare's usage in particular. The critic of
Hamlet will have to ponder irregularities in spelling and
punctuation, just as he will have to reconcile himself with
the Elizabethan habit of punning and quibbling. Thus, if one
wants to judge *Hamlet* by the standards of its own time
(which does not mean to judge it for all that it is worth), he
must immerse himself in the cultural history of Shakespeare's time and nation.

Another historical approach to literature, which proved
especially popular with scholars in the positivistic nineteenth
century with its fondness for factual evidence, bears the
multiple name of *Stoff-, Motiv-* and *Quellengeschichte,* i.e.
the study of earlier versions, of related motifs and subjects,
and of the immediate sources of a particular work or group
of works. The roots of Shakespeare's *Hamlet* can be traced
to the Icelandic Ambales saga, while among the direct
antecedents of his drama the *Historia Danica* of Saxo Gram-
maticus and Belleforest's *Histoires Tragiques,* its French
derivative—a knowledge of which, either in translation or
in the original, must be presupposed in the author of the
Ur-Hamlet, if not in Shakespeare himself—are the most
important ones.[6] The question of the exact relationship between a work of art and its source or sources is vital if an
artist's originality and his personal contribution to a "Stoff"
are to be measured. Only when all the material bearing on
this relationship has been gathered does it become meaningful for the critic to seek an explanation for the causes and
symptoms of Hamlet's madness (which in the chronicles is

obviously feigned but becomes ambiguous in the drama) and such other changes as have been wrought by Shakespeare.

Often the search for sources leads to the discovery of parallel stories and motifs, which offer themselves for comparison with the work in question. A number of *Hamlet* scholars have dwelt on the similarities which exist between the story told by Saxo and the Brutus legend found in Livy. Linguists have come to their support by showing that the names of the two protagonists share one meaning, namely that of dullard. Whatever the truth of their contention in this particular instance, it brooks no doubt that those who abandon the search for historically identifiable sources and their transformation in the finished product in order to hunt for parallels and analogies are in danger of leaving the straight road of objective scholarship for the crooked path of speculation.

Once he has established and analyzed the sources of a work, the critic-historian will come up against the task of finding its literary models as well as studying all the available drafts, sketches and discarded versions, since all of these are likely to contribute to an understanding of its genesis. Dramas of the *Hamlet* type occur with some frequency among the Senecan revenge tragedies with their enormous appeal to the Elizabethan audiences. Critics are nearly unanimous in believing that Thomas Kyd concerned himself with the Hamlet motif. No traces of his play can now be found, however, unless one assumes, as a number of scholars are inclined to do, that parts of it were incorporated into, and thus form part of, the Shakespearean drama in its present shape. Moreover, the existence and performance of an earlier version of *Hamlet*, probably by the hand of Shakespeare himself, can be inferred from Thomas Nash's preface to Greene's novel *Menaphon* (1589), from an entry in Henslowe's diary of 1596, and from an allusion contained in Lodge's *Wits Miserie* of the same year.[7]

It is, naturally, impossible to tell exactly what this mysterious *Ur-Hamlet* may have looked like; but it is tempting to assume that certain of its features have been preserved in *Der bestrafte Brudermord,* a German adaptation of the play known to have been performed on the continent in the third decade of the seventeenth century.[8] In all likelihood this work harks back to an English play imported and acted by traveling English comedians. Unfortunately, the written manuscript of *Der bestrafte Brudermord* dates from a much later period so that, considering the many corruptions and emendations that are likely to have taken place in the intervening years, we are prevented from fashioning solid links between the German play and the lost *Ur-Hamlet.* As it is, the former differs in many puzzling ways from Shakespeare's drama; and one would give much to know by whom and under what circumstances a prologue was added and what led to the removal of the soliloquies and the alteration of characters together with their names. The German *Hamlet,* which is full of farcical matter, suffers much from the often ludicrous nature of its action.

Extending their search beyond the confines of *Motivgeschichte* (which marks the utmost limit of the domain reserved for the literary historian), mythologists and folklorists endeavor to trace significant archetypal relationships between historically unrelated subjects. Their aim is not primarily an aesthetic one, since, instead of seeking to show what is unique in *Hamlet* and what constitutes Shakespeare's artistic genius, they desire to demonstrate what makes a work universal, what it has in common with others, and in what sense it reflects certain of man's basic experiences. In performing this act of identification, which is in itself a ritual, the individual preoccupied with the mythological aspects of a work ceases to be a literary critic: For as such he would hardly be content with proving that a work is merely the variant of what Webster's calls "a story, the origin of which is forgotten, ostensibly historical but usually such as to explain some practice, belief, institution or natural phenomenon." In his *Hamlet* essay in *The Idea of a Theater* Francis Fergusson has deftly avoided this pitfall by treating the play as a dramatic structure based on the dichotomy of ritual and improvisation.

As for *Hamlet's* mythological extensions, the Orestes parallel, which Nicholas Rowe in his *Preface to Shakespeare* of 1709 was perhaps the first to mention, is most elaborately treated by Gilbert Murray in a British Academy lecture, which rests on the hypothesis that there exists

a great unconscious solidarity and continuity, lasting from age to age, among all the Children of the Poets, both the Makers and the Callers-forth, both the artists and the audiences. In artistic creation, as in all the rest of life, the traditional element is far larger, the purely inventive element far smaller, than the unsophisticated man supposes.

Further, it implies that in the process of tradition . . . a subject sometimes shows a curious power of almost eternal durability. It can be vastly altered; it may seem utterly transformed. Yet some inherent quality still remains, and significant details are repeated quite unconsciously by generation after generation of poets.[9]

Oddly enough, the Shakespearean *Hamlet* himself became the idol of a cult, and his story the core of a myth, in nineteenth-century French literature.[10] *Hamletisme*, whose obituary was written by Max Jacob in his *Art Poétique*, had its devotees in writers like Baudelaire, Mallarmé (who spoke of Hamlet as "le seigneur latent qui ne peut devenir, juvénile ombre de tous, ainsi tenant du mythe" and of his problem as "l'antagonisme de rêve chez l'homme avec les fatalités à son existence départies par le malheur" [11]), Théodore de Banville and Jules Laforgue, one of whose *Moralités Légendaires* owes its title to the Danish prince.

No systematic study of the folkloristic aspects of Shakespeare's play (folklore being defined by Webster's as "traditional customs, beliefs, tales or sayings, preserved unreflectively among a people") has so far been undertaken, much less an explanation of its structure in terms of such ingredients. However, in his essay "Folk-Play and Ritual in *Hamlet*," William Montgomerie has made at least an effort to collect some of the evidence, his conclusion being that *"Hamlet,* especially in the play-within-the-play, has many connexions with the folk-play, as well as with traditional ritual." [12] Like the mythologist, the folklorist is not concerned with showing what an individual artist has done to raise tribal or national customs above the level of anonymity but contents himself with demonstrating to what extent specific works of art are rooted in, and reflect, such customs.

From the folkloristic-mythological approach to literature it is only a step—though certainly a major one—to that which entails the treatment of fictional characters as summations of national characteristics or as representatives of entire cultures. Turgenev thought of Hamlet and Don Quixote as artistic expressions of two basic modes of human behavior, the former being considered a man who constantly challenges mankind's ideals, the latter as one satisfied with receiving such ideals readymade.[13] In a recent speech before the Modern Language Association of America, Hans Egon Holthusen pointedly referred to Oedipus, Hamlet, Don Quixote,

Don Juan and Faust as incarnations of our Western mentality (as opposed to Eastern ways of thought) with the assumption that "there is something so immediately true about them that they transcend the literary medium in which they were created" and that "their destinies symbolize destiny-laden humanity as a whole, in so far as humanity has not yet straitened and distorted itself through its wilful captiousness, but still has roots reaching to the ground-water of the soul through which we all communicate with one another." [14] Obviously here we have again passed beyond the limits of literary criticism.

Losing himself altogether in the realm of abstract speculation, where every conclusion holds water, William Robbins reads *Hamlet* as an allegory of human nature and existence, one way of viewing which is

> to place emphasis upon six of the characters, and to balance them three against three. On the one side are the Ghost, the King and Hamlet, on the other the Queen, Ophelia and Horatio. In the former three, we have human nature obsessed, distorted, fanatical, embodying the dynamism which, whatever its motives, is destructive of peaceful equilibrium. In the latter three we have human nature tolerant, acquiescent, rational, by its limitations as much as by its virtues preservative of harmony and stability. [15]

After this flight into fancy, where all wings carry, we return once more to the terra firma of the historical-critical approach to literature. Many patient hours of documentary research have gone into the study of the historical setting of Shakespeare's play, the intention of the scholar being to catch topical allusions or anachronisms and to identify, if possible, the historical models for its principal characters. Admittedly this can be a very valuable method of investigation, especially if it is practised with discretion. Those scholars, however, who aim solely at reconstructing the author's intentions at the moment of inception and in the process of writing—most of which simply can no longer be verified— act like intelligence agents bent upon deciphering a coded message rather than like the literary critics they sometimes consider themselves to be.[16]

A good example of the fallacy involved in trying to read Hamlet as a *drame à clef* is furnished by Lilian Winstanley in her *Hamlet and the Scottish Succession.*[17] Having ascertained that "at the period when *Hamlet* was written, the two great subjects of universal interest were the question of the Scottish succession and the fate of the Essex conspirators" and "that the two subjects were so intimately connected that they formed but one in the popular mind," she boldly concludes that "in treating them as one, Shakespeare would be simply working to a unity already existing in the minds of his audience." The absurdity of this sequitur is revealed when Miss Winstanley proceeds to ascribe double or triple identities to the principal dramatic figures. Hamlet, in her opinion, is "mainly James I, but there are certainly large elements in his character and story taken from Essex, and probably some from Southampton." Claudius, "in the murder portion of the story, represents the elder Bothwell, in his relations to Hamlet the younger Bothwell; his attitude towards Laertes and Hamlet is that of Robert Cecil towards Raleigh and Essex." Polonius, finally, "in most of the relations of his life is a minute and careful study of Burleigh, but his end is the dramatic end of Rizzio." [18]

What Miss Winstanley has done, in effect, is to place such heavy emphasis on the political overtones of *Hamlet* as to cancel out all aesthetic considerations with regard to it, except in so far as she is trying to explain the ambiguity of its characters. None of her identifications sits like a tightly fitting coat on Shakespeare's figures. Hence, if he is to follow her precedent, the critic will be forced to acknowledge the impossibility of interpreting the play as an integrated whole. An analysis based on such an assumption, however, will inevitably result in the "proof" that *Hamlet* is an artistic failure, even though it may be a fascinating historical document.

In speaking of the numerous variations of the historical approach to *Hamlet,* one should not forget to call attention to the more or less successful attempts that have been made to read the play as an apology for Protestantism or Catholicism or to ascribe to Montaigne, Giordano Bruno, Pico della Mirandola, Castiglione and Ludwig Lavater the roles of spiritual godfathers to the whole work or certain of its aspects.[19] Nor should one overlook the many books and articles devoted to the study of *Hamlet* as an illustration of the doctrine of humors, and especially those concerned with Hamlet as a melancholic man such as they are described by Dr. Timothy Bright in his *Treatise on Melancholy* and by Thomas Burton in his *Anatomy of Melancholy.*[20] Mention might also be made of Salvador de Madariaga's [21] discussion of Hamlet as a typical Renaissance man and fellow-at-arms of Cesare Borgia, whose "scale of values is not one of merit, virtue, but of power, virtù." Madariaga discovers in Hamlet the "Renaissance-Borgian indifference to any other human being than himself" and concludes that he "thought everything permissible to the powerful for the sake of power." This line of argument throws into relief the danger inherent in the attempt to explain a fictional character on the basis of a single quotation, however pithy, that is shorn of its dramatic context—a danger to which even the most cautious critics show themselves now and then to be susceptible. In the present instance, the statement in question is, of course,

Hamlet's famous remark that "there is nothing either good or bad but thinking makes it so."

Turning from the historical approach with its penchant for external evidence to those critical procedures which feed on material quarried from the work of art itself, I shall group them according to the Aristotelian categories insofar as they are applicable to *Hamlet*. First, then, we must turn our attention to plot and the neoclassical concern with purity of kind and the dramatic unities, which goes hand in hand with it. When used as a yardstick for Shakespeare's drama, the neoclassical theory gives rise to such pronouncements as that of Voltaire, who charges *Hamlet* with being "une pièce grossière et barbare, qui ne serait pas supportée par la plus vile populace de la France et de l'Italie," [22] and who, after listing all those irregularities which offend the neoclassicist's sense of decorum and propriety, denounces the piece as "le fruit de l'imagination d'un sauvage ivre." Yet, in his heart of hearts Voltaire could not help but admire some of the irregularities as "traits sublimes, dignes des plus grands génies." He was especially taken by the skill with which Shakespeare handled the appearance of the ghost of Hamlet's father, a scene which he admitted to be "un des coups de théâtre les plus frappants" and which he promptly imitated in one of his own plays (see the eleventh and twelfth letter in Lessing's *Hamburgische Dramaturgie*). Friedrich Gundolf has shown how slowly Shakespeare's dramaturgical innovations were accepted in Germany and how many successive changes in attitude were needed to make his works acceptable to a generation reared on Gottsched's theories.[23]

Among the literary critics of our own time, so many of whom are antagonistic toward the use of external evidence, some have shown an interest in structural matters. However, whereas the neoclassicists found the greatest virtues of a play to reside in the simplicity of its design, the adherents of the modern school take pride in a plot's complexity and in the proliferation of analogies among its ingredients. Francis Fergusson, two sections of whose essay on *Hamlet* are superscribed "Hamlet as Multiple Plot" and "Analogous Action" respectively, approvingly quotes from Henry James when describing the play as "a circle consisting of a number of small rounds disposed at equal distance about a central object." [24]

Combining the structural approach with the historical, T. S. Eliot—following J. M. Robertson, who claimed that "the difficulty was that Hamlet went on doing things done by the barbaric Hamlet before him" and that "this persistent incongruous action partly undid the emotional assent by obtruding perplexity" since "Shakespeare was but transmuting an old play without reconstructing it"—accounts for the "failure" of the play in terms of the missing objective correlative. He, too, leaves no doubt that, as far as he is concerned, "the play's the thing," and that the hero's failure to act (which is surely the knottiest problem in the voluminous *Hamlet* literature) is due more to Shakespeare's inability to impose "the effect of the mother's guilt upon her son on the intractable material of the old play" than to a flaw in his character.[25]

By far the most widely used approach to the problem of *Hamlet* is that of regarding it as the problem of Hamlet's character, a mode which presupposes an elaborate psychological, or even psychoanalytical, study and which, principally aiming at an explanation of behavior, usually stops short of literary criticism. Among the leading exponents of the psychological theory we find Goethe, the brothers Schlegel and S. T. Coleridge. In his novel *Wilhelm Meisters*

Lehrjahre Goethe [26] offers the following solution to the problem:

To me it is clear that Shakespeare meant to represent the effects of a great action laid upon a soul unfit for the performance of it. In this sense the piece seems to be composed throughout. Here is an oak-tree planted in a costly jar, which should have borne only lovely flowers in its bosom; the roots expand, the jar is shivered.

A beautiful, pure, noble and highly moral being, without the strength of nerve which makes the hero, sinks beneath a burden which it can neither bear nor cast away. All duties are sacred to him; the present one is too hard. He is to do the impossible; not what is impossible as such, but impossible to him.

Friedrich Schlegel disagrees with Goethe when, writing to his brother August Wilhelm, he characterizes the Danish prince as a man suffering from hypertrophy of the intellect rather than as a weak-willed individual: "The theme and the effect of this play is heroic despair, i.e. a profound disturbance in the highest faculties. The reason for his spiritual death lies in the greatness of his mind. If he were less great, he would be a hero. It is not worth his while to be a hero. If he wanted to be one, it would be a child's game for him." [27]

Coleridge,[28] on the other hand, who believed that "the character of Hamlet may be traced to Shakespeare's deep and accurate science in mental philosophy," saw the key to his failure in a condition resulting from an "overbalance in the contemplative faculty," whereby man becomes "the creature of mere meditation" and is thus robbed of his natural power of action. Coleridge's theory, in fact, brings us back to the Elizabethan doctrine of the humors, according to which character is not so much self-induced or acquired by experience as physiologically conditioned by the mixture of juices in the blood.

Whatever the effort expended in the study of Hamlet's personality and in the interpretation of the whole play as a character drama, its value is questioned by Benedetto Croce,[29] who mocks the habit of treating fictional characters as if they were live human beings and could be analyzed accordingly. Croce once and for all rejects any attempt to break up the *Gestalt* of the work of art by extending it into life proper. Like the New Critics, whose views he partly anticipated, he wants us to concentrate on the text itself rather than its ramifications:

Historians, psychologists, lovers of amorous adventures, gossips, police spies, criminologists investigate the character, the intentions, the thoughts, the affections, the temperament, the previous life, the tricks played, the secrets hid, the family and social relations, and so, without any real claim to do so, round the "characters of Shakespeare," detaching them from the creative centre of the play and transferring them into a pretended objective field, as though they were made of flesh and blood.

In thus denouncing a whole family of critical approaches, Croce echoes a statement which appears in Edgar Allan Poe's review of William Hazlitt's *Characters of Shakespeare*. Poe castigates the people who attempt to expound Shakespeare's characters "not as if they were the coinage of a human brain, but as if they had been actual existences upon earth." "We talk of Hamlet the man," Poe continues "instead of Hamlet the *dramatis persona*—of Hamlet that God, in place of Hamlet that Shakespeare created." [30]

Special application of the psychological method outlined in the preceding paragraphs is made in the writings of the Freudian school, whose members seek for explanations via a hypothetically reconstructed infantile phase in the fictional character's existence. Prompted by Sigmund Freud's reference to Hamlet's frustrations as a variant of the Oedipus complex—a reference first made in a letter to Wilhelm Fliess and later expanded in Freud's book *Die Traumdeutung*— Ernest Jones felt called upon to dispel the aura of mystery surrounding the drama.[31] Denying the validity of Poe's and Croce's premise, Jones positively affirms that "no dramatic criticism of a person in a play is possible except under the pretence that they are living people." Once this premise is granted, nothing will prevent the reader from realizing that *Hamlet* is the highly elaborated and disguised account of a boy's love for his mother and of hatred toward his father. Jones further insists that "in recognizing Hamlet's non-consciousness of the cause of his repugnance, we are nearing the core of the mystery," for whereas "Hamlet's advocates say he cannot and his detractors he will not . . . the truth is that he cannot will." Hinting at Shakespeare's personal involvement in this struggle and his apparent inability to state Hamlet's problem unequivocally, Jones assures us that this is due to the fact that "he himself was unaware of its nature."

In an important passage of his *Traumdeutung* Freud[32] had commented on what he considered to be the autobiographical nature of the play by stating:

It can, of course, be only the poet's own psychology with which we are confronted in *Hamlet;* and in a work on Shakespeare by Georg Brandes (1896) I find the statement that the drama was composed immediately after the death of Shakespeare's father (1601) —that is to say, when he was still mourning his loss, and during the revival, as we fairly assume, of his own childish feelings in respect of his father. It is known, too, that Shakespeare's son, who died in childhood, bore the name of Hamnet (identical with Hamlet).

The autobiographical approach to *Hamlet* from a historical rather than psychoanalytical point of view was defended by Frank Harris, whose book *The Man Shakespeare and his Tragic Life Story* [33] contains a chapter on dramas of revenge and jealousy, in which the author sets out to show that the play is a reflection of the Bard's love for Mary Fitton and his subsequent betrayal by Lord Herbert. Expanding the framework of this theory, Harris identifies Hamlet with Shakespeare as he was, "irresolute and shrinking from bloodshed," and Laertes with Shakespeare as he should have liked to be, "instant and determined . . . in taking murderous revenge." The role of Claudius is given to Lord Herbert, and that of Queen Gertrude to Mary Fitton. The basic assumptions underlying Harris' argument *ad hominem* are exploded by C. J. Sisson in his British Academy lecture on "The Mythical Sorrows of Shakespeare," where strong exception is taken to the belief "that dramatists write tragedies when their mood is tragic, and comedies when they are feeling pleased with life." [34]

Proceeding from our survey of the various modes of structural and character analysis to the discussion of that portion of *Hamlet* criticism which results from a close study of the play's poetic imagery, we take note that this approach, so blandly preferred by the New Critics, most easily lends itself to the interpretation of the shorter lyric, whereas complementary techniques are required for the exegesis of narrative, dramatic and epic literature. Caroline Spurgeon,[35] who, together with Wolfgang Clemen,[36] has pioneered in the study of patterns of imagery in Shakespeare's dramas, ventures the following observation with regard to *Hamlet:*

To Shakespeare's pictorial imagination the problem of *Hamlet* is not predominantly that of will or reason, of a mind too philosophical or a nature temperamentally unfitted to act quickly; he sees it pictorially not as the problem of an individual at all, but as something greater and even more mysterious, as a condition for which the individual himself is apparently not responsible any more than the sick man is to blame for the infection which strikes and devours him, but which nevertheless, in its course and development, impartially and relentlessly annihilates him and others, innocent and guilty alike.

She finds *Hamlet* replete with images bearing on sickness or blemishes of the body and concludes her argument by stating that "the idea of an ulcer or tumor, as descriptive of the unwholesome condition of Denmark morally is, on the whole, the dominating one."

Promising as this approach to *Hamlet* may seem at first glance, it actually represents prima facie evidence for reasoning in a vicious circle. For we do not have to scrutinize the play's imagery in order to discover that something is rotten in the state of Denmark; and if something is rotten in that state, we can count on the use of apposite imagery. Miss Spurgeon's method—which is at worst statistical—will serve the cause of literary criticism only in cases where the imagery of a work reveals its hidden meaning, i.e. where it presents an objectivation of the author's subconscious.

In a well-written and highly suggestive essay concerned with Robert Heilmann's study of *King Lear*, W. R. Keast [37] deplores the excesses indulged in by certain of Miss Spurgeon's followers who "have taken the recurrent images of the plays as their primary data, often with the more or less explicit assumption that a careful study of these apparently less obvious and calculated elements is likely to bring us nearer to Shakespeare or his meaning than is the study of such more obvious elements as plot, character and thought." Having weighed this approach with all those previously mentioned, Keast arrives at the conclusion that nothing in the text of the play [*Lear*], nothing in Shakespeare's habits as a dramatist, nothing in the circumstances of its composition and production, nothing in Elizabethan dramatic practice, nothing in the dramatic critics of Shakespeare's day, nothing, in short, internal or external, suggests, or has been thought until recently to suggest, that a literal reading of *Lear* will fail to account for essential features of the play and that the tragedy must, therefore, be interpreted as an organized body of symbols.

Moving within the orbit of stylistic criticism, Harry Levin [38] treats the play as "primarily and finally a verbal structure" since he feels that "our scrutiny is most concretely rewarded at the level of phrase and emphasis." Levin looks for the key to the *Hamlet* mystery in three figures of speech and thought—*interrogatio, dubitatio* and *ironia*—all of them characterized by a leaning toward ambiguity. Levin's choice, though historically defensible, is arbitrary in so far as a considerably larger reservoir of rhetorical devices was available for use by the Elizabethan dramatists. A more orthodox, because historically oriented, stylistic analysis is offered by Wilhelm Michels, whose comparative study of Shakespeare and Calderon [39] lists numerous devices used by the two authors as representatives of the Baroque (just as Wylie Sypher was later to do,[40] though much less convincingly, with the Manneristic elements in *Hamlet*). Michels' extensive list includes such terms as euphuism, antithesis, parallelism, "Schwulst," "Schraubung" and "Sezierung."

Without pretending to exhaust the issue, I should like to conclude my survey with a brief discussion of one among many possible ways of looking at *Hamlet* as an expression of *Weltanschauung*, i.e. as a work illustrative of political, philosophical or socio-economic ideas. Of special interest to the student of literature is the development of a Marxist-Communist aesthetics, from the scattered comments by Marx and Engels to a full-fledged "theory" of social realism.[41] Marx himself did not subscribe to any one narrow doctrine in artistic matters; he did, however, indicate his predilection for the use of representative as compared with individualistic characters. (The crucial point in any discussion of social realism is reached when a definition of the words *type* and *typical* is needed.) In his correspondence with Lassalle, Marx praises the latter's drama *Franz von Sickingen*, because in it "the characters are representatives of specific classes and tendencies, that is to say, of specific ideas of their time, and they are motivated not by petty individual desires but by the historical current upon which they are borne." [42] Here, then, is the basis for a Marxist brand of literary criticism.

The social realist among Shakespearean critics will tend to stress the transitional nature of the age in which the Bard created his masterpieces. When reading *Hamlet*, he may look at the hero's plight as one resulting from the incompatibility of his "modern" point of view with that of a feudalistic society in which vendetta is still *de rigueur*. The critique derived from such an observation would rest on the belief in the literal truth of Hamlet's remark to the effect that "the time is out of joint." Georg Lukacs,[43] the dean of Marxist critics and a writer of great perspicacity, embraces this view when arguing:

The great tragedies of Shakespeare's mature period (*Hamlet, Macbeth, Lear,* etc.) use legendary-anecdotic material from the old chronicles, in order to present certain social and moral problems of this transitional period in a more concentrated form than would be possible if actual historical events were used. . . . The great tragic figures of Shakespeare's mature period are, therefore, the most forceful historical types of this transitional period. Precisely because Shakespeare was able to proceed in keeping with the action—with greater dramatic concentration and with greater "anthropological" accuracy in the characterization of individuals than was possible in the history plays—these great tragedies are, from Shakespeare's point of view, historically more profound and faithful than the historical dramas.

While writers like Lukacs do not necessarily exclude the aspect of timelessness in the typical, Stalinist critics aim at reducing it to the topical, i.e. to contemporary figures which not only serve as the lowest common denominators of their class or society but also foreshadow future trends of development. In the thirties a Russian critic, A. Voransky, could still observe that "a great writer is apt to transcend the limitations of his milieu" and that "guided by his intuition and bolstered by his creative integrity he often cannot help but see and embody in his work certain truths which run counter to his own conscious bias and which are damaging to the interests of his class." [44] But Voransky's successors are not likely to sympathize with the works of socialist-realists against the grain, whose unconscious has gotten the better of their conscious minds. They would consider Hamlet's failure to act as being socio-politically inexcusable. [45] For this type of dogmatist Shakespeare's *Timon*, because of the economic theories supposedly illustrated by it, [46] would appear to be more valuable and more accomplished a play than the drama of procrastination which Western critics have come to regard as the Bard's most distinguished contribution to world literature.

NOTES AND INDEX

1 DEFINITION AND FUNCTION

1. The approach deliberately chosen in this essay is descriptive and synchronic, not historical and genetic. A combination of both approaches would have gone beyond the intent and proportions of this volume, but remains an ultimate desideratum. Nor are this study or the bibliography concerned with the status of comparative-literature research and programs in particular universities and countries except to the extent that they bear directly on the basic question of definition.

2. Represented by such leading scholars as the late Fernand Baldensperger, Jean-Marie Carré, Paul Hazard, Paul Van Tieghem, as well as Marcel Bataillon, Charles Dédéyan, Henri Roddier, Basil Munteano, M.-F. Guyard, and others. Van Tieghem, Carré and Guyard have been responsible for the principal formulations of contemporary French comparative theory and policy (see bibliography). Although care has been taken to concentrate in this essay on problems not covered in my *Yearbook* 1960 contribution (see bibliography), there is occasional slight overlapping with it in those portions contrasting American with European trends.

3. In weighing the possibility of coincidence against the possibility of influence, the comparatist could learn a great deal from the techniques of the folklorist who has long had to face this problem in his examination of motifs. Many folklore studies are comparative par excellence.

4. A few sentences in this paragraph have been taken from my review of Fritz Neubert, *Studien zur vergleichenden Literaturgeschichte*, in *Modern Language Forum*, xxxix (1954), 154–55.

5. Even in theory, we find some signs of wavering. Late in his survey (see bibliography), Guyard reports that recently there has been a movement toward a more aesthetic appreciation of literature (p. 121). He also concedes that influence studies and vast syntheses, though perilous, are necessary (pp. 77, 108–9), and even sees a place for "coincidence" studies (p. 24). Van Tieghem, while excluding "coincidental" comparisons from Comparative Literature, somewhat

arbitrarily welcomes them to "General Literature" (p. 174). More recently still, certain French scholars (Bémol, Etiemble, etc.) have challenged the traditional goals of French comparatism, either in writing or in the debates of the First French Congress of Comparative Literature (Bordeaux, 1956) and of the Second International Comparative Literature Congress (Chapel Hill, 1958). Moreover, such prominent French spokesmen at the latter meeting as Frappier, Roddier, Munteano, Escarpit, etc., while defending the basic soundness of the French comparative tradition, are cognizant of its past and potential abuses and are suggesting new applications of their methods that incorporate some of the tenets of the "American school."

6. In America, too, theory and practice are not identical. It seems safe to say that the majority of American scholars, including those in comparative literature do their actual research along more or less traditional historical lines regardless of their theoretical adherence or nonadherence to Criticism.

7. At the First French Congress of Comparative Literature held in Bordeaux in March of 1956, Basil Munteano assigned the relationship between literature and the other arts to "general literature" (*Littérature générale et Histoire des idées*, 1957, p. 25).

8. The Italian and English concepts of comparative literature follow French ideas quite closely. English comparative scholarship seems, however, somewhat less restrictive than French in its greater attention to the literature of the middle ages, although the original French position which excluded antiquity and the middle ages from comparative literature has undergone a revision in the last fifteen or twenty years (see Jean Frappier, "Littératures médiévales et littérature comparée: problèmes de recherche et de méthode," in the *Proceedings* of the Second Congress of the International Comparative Literature Association, Chapel Hill, 1959, I, 25–35). Italian comparatists, no doubt due to the influence of Croce, do not hesitate to emphasize the aesthetic side of literature despite their general adherence to French models. The trend in Germany, as in the United States, is very decidedly in the direction of literary criticism. Japan, long beholden to the French tradition, is veering in the American direction. For details on the situation of Comparative Literature in various countries, see the *Yearbooks of Comparative and General Literature*, the *Forschungsprobleme der Vergleichenden Literaturgeschichte* I and II, the *Revue de littérature comparée*, January–March, 1953, and the Congress *Proceedings*.

9. To the American comparatist, such a "lack of logical co-

herence" would be more apparent than real, for he would see a fundamental connection between the inclusion of "literature and the arts," "literature and music," etc. in Comparative Literature, and the "analogy *inside* literature" approach recognized by American practicioners: in both cases, comparison (whether "pure" or causally connected) brings out inherent or potential characteristics of literature.

10. The quarterly bibliographies of the *Revue de littérature comparée* contribute to the same confusion. What are such titles as *Erzählformen in den Werken Gerhart Hauptmanns* or *Zur erlebten Rede im englischen Roman des 20. Jahrhunderts* doing in a comparative bibliography (XXXIII, 148–49, January–March, 1959)?

11. The terms "international literature" and "universal literature" are more or less synonymous with world literature, but have not been able to establish themselves. The Dutch scholar J. C. Brandt Corstius gives, in his *De Muze in het Morgenlicht*, Zeist, 1957) pp. 149–70, an excellent account, both descriptive and critical, of the evolution of the term "world literature" from the threshold of history via Herder and Goethe to the twentieth century.

12. August Wilhelm von Schlegel's pioneering *Lectures on Dramatic Art and Literature* (1808) may serve as an illustration. They belong to comparative literature not because he covers the literatures of Greece and Rome in the first, and the literatures of Italy, France, England, Spain and Germany in the second volume, although, were they restricted to independent discussions of these literatures, his essays would still provide a rich nutrient for comparative literature. They *are* comparative literature because, e.g., in his first lecture, he compares not only Greek with Latin drama but the classical with the romantic drama, and brings in the Spanish, Portuguese and German drama; because he constantly refers back to the classical literatures when he treats, e.g., Italian and French literature; because he avails himself of every opportunity to draw general comparisons (between the dramatic literatures of England and Spain, of Spain and Portugal, of France and Germany, etc.); because he consistently keeps the general polarities of the drama in mind (tragic-comic, poetical-theatrical, "Ernst und Scherz" etc.); because, wherever possible, he directs attention to the fine arts. It is the combination of these factors which makes this work clearly comparative. But not every one of his chapters would (or need) qualify for the overall label "comparative": e.g., his eleventh lecture is completely limited to France, his thirteenth to England.

13. Julius Petersen makes the interesting point that *any* treatment

of a foreign literature is, in a way, comparative, inasmuch as it utilizes, consciously or unconsciously, criteria derived from the writer's own national environment. (*Die Wissenschaft von der Dichtung*, Berlin, 1939, I, 7). This is a valid observation, but it is clear that the comparative angle of a literary study must be explicit rather than implicit if we are going to have standards at all.

14. Sometimes Van Tieghem uses the alternate term "Synthetic Literature."

15. This definition was suggested by Professor Craig La Drière in addressing the Comparative Literature section of the Modern Language Association of America, New York, December, 1950, and elaborated on by him in the *Proceedings* of the Second Congress of the International Comparative Literature Association, I, 160–75.

16. Equally unacceptable, because artificial, is Werner P. Friederich's compromise suggestion that comparative-literature scholars might well restrict themselves to the "French system" in teaching but could indulge in the "American point of view" in their researches ("Zur Vergleichenden Literaturgeschichte in den Vereinigten Staaten" in *Forschungsprobleme der Vergleichenden Literaturgeschichte*, II, eds. Fritz Ernst and Kurt Wais, Tübingen, 1958, 186.

2 ON DEFINING TERMS

1. Among others Meyer H. Abrams, *A Glossary of Literary Terms* (New York, 1957), based on earlier edition by Daniel S. Norton and P. Rushton (New York, 1953); William R. Benét, *The Reader's Encyclopedia* (New York, 1955); Cassell's *Encyclopœdia of Literature* (London, 1953); *Columbia Dictionary of Modern European Literature* (New York, 1947); Charles Duffy and Henry J. Pettit, *A Dictionary of Literary Terms*, rev. ed. (New York, 1952); H. W. Fowler, *A Dictionary of Modern English Usage* (Oxford, 1926); Cardinal Georges Grente, *Dictionnaire des lettres françaises. Le Seizième Siècle* (Paris, 1951); *Le Dix-septième Siècle* (Paris, 1954); Heinz Kindermann and Margarete Dietrich, *Lexikon der Welt-literatur* (Wien and Stuttgart, 1950); Laurie Magnus, *A Dictionary of European Literature* (New York, 1927); Paul Merker and Wolfgang Stammler, *Reallexikon der deutschen Literaturgeschichte* (Berlin, 1925–1931); Margaret Nicholson, *Dictionary of American-English Usage* (Oxford, 1957), based on Fowler; *The Oxford Companion to English Literature* (Oxford, 1953); Mario Pei and Frank

Gaynor, *Liberal Arts Dictionary* (New York, 1952) ; Federico Carlos
Sainz de Robles, *Ensayo de un diccionario de la literatura*. Vol. I:
Términos y conceptos literarios (Madrid, 1949) ; Joseph T. Shipley,
Dictionary of World Literary Terms (London, 1955), and *Dictionary
of World Literature* (New York, 1953) ; William F. Thrall, *A
Handbook to Literature* (New York, 1936) ; H. L. Yelland and
others, *A Handbook of Literary Terms* (London, 1950).

2. *Works* (London, 1764), II, 136.

3. Cf. Emile Deschanel, *Le Romantisme des classiques* (Paris,
1885–98) ; Ferdinand Brunetière, "Classiques et romantiques," in
Etudes critiques sur l'histoire de la littérature française, 3ᵉ série
(Paris, 1898), pp. 291–326; Pierre Moreau, *Le Classicisme des romantiques* (Paris, 1932).

4. Thus we find, in France, the earliest use of *pittoresque*, in
the Romantic sense of that quality "which speaks to the soul and
inspires melancholy ideas," in Letourneur's preface to his translation of Shakespeare (1776), the year before Rousseau applied the
term to landscape in *Les Rêveries du promeneur solitaire* ("Cin-
quième Promenade").

5. Part 1, Sec. 1, Member 3, Subsection 4.

6. *L'Amour médecin* (1666), III, viii; *Le Malade imaginaire*
(1673), II, ix.

7. *Portraits contemporains*, new ed. (Paris, 1891), I, 174.

8. E.g., by Philarète Chasles, cited in Joachim Merlant, *Sénan-
cour* (Paris, 1907), p. 303. Merlant credits the *Night Thoughts*
with Senancour's taste for "l'expression lugubre" (p. 100), and
suggests that some of his pessimism and stoicism was derived from
Voltaire, Rousseau, and Hindu literature.

9. André Monglond, *Vies préromantiques* (Paris, 1925), pp.
153–54.

10. *Impressions et souvenirs*, 3rd ed. (Paris, 1873), p. 39.

11. Cf. *Lettres d'un voyageur*, new ed. (Paris, 1869), p. 138; also
her letter to Musset, June 26, 1834: "Ce sont de ces choses-là qui
me donnent le spleen et qui réveillent mon idée de suicide, la
triste compagne cramponnée après moi"; another to the same,
May 12, 1834; to Duleil, Feb. 15, 1831; to Mme D'Agoult, July 10,
1836, etc.

12. Edmond Estève, *Byron et le romantisme français* (Paris, n.d.),
p. 164.

13. Cf. Théophile Gautier's lines describing his own youth, in
Poésies complètes (Paris, 1882–84), I, 103:

J'étais sombre et farouche;
Mon sourcil se tordait sur mon front soucieux
Ainsi qu'une vipère en fureur, et mes yeux
Dardaient entre mes cils un regard fauve et louche.
Un sourire infernal crispait ma pâle bouche.

14. *Le Préromantisme français* (Grenoble, 1930), ɪ, 18, 245.

15. *Mémoires pour servir à l'histoire des mœurs et usages des Français* . . . (Paris, 1827), ɪɪɪ, 360.

16. For example, H. S. Canby, *Definitions* (New York, 1922; second series, 1924); Stuart Chase, *The Tyranny of Words* (New York, 1938); Louis Grudin, *A Primer of Aesthetics* (New York, 1930); Martin Kallich, *The Association of Ideas and Critical Theory in Eighteenth-Century England* (Baltimore, 1945); also in *ELH*, xɪɪ (1945), 290–315; Abraham Kaplan, "Definition and Specification of Meaning," *Journal of Philosophy*, xLɪɪɪ (1946), 281–88; I. A. Richards, *Principles of Literary Criticism* (New York, 1930); Wilbur Marshall Urban, *Language and Reality. The Philosophy of Language and the Principles of Symbolism* (New York, 1939).

17. H. N. Lee, "The Use and Abuse of Words," *Journal of Philosophy*, xxxɪx (1942), 625.

3 LITERARY INDEBTEDNESS

1. For example, Dmitry Čiževsky attacks the "genetic method" as it has been used in the study of Slavic literatures (*Outline of Comparative Slavic Literatures*—Boston, 1952—p. 134), and states that "after decades of raptures over the search for 'borrowings' and 'influences,' historians of literature have, fortunately, lost interest in investigations of this kind" ("A Comparativist Looks at Mickiewicz," *Adam Mickiewicz: Księgu w stulecie zgonu*—London, n.d.— p. 481). Harry Levin states that good examples of source study are rare, "et des signes de plus en plus nombreux indiquent que la chasse aux sources et aux influences ne rapporte plus grand'chose. En ce moment les traditions et les mouvements attirent de plus et plus l'interet" ("La Littérature Comparée: Point de vue d'Outre Atlantique," *Revue de Littérature comparée*, xxvɪɪ—1953—25). Henri Peyre, though not denying the validity of influence studies, suggests that "studies of countries and relations between two or more writers would be well advised to give up in most cases the search for causes or influences, and to engage in the exploration of families of minds and of fortuitous analogies linking authors who

had no awareness of one another" (*Yearbook of Comparative and General Literature* [hereinafter cited as *YCGL*], I—1952—7).

2. See, for example, David H. Malone, "The 'Comparative' in Comparative Literature," *YCGL*, III (1954), 13–20, and especially p. 17. Also see Čiževsky's articles cited above in note 1.

3. See R. M. Samarin, "Sovremennoe sostojanie sravnitel'nogo literaturovedenija v nekotoryx zarubežnyx stranax," *Izvestija Akademii nauk SSSR: Otdelenie literatury i jazyka*, XVIII (1959), 334–47.

4. Boris Ejxenbaum, *Lermontov* (Leningrad, 1924), pp. 28–34. On this basis he denies any meaningful influence of Byron on Lermontov's verse tales, in that Pushkin had already naturalized the genre in Russia, and hence Lermontov is acting within the "needs" of the new Russian genre. Viktor Žirmunskij, *Bajron i Puškin* (Leningrad, 1924), does not deny influence in international literary relationships, but argues that it is demonstrable only in the influence of literary works upon literary works; he shows how Pushkin took the genre of the romantic or Byronic verse tale from Byron and what he did with it.

5. Ihab H. Hassan, "The Problem of Influence in Literary History: Notes Toward a Definition," *Journal of Aesthetics and Art Criticism*, XIV (1955), 66–76.

6. For example, see the annual *PMLA* bibliographies, or F. Baldensperger and W. Friederich, *Bibliography of Comparative Literature* (Chapel Hill, 1950), and annual supplements in *YCGL*.

7. Haskell M. Block points this out in an able apologia for "The Concept of Influence in Comparative Literature," *YCGL*, VII (1958), 30–37.

8. For example, see Paul van Tieghem, *La Littérature comparée* (3rd ed., Paris, 1946), and such handbooks as André Morize, *Problems and Methods of Literary History* (Boston, c. 1922), and Gustave Rudler, *Les Techniques de la critique et de l'histoire littéraires en littérature française moderne* (Oxford, 1923). All these works discuss reception, though often using different phraseology, and all discuss influence, though often, as in Morize, there is confusion between reception and influence.

9. Renato Poggioli, "The Added Artificer," in *On Translation*, ed. Reuben A. Brower (Cambridge, Mass., 1959), p. 141. Two articles in this stimulating book discuss how translations differ with various ages and reflect them: Reuben A. Brower, "Seven Agamemnons" (pp. 173–95), and Douglas Knight, "Translation: The Augustan Mode" (pp. 196–204).

10. Pushkin wrote these words in 1836, the year before he died, and of a young author who had echoed the "farewell" lines from Byron's *Childe Harold*, Canto I. Pushkin was no doubt remembering that he himself had echoed the same lines in a poem ("Pogaslo dnevnoe svetilo") fifteen years earlier and was thinking how far he had developed since that time. The discussion is from Pushkin's review, "Frakijskie èligii: Stixotvorenija Viktora Tepljakova, 1836," in *Polnoe sobranie sočinenij* (16 vols. in 20, Ak. nauk, SSSR, 1937–49), XII, 82.

11. Žirmunskij, *Bajron i Puškin.*

12. N. Otzoupe, "Vigny's *Éloa* and Lermontov's *Demon*," *Slavonic and East European Review*, XXXIV (1956), 311–37. That Lermontov knew of Vigny's *Éloa* in 1841, the date of the last version of the *Demon*, is shown by his rejecting an "improvement" suggested for his poem, as "smacking" too much of Vigny. See A. P. Šan-Girej, "M. Ju. Lermontov," in E. K. Xvostova (Ekaterina Suškova), *Zapiski: 1812–41*, ed. Ju. G. Oksman (Leningrad, 1926), p. 361. For discussion see my "Lermontov's *Demon* and the Byronic Verse Tale," *Indiana Slavic Studies*, II (1958), 178.

13. See Block, paper cited, *YCGL*, VII, 35–36.

14. See my paper cited above in note 12, and my "Byron, the Byronic Tradition of the Romantic Verse Tale in Russian, and Lermontov's *Mtsyri*," *Indiana Slavic Studies*, I (1956), 165–90.

15. See N. I. Konrad, "Problemy sovremennogo sravnitel'nogo literaturovedenija," *Izvestija Akademii nauk SSSR: Otdelenie literatury i jazyka*, XVIII (1959), 315–33.

16. Edmond Estève, *Byron et le romantisme français* (Paris, 1907).

4 THE ART OF TRANSLATION

1. *The British Academy Third Annual Shakespeare Lecture* (London, 1913), p. 11.

2. See Friedrich Gundolf's preface to his edition of *Shakespeare in deutscher Sprache* (Berlin, 1920), I, 5–7.

3. *Faust II* (Boston and New York, 1871), v. vi.

4. *Faust* (New York: H. M. Caldwell, n.d.), p. 4.

5. W. H. Van der Smissen, *Goethe's Faust: Done into English Verse in the Original Metres with Commentary and Notes* (London, 1926), p. xviii.

6. *Ibid.*, p. xiii.

7. *Faust* (New York, 1941), p. iv.

8. *Faust: Part I* ("Rinehart Editions," 75—New York, 1955), p. xxxv.

9. Alfred McKinley Terhune, *The Life of Edward FitzGerald* (New Haven, 1947), p. 223.

10. *North American Review,* cix (Oct. 1869), 575–76.

11. Terhune, *Life of FitzGerald,* p. 222.

12. George Sampson, *The Concise Cambridge History of English Literature* (Cambridge, England, 1941), p. 724.

13. Theodore Savory, *The Art of Translation* (London: Cape, 1957), p. 39. See also F. O. Matthiessen, *Translation, an Elizabethan Art* (Cambridge, Mass., 1931).

14. Savory, *Art of Translation,* p. 101.

15. Edmond Cary, *La Traduction dans le monde moderne* (Geneva, 1956), p. 185.

16. *Ibid.,* p. 165.

17. *Ibid.,* p. 62.

18. Samuel Putnam, *The Portable Rabelais* (New York, 1946), p. 5.

19. *Ibid.,* pp. 6–41.

20. Cf. Pauline Steiner and Horst Frenz, "Anderson and Stalling's *What Price Glory?* and Carl Zuckmayer's *Rivalen,*" *German Quarterly,* xx (Nov. 1947), 239–51.

21. Cf. Putnam, *Portable Rabelais,* p. 10, note.

22. Hermann Sudermann, *The Joy of Living* (New York, 1902), p. 56.

23. See my article on "Eugene O'Neill in Russia," *Poet Lore,* xlix (Autumn, 1943), 242–47.

24. Cf. Douglas Bub's review in *Yearbook of Comparative and General Literature,* iii (1954), 99–101.

25. *New York Times Book Review,* Nov. 19, 1950, p. 45.

26. *Flowers of Evil* (New York, 1936), p. vii. Cf. Jackson Matthews' opinion on this point in *On Translation,* ed. R. A. Brower (Cambridge, Mass.: Harvard University Press, 1959), p. 68.

27. *Dante. The Divine Comedy. I: Hell* ("Penguin Classics," L 6—Harmondsworth, Middlesex, 1954), p. 56.

28. *Dante. Inferno.* ("Mentor Book," MD113—New York, 1959), translator's note.

29. *The Aeneid of Virgil* (New York: Charles Scribner & Sons, 1951), p. xii.

30. *Aeneid* ("Doubleday Anchor Book," A 20—New York, 1952), p. 8.

31. *The Theban Plays* (New York: Oxford University Press, 1956), p. xvi.

32. *Euripides. Alcestis and Other Plays* ("Penguin Classics," L 31—Harmondsworth, Middlesex, 1953), pp. 24–25.

33. *The Antigone of Sophocles* (New York: Oxford University Press, 1951), p. vii.

34. *Oedipus Cycle of Sophocles* ("Harvest Books," HB 8—New York, 1949), pp. 239–40.

35. *The Aeneid of Virgil*, p. xii.

36. *The Song of God: Bhagavad-Gita* ("Mentor Book," M 103—New York, 1951), pp. 10–11.

37. *Flowers of Evil*. p. vii.

38. *Homer. The Odyssey* ("Mentor Classics," M 21—New York, 1949), pp. vii and 278 respectively.

39. *Ibid.*, p. vii.

40. Lawrence, *The Odyssey of Homer* (London: Oxford University Press, 1955), p. 440.

41. *Homer. The Odyssey* ("Penguin Books," 613—New York, 1946), p. ix.

42. *Virgil. The Pastoral Poems* ("Penguin Classics," L 8—Harmondsworth, Middlesex, 1949), p. 16.

43. *Dante. The Divine Comedy* ("Rinehart Editions," 72—New York, 1954), p. xiii.

44. *Goethe. Faust I* ("The Library of Liberal Arts," LLA 33—New York, 1954), p. viii.

45. *The Autobiography of Benvenuto Cellini* ("Penguin Classics," L 49—Harmondsworth, Middlesex, 1956), p. 13.

46. *Thucydides. The Peloponnesian War* ("Penguin Classics," L 39—Harmondsworth, Middlesex, 1954), p. 9.

47. *Plato. The Republic* ("Penguin Classics," L 48—Harmondsworth, Middlesez, 1955), p. 48.

48. Samuel Putnam (trans.), *The Ingenious Gentleman Don Quixote de la Mancha by Cervantes* (New York: The Viking Press, 1949), pp. xvi, xviii.

49. *Voltaire. Candide* ("Penguin Classics," L 4—Harmondsworth, Middlesex, 1951), pp. 13–14. Cf. Vladimir Nabokov's reference to Butt's translation as an "execrable English version of *Candide*" in *On Translation*, p. 110.

50. *Honoré de Balzac. Old Goriot* ("Penguin Classics," L 17—Harmondsworth, Middlesex, 1951), p. 23.

51. *Cervantes. Don Quixote* ("Penguin Classics," L 10—Harmondsworth, Middlesex, 1950), p. 11.

52. "Mentor Book," MD 113, translator's note.

53. *Inferno* ("Croft's Classics"—New York, 1948), p. xii.

54. "Penguin Books," 613, pp. vii and xiv respectively.

55. *Tacitus on Imperial Rome* ("Penguin Classics," L 60—Harmondsworth, Middlesex, 1956), pp. 23–24.

56. *Henrik Ibsen. Three Plays* ("Penguin Classics," L 16—Harmondsworth, Middlesex, 1950), p. 22.

57. *Émile Zola. Germinal* ("Penguin Classics," L 45—Harmondsworth, Middlesex, 1954), p. 14.

58. "Il est assez remarquable que la théorie de la traduction . . . fleurisse en Union Soviétique." (Cary, *La Traduction*, p. 73, note.)

59. I am indebted for this description to Dr. Kurt Heinrich Hansen, translator of William Faulkner's *A Fable* and other American works into German.

60. This is a paraphrase of a definition by Ludwig Fulda, "Die Kunst des Uebersetzens," *Aus der Werkstatt* (Stuttgart and Berlin, 1904), p. 162.

61. André Gide, *Divers* (Paris: Librairie Gallimard, 1931), p. 189.

6 IDEAS AND LITERATURE

1. R. G. Collingwood, *Outlines of a Philosophy of Art* (London, 1925), pp. 98–99.

2. R. G. Collingwood, *The Idea of History* (London, 1948), p. 252.

3. The student will find a theory of unit-ideas ably set forth by such writers as A. O. Lovejoy and George Boas. See especially Lovejoy's *The Great Chain of Being* (Cambridge, Mass., 1936), pp. 3–24. Although I cannot accept their theory, I am ready to admit that their practice is often unaffected by its shortcomings. The term "unit-idea" is, however, a dangerous one that can often mislead the student by its unfortunate connotation. Nonetheless, Lovejoy's *The Great Chain of Being* is a classic in its field and should be read in its entirety by anyone interested in the history of ideas and in the relations of philosophy and literature. This study might well be supplemented by readings in some of the less technical histories of philosophy. For descriptive bibliography including such books see N. P. Stallknecht and R. S. Brumbaugh, *The Spirit of Western Philosophy* (New York, 1950), pp. 511–30; also Wellek and Warren, *Theory of Literature,* Chap. X.

4. In recent years there have been many excellent studies of the way in which scientific hypotheses newly accepted in a given period have been reflected in its literature. Professor Marjorie H. Nicolson's studies of the influence of the new astronomy and physics of the seventeenth century are among the most distinguished of these investigations. She has made very vivid the new sense of spatial orientation, of distance and of scale, that followed upon the theoretical revolution in astronomy and upon the use of telescope and microscope. This new orientation is gradually recognized and makes itself felt in diverse ways in the work of many authors, as for instance in Milton, Donne, Swift, and Pope among major British writers. In each case, however, it is not newly discovered facts or newly established hypotheses that by themselves capture the literary imagination and "command the muse." It is rather the relation of certain discoveries or points of view to an inclusive *Weltanschauung* of philosophical, even of mythological, origin. Professor Nicolson has done much to make this apparent (see especially her Science and Imagination, Ithaca, N.Y., 1956). In so far as scientific ideas influence the self-consciousness of the individual by reshaping his orientation in the world and his sense of his own destiny, they will appeal to the imagination of the serious writer. Otherwise their significance lies primarily in their amusement value as curiosities and approaches that in run-of-the-mill science fiction. Indeed thoughtful science fiction might better be called "philosophical fiction," as would seem to be true in the case of Aldous Huxley's *Brave New World*. Furthermore, in our age when scientific investigation assumes great importance and enjoys an increasing prestige, the personal and professional problems of the scientist, considered as a human individual, may well appeal to the novelist. Consider Sinclair Lewis' *Arrowsmith* and the recent novels of C. P. Snow. But here it is clear that the situations described and the problems faced are moral rather than strictly scientific in nature.

5. See Plato, *Phaedrus*, 264, and Aristotle, *Poetics*, VII, 1450b.

6. Simone De Beauvoir, *Le Sang Des Autres* (Paris, 1945); translation taken, with minor changes in the last sentences, from English version by Roger Senhouse and Yvonne Moyse (New York, 1948), p. 83.

7. The application of this notion to the theory of tragedy is interesting. Consider from this point of view Sartre's play *Les Mouches*, an existentialist adaptation of the Electra story. Here we find the classical standards of value boldly inverted. *Hybris* or extreme independence on the part of the individual becomes a virtue. See

Albert W. Levi, *Philosophy and the Modern World* (Bloomington, Indiana, 1959), chap. X, "The Drama of Choice: Karl Jaspers and Jean Paul Sartre."

8. Henri Bergson, *The Two Sources of Morality and Religion*, trans. R. A. Audra and C. Brereton (New York, 1935), chap. II.

9. D. A. Traversi, *An Approach to Shakespeare* (Garden City, N.Y., 1956), pp. 10–11.

7 LITERATURE AND THE ARTS

1. See, for example, John Crowe Ransom's *The World's Body* (London and New York, 1938) and Francis Fergusson's *The Idea of a Theater* (Princeton, New Jersey, 1949). Others associated with the new criticism as well as other critics have been sensitive to this problem of communication and analysis. Such works as I. A. Richards' *The Meaning of Meaning* (London and New York, 1923), William Empson's *Seven Types of Ambiguity* (London, 1930), and Cleanth Brooks' and Robert Penn Warren's *Understanding Poetry* (New York, 1938) and *Understanding Fiction* (New York, 1943) illustrate this awareness of the need for clarification of the use of language in criticism.

2. The subjects or art forms which lend themselves to this category are obviously the opera and the ballet, depending as they must upon the combined efforts of writers, musicians, choreographers, set and costume designers, etc. No such studies will be discussed in this paper, but the reader is referred to Calvin Brown, "The Dilemma of Opera," in *Music and Literature* (Athens, Georgia, 1948), pp. 87–99, and Joseph Yasser, "The Variation Form and Synthesis of Arts," *JAAC*, XIV (1956), 318–23, as two examples which deal with these art forms.

3. New York, 1949.

4. *The Aeneid*, trans. J. W. MacKail (New York, 1934), bk. II.

5. *Laokoön*, trans. E. C. Beasley (London, 1913), p. 14.

6. "Spatial Form in Literature," *Sewanee Review*, LIII (1945), 225. Mr. Frank states that his intention in his essay is "to apply Lessing's method to modern literature."

7. One third of Mr. Frank's essay is a detailed analysis of this novel as it illustrates the principle of reflexive reference.

8. *Selected Prose*, ed. John Hayward (Harmondsworth, Middlesex: Penguin, 1953), pp. 66–67.

9. *The Art of T. S. Eliot* (London, 1949), pp. 37–48.

10. *Selected Prose*, p. 60.

11. For a wholly different analysis of Eliot's *Four Quartets* in terms specifically keyed to Beethoven's *Quartet in A Minor*, Opus 132, see Howard Howarth, "Eliot, Beethoven and J. W. N. Sullivan," *Comparative Literature*, IX (1957), 322–32. Mr. Howarth is convinced that Eliot was drawn to this particular quartet as a "holy thanksgiving to Godhead for recovery" and tries to show Eliot's varying degrees of success in a formal reproduction of Beethoven's pattern in the respective poems comprising the *Four Quartets*. He then proceeds to show also how ideas, even exact phrases from Sullivan's biography of Beethoven crop up in the poems. In contrast to Helen Gardner's point that Eliot conceived the *Four Quartets* at the outset as a unity, Howarth sees them as gradually evolving along the five-movement pattern of the Beethoven *Quartet* over a period of several years. Howarth's study is provocative for the influences he contends operated upon Eliot, but it is based too much upon "supposition," "perhaps," "probably," "speculation," and "if" to be wholly dependable.

12. Herbert Read, *The Philosophy of Modern Art* (New York, 1955), pp. 143–48.

13. Helmut Hatzfeld, *Literature Through Art* (New York, 1952), pp. v, 211–23.

14. *Music and Literature: A Comparison of the Arts* (Athens, Georgia, 1948).

15. *Wechselseitige Erhellung der Künste* (Berlin, 1917).

16. *Deutsche Klassik und Romantik, oder Vollendung und Unendlichkeit* (Munich, 1922).

17. *Four Stages of Renaissance Style: Transformations in Art and Literature, 1400–1700* (New York, 1955).

18. R. Wellek and A. Warren, *Theory of Literature* (New York, 1956).

19. H. Hungerland, "The Aesthetic Response Reconsidered," *JAAC*, XVI (1957), 32, 43.

20. K. Aschenbrenner, B. C. Herl, in *JAAC*, XVIII (1960), 108, 393.

21. A. R. Neumann, *Literature and the Other Arts: A Select Bibliography 1952–1958* (New York, 1959).

9 TRAGEDY AND MORALISM

1. For the reader unfamiliar with this material, the following items are essential: Euripides, *Hippolytus*, trans. David Grene, in

The Complete Greek Tragedies (Chicago, 1959), III, 163–221; Seneca, *Hippolytus*, trans. F. J. Miller, in *Seneca's Tragedies* (Loeb Classical Library—London, 1917), I, 321–423; Seneca, *On Anger*, trans. J. W. Basore, in *Seneca, Moral Essays* (Loeb Classical Library—London, 1928), I, 107–65; H. D. F. Kitto, *Greek Tragedy: A Literary Study*, Anchor Book, pp. 210–18. I am indebted to Professor Kitto's ideas about the Euripidean *Hippolytus*.

2. *The Idea of a Theater*, Anchor Book, pp. 38–39, 31.

3. The following five quotations are from Grene's translation, pp. 219, 216, 208, 215, 179–80.

4. *Greek Tragedy*, p. 217.

5. "The Stoic Base of Senecan Drama," *Trans. Am. Philol. Ass.*, vol. 79 (1948) pp. 1–11.

6. Basore's translation, p. 107.

7. Miller's translation, p. 333.

8. *Ibid.*, pp. 357–61.

9. *Ibid.*, pp. 333–35.

11 ROMANTICISM

1. We could find no generally accepted guide regarding the capitalization or noncapitalization of "Romantic" and "Romanticism." We decided to use upper case whenever speaking of the (supposed) period movement, but lower case when alluding to the psychological inclination. Other similar terms were treated in the same manner.

Authors and titles not identified in the notes or described and evaluated in the critical bibliography at the end of the essay can be found in the bibliographies and indices of the larger works listed.

2. *PMLA*, LXVI (March 1951), 5–23. Although Peckham states (p. 5) that "such a theory . . . must show that Wordsworth and Byron, Goethe and Chateaubriand, were all part of a general European literary movement," his article contains practically no reference to German or French Romanticism; cursory mentions of Kant, Leibniz, Beethoven, Mozart, Haydn, Eduard von Hartmann and Picasso can hardly compensate for this omission.

3. Italo Siciliano, *Il Romanticismo Francese* (Venice, 1955). Mario Marcazzan, "Decadenza Romantica e Decadentismo," *Humanitas* (Brescia), XI (1956), 543–57. Ladislao Mittner, *Ambivalenze Romantiche* (Messina, 1954).

4. For the whole question of literary periodization (including Romanticism), the reader may still consult with profit the papers

and recorded discussions of the second International Congress of Literary History (Amsterdam, 1935) devoted to this problem (*Bulletin* of the International Committee of Historical Sciences, IX, no. 36, September 1937, pp. 255–408).

5. These critics include F. J. Billeskov Jansen in Denmark, J. G. Robertson, L. P. Smith, and Tymms in England, Bremond, Carré, Desprès, Dubois (*Globe*), Mercier, Moreau, Roddier, van Tieghem, and Valéry in France, Nicolai Hartmann, Hatzfeld, Klemperer, Milch, Nadler, Petersen, Franz Schultz, and Wais in Germany, Teesing in Holland, Croce, Farinelli and Gioberti in Italy, Eckhoff in Norway, Folkierski in Poland, and Bernbaum, Chew, Lovejoy, Nitchie, Peyre, Wimsatt and Brooks in the United States. The positions taken by these and other scholars must be reduced to their barest common denominators for the sake of our argument. Such a procedure obviously cannot do justice to the subtlety and differentiation of their dialectics. Nor do we aim at anything even remotely approaching completness in reporting the multitude of attitudes taken on this hotly contested question. All we can hope to do is to outline a few representative views.

6. See, e.g., Artufo Farinelli, *Il Romanticismo nel Mondo Latino* (Turin, 1927), I, 4 ff., and John E. Smith, "Rousseau, Romanticism and the Philosophy of Existence," *Yale French Studies*, no. 13 (Spring-Summer 1954), p. 52.

7. In this last article, while continuing to insist that it is futile to seek to define "romanticism," Lovejoy does, however, pick "out of the many new [German] ideas of the 1780's and 1790's" (p. 272), which he holds to be "in large part heterogeneous" (p. 261), three notions: organicism, dynamism and diversitarianism—terms on which Peckham will pounce in order to save the positive Lovejoy from the negative Lovejoy.

8. *Essays in the History of Ideas* (Baltimore, 1948), p. xvi.

9. In his paper, "Perspectives on Romanticism," read at the December 1950 meeting of the Modern Language Association. Speaking about Spanish Romanticism, Tarr has made a parallel assertion: The real Spanish Romantic school in the nineteenth century is, he suggests, not represented by the generation of Espronceda and Larra (about 1830–40), but by the "Generation of 1898": Unamuno, Baroja, Azorín, etc. "Romanticism: A Symposium," *PMLA*, LV (March 1940), 1–60.

10. In his "Romantic Poetry and Rhetoric," *Yale French Studies*, no. 13 (Spring-Summer, 1954), pp. 39–40, Peyre underscores the gap between French Romanticism, on the one hand, and German

and English Romanticism, on the other, and breaks up the French phenomenon into several waves or ripples, beginning with Preromanticism (1760–75) and ending with Symbolism.

11. While this radical simplification of Croce's views gives, we hope, a rough idea of the direction of his impact on modern criticism, it must not convey the impression that Croce's interests were restricted. He was far from neglecting the fields of history, biography, politics, etc.; in fact, he is the most encyclopedic European intellectual of the first half of the twentieth century.

12. Professor Orsini, who has read this essay in manuscript, takes strong exception to the picture of Croce presented here. He states that Croce built up a masterly synthesis of Romanticism in his *History of Europe in the 19th Century* (1932), was by no means averse to grouping authors and works according to place and time in his works on the Italian Renaissance (1951), the Italian Baroque (1929) and Italian literature from 1870 to 1900 (1915), and arrived, in his work on poetry (*La Poesia*, 1936), at "a complete methodology for the definition of an artist's aesthetic personality, as evidenced by *the whole* of his work."

I intend in no way to give a just and balanced appreciation of the totality of Croce's thought; this will have to await the forthcoming publication of Professor Orsini's own book on Croce. Rather, I tried to pinpoint one particular aspect of his incredibly vast and versatile output that seems to have had the most obvious impact on contemporary criticism outside of Italy. The meaning attributed to his theory by these readers may have been a gross simplification or even falsification, but this is not relevant in *this* context; what counts is the nature of the influence. Rousseau suffered a similar fate.

13. Italian Romanticism has likewise been held to be nonexisting; see Gina Martegiani's *Il Romanticismo Italiano non esiste* (Florence, 1908).

14. Werner P. Friederich and David H. Malone, *Outline of Comparative Literature* (Chapel Hill, 1954), p. 256. Irving Babbitt suggests that those telling us that the terms "classic" and "romantic" cannot and need not be defined are themselves romantic, representing just another facet of the movement from Rousseau to Bergson attempting to discredit the analytic intellect (*Rousseau and Romanticism*—Boston, 1919—p. 1) See also John G. Robertson, *The Reconciliation of Classic and Romantic* (Cambridge, England, 1925).

15. Ernest Bernbaum lists twenty-eight well-known definitions (*Guide Through the Romantic Movement*—New York, 1948—p.

301). See also Lovejoy, *Essays in the History of Ideas*, 228–31; and Jacques Barzun, *Romanticism and the Modern Ego* (Boston, 1943), pp. 16, 19, 20, 213–30.

16. Croce is quick to add, however, that the great artists and the great works (or rather the strong parts of these works) are classical as well as romantic, representational as well as sentimental. Lucas and Guérard agree with this position. It is quite clear that Croce's and Farinelli's ideas on classicism and romanticism are deeply colored by what they consider the admirable fusion of both elements in their compatriot, Manzoni.

17. Many definitions and often critical characterizations of romanticism, especially but not only in France, have political, social, religious and ethical tinges and biases, e.g. those of Barrès, Léon Daudet, Faguet, Lasserre, Maurras, Louis Reynaud, and Seillière.

18. Note also Croce's tripartite division of Romanticism into three distinct categories: moral, artistic and philosophical.

19. Not in the sense of Zola, of course, but as a new penetration and cult of nature.

20. Wellek's theory has undoubtedly found much support (e.g. R. H. Samuel, "Romanticism," Cassell's *Encyclopedia of World Literature*), though not everywhere (e.g. Ronald S. Crane in *Philological Quarterly*, XXIX—1950—257–59. Wellek's more general approach to literature, of which his concept of Romanticism is an important part, has subsequently been endorsed by Mario Praz ("Literary History," *Comparative Literature*, II—Spring 1950—97–106) and Manfred Kridl ("The Integral Method of Literary Scholarship: Theses for Discussion," *Comparative Literature*, III—Winter 1951—18–31, among others. His physical and ideological proximity to such "new critics" as Brooks and Wimsatt may well have something to do with his emphasis of symbol and myth as cardinal features of European Romanticism.

21. Friederich (*Outline of Comparative Literature*, p. 257), e.g., has been chipping away at "organicism," which, he says, does not chime in with the Romantic fondness for Catholicism or Neoplatonism with its insistence on absolute values and forms. Be it noted that in the sequel to his first article on Romanticism Peckham qualifies his former antithesis between Enlightenment and Romanticism. We wish to acknowledge Professor Peckham's kindness in giving us access to the manuscript of his second paper on the subject.

22. Sometimes phraseology will give the scholar away, as Wellek's constantly repeated, gleeful assertion that this or that author "fits [ties] into our scheme [pattern]." "The Concept of 'Romanti-

cism' in Literary History," *Comparative Literature*, I (1949), 149, 154, 155, 157, 158, 170.

23. We have already examined the nature of the involvement of Lovejoy, Peyre, Croce and Wellek. As to other definers: Carlyle was certainly far from being objective; in Fairchild one senses a certain insularism and religious proclivities which might have had a bearing on his attitude toward Romanticism; and Peckham, in a forthright confession at the end of his first article, avows that he, himself, is a "positive romanticist."

24. The desirability, necessity or difficulties of such an undertaking have been referred to or dwelled on by Kaufmann, Lovejoy, Nitchie and Wellek. A good beginning has been made by Farinelli and Van Tieghem. But Farinelli takes in Latin countries only (particularly France, Italy and Spain), and in the thirty years since the appearance of his work a tremendous amount of scholarship on the subject has been added. Since the publication of Van Tieghem's synthesis in 1948, important suggestions have been made. Neither Farinelli's three volumes nor Van Tieghem's 560 pages lend themselves to the graphic survey which we have prepared for this essay.

25. Each "verdict" was arrived at after careful consideration of evidence which, by necessity, had to be largely secondhand. It is impossible, in a summary of this kind, to retrace the steps leading up to each of the decisions.

26. "Au temps du romantisme, les idées littéraires circulaient avec une force et une rapidité inconnues jusque-là. Les nations européennes échangeaient sans cesse leurs thèmes et leurs formes littéraires." (F. J. Billeskov Jansen, *L'Age d'Or*—Copenhagen, 1953 —pp. 36–37.)

27. Van Tieghem and Wellek have initiated coverage of these literatures as part of the European picture.

28. The political ambiguity of Romanticism, as we have found it, bears out Peckham's note of caution on the subject (paper cited, *PMLA*, LXVI, 5). Wellek, too, is aware of it ("The Concept of 'Romanticism,'" p. 171), but feels that political criteria are not paramount.

29. To prevent any misunderstanding, we should like to state that after the clarification of the more specific components of Romanticism, after the analytical and "additive" spade work has been done, the justification of and need for a "key" approach still exists, but this key may be a different one in the light of the preceding analysis.

12 MODES OF CRITICISM

1. New York, 1949, p. 30.

2. Paul S. Conklin has written a *History of Hamlet Criticism 1601–1821* (New York, 1957) and Augustus Ralli a *History of Shakespearean Criticism* (London, 1932) in two volumes. *Hamlet* criticism has been collected by Claude H. Williamson in his *Readings on the Character of Hamlet* (London, 1950) and, less exhaustively, in three recent casebooks: C. Sachs & E. Whan (eds.), *Hamlet: Enter Critic* (New York, 1960); R. E. Leavenworth (ed.), *Interpreting Hamlet: Materials for Analysis* (San Francisco, 1960); and J. C. Levenson (ed.), *Discussing Hamlet* (New York, 1960).

3. The textual problems in *Hamlet* scholarship are fully discussed in J. Dover Wilson's painstaking two-volume study *The Manuscript of Shakespeare's Hamlet and the Problems of its Transmission* (London, 1934). See also H. de Groot's *Hamlet, its Textual History* (Amsterdam, 1923) and A. P. van Dam, *The Text of Shakespeare's Hamlet* (London, 1924).

4. For a description of Sievers' method, which, to my knowledge, has never been applied to *Hamlet*, see his article "Ziele und Wege der Schallanalyse" in *Stand und Aufgabe der Sprachwissenschaft: Festschrift Wilhelm Steinberg* (Heidelberg, 1924). The latter technique is described in G. U. Yule's *The Statistical Study of Literary Vocabulary* (Cambridge, Mass., 1944).

5. "He's fat and scant of breath" forms the basis of Jules Derocquigny's article "L'Embonpoint d' Hamlet" in the *Revue Anglo-Americaine,* IV (1926), 527–29. This is one of the "thirty-two cruxes" which J. Dover Wilson discusses in the second volume of his study.

6. Pertinent material can be found in Sir Israel Gollancz' book *The Sources of Hamlet, with an Essay on the Legend* (London, 1926). Literary and other parallels to *Hamlet* were collected by J. Schick in the four published volumes of his *Corpus Hamleticum: Hamlet in Sage und Dichtung, Kunst und Musik* (Leipzig, 1922). See also Kemp Malone, *The Literary History of Hamlet: I. The Early Tradition* (Heidelberg, 1923). The question of the *Ur-Hamlet* was discussed by F. J. Boas in *The Ur-Hamlet* (Oxford, 1907) and by A. E. Jack, "Thomas Kyd and the *Ur-Hamlet*," *PMLA*, XX (1905), 729–48.

7. Nash states: "It is a common practice now a daies amongst a sort of shifting companions that runne through every arte and

thrive by none to leave the trade of *Noverint* whereto they were borne, and busie themselves with the endivours of art, that could scarcelie latinize their neckeverse if they should have neede; yet English Seneca read by candle-light yeeldes manie good sentences, as *Bloud is a begger* and so foorth; and if you intreate him faire in a frostie morning, he will affoord you whole Hamlets, I should say Handfulls of tragical speeches." Lodge uses the phrase "as pale as the visard of ye ghost which cried so miserally at ye theator, like an oisterwife, Hamlet revenge." Quoted from Vol. IV, pp. 5 and 9 respectively, of the Variorum Edition.

8. For a discussion of the German play and its relation to *Hamlet* see M. Blakemore Evans' monograph *Der bestrafte Brudermord —Sein Verhältnis zu Shakespeares Hamlet* (Leipzig, 1910). The text of the play is reproduced in the Variorum Edition as well as in Volume 23 of Kürschner's *Deutsche National-Literatur*. See also R. Freudenstein, *Der bestrafte Brudermord: Shakespeares Hamlet auf der Wanderbühne des 17. Jahrhunderts* (Hamburg, 1958).

9. *Proceedings of the British Academy*, VI (1913/14), 410.

10. Hamletism is discussed by René Taupin in an essay entitled "The Myth of Hamlet in France in Mallarmé's Generation," *Modern Language Quarterly*, XIV (1953), 432–47.

11. *Divagations* (Geneva, 1943), p. 154. Mallarmé wrote the piece on the occasion of Mounet-Sully's interpretation of Hamlet.

12. *Folk-Lore*, LXVII (1956), 227.

13. "Hamlet and Don Quixote" in *The Anatomy of Don Quixote*, eds. Bernadete & Flores (Ithaca, N.Y., 1932).

14. "A Concept of Human Destiny in Western Literature," *PMLA*, LXXV/2 (May, 1960), 1.

15. "Hamlet as Allegory," *University of Toronto Quarterly*, XXI (1951/52), 218.

16. Wellek and Warren contend that "if we should really be able to reconstruct the meaning which *Hamlet* held for its contemporary audience, we would merely impoverish the legitimate meanings which later generations found in it" (*Theory of Literature*, p. 34). Their use of the term "legitimate" in this connection would seem to be somewhat objectionable.

17. London, 1921, p. 173. A similar reconstruction was attempted by Percy Allen in *De Vere as Shakespeare* (London, 1932).

18. Even J. Dover Wilson, however, inclines to the belief that Hamlet is "a really detailed reflexion of the inner Essex." *The Essential Shakespeare* (London, 1932).

19. See Elisabeth Gerkrath's *Hamlet—Das dramatische Meisterwerk des Protestantismus* (Berlin, 1918); W. J. Devlin's "A Catholic View of *Hamlet*," *American Catholic Quarterly Review*, XXIII (1907), 239–50; Max Deutschbein, "Shakespeare's *Hamlet* and Montaigne," *Shakespeare-Jahrbuch*, LXXX/LXXXI (1944/45), 70–107; Wilhelm König, "Shakespeare und Giordano Bruno," *Shakespeare-Jahrbuch*, XIII (1876), 97–139; Frank M. Caldiero, "The Source of Hamlet's 'What a piece of work . . .'," *Notes and Queries*, CXLVIII (1951), 421–24; W. B. Henderson, "Hamlet as Castiglionean Courtier," *The McGill News*, XV (1937), 15–17. Ludwig Lavater's book *Of Ghosts and Spirits Walking by Night*, which was published in 1570, is commonly held to have inspired Shakespeare's use of the ghost in *Hamlet*.

20. See Mary O'Sullivan's article "Hamlet and Dr. Timothy Bright," *PMLA*, XLI (1926), 667–79. Lilian Campbell gives a somewhat different interpretation in her book *Shakespeare's Heroes, Slaves of Passion* (London, 1930). See also E. E. Stoll, "Shakespeare, Marston and the Malcontent Type," *Modern Philology*, III (1906), 1–23.

21. *On Hamlet* (London, 1949), p. 22, 18.

22. This and the following quotes are taken from Voltaire's "Dissertation sur la Tragédie" (preface to *Sémiramis*, 1748) in *Oeuvres Complètes* (Paris, 1877), IV, 501 ff.

23. "Erstes Stadium: Gegner: Shakespeare wird als regellos schlechthin abgelehnt (Gottsched). Zweites Stadium: Entschuldiger: Shakespeare wird wegen gewisser ausserhalb der Regeln liegender Vorzüge, die den Gehalt betreffen, entschuldigt (Elias Schlegel) oder gelobt (Bodmer). Drittes Stadium: Verteidiger: Shakespeare wird anerkannt als Vertreter der richtig begriffenen Regeln (Lessing). Viertes Stadium: Panegyriker: Shakespeare gepriesen als Schöpfer eigener Welt mit eigenen Regeln (Herder). Fünftes Stadium: Schwärmer: Shakespeare vergöttert wegen seiner Regellosigkeit (Stürmer und Dränger)." *Shakespeare und der deutsche Geist* (new edition; Godesberg, 1947), p. 286.

24. *The Idea of a Theater* (Princeton, 1949), p. 120.

25. J. M. Robertson, *Hamlet Once More* (London, 1923). T. S. Eliot, "Hamlet" in *Selected Essays* (2nd ed.; London, 1934), p. 145. The objective correlative is defined by Eliot as a "set of objects, a situation or chain of events, which shall be the formula of a particular emotion; so that when the external facts, which must terminate in sensory experience, are given, the emotion is immediately evoked."

26. *Gedenkausgabe der Werke, Briefe und Gespräche,* ed. Ernst Beutler (Zürich, 1948), VII, 265.

27. Letter of June 19, 1793, my translation. See Schlegel's *Briefe an seinen Bruder August Wilhelm,* ed. O. Walzel (Berlin, 1894), p. 95.

28. *Complete Works,* ed. W. G. T. Shedd (New York, 1884), IV, 145.

29. *Ariosto, Shakespeare e Corneille* (3rd. revised ed.; Bari, 1944), p. 191.

30. The review was originally published in the *Broadway Journal* of August 16, 1845. It can be found in Poe's *Complete Works,* ed. J. A. Harrison (New York, 1902), XII, 226.

31. The letter to Fliess, dated October 15, 1897, is included in Freud's *Aus den Anfängen der Psychoanalyse* (London, 1950), p. 238. Ernest Jones, *Hamlet and Oedipus* (New York, 1954), pp. 20, 55, 59, 57; a shorter version of this essay appeared in the January, 1910, issue of the *American Journal of Psychology,* a second expanded one in Jones' *Essays in Applied Psycho-Analysis* (New York, 1923).

32. *Gesammelte Werke* (London, 1942), II/III, 272, my translation.

33. New York, 1909, p. 262.

34. *Proceedings of the British Academy,* XX (1934), 47.

35. *Shakespeare's Imagery and What it Tells Us* (London, 1935).

36. *Shakespeares Bilder, ihre Entwicklung und Funktion im dramatischen Werk* (Bonn, 1936).

37. "The New Criticism and *King Lear*" in *Critics and Criticism,* ed. R. S. Crane (Chicago, 1952), p. 136.

38. *The Question of Hamlet* (New York, 1959), p. 13.

39. "Barockstil bei Shakespeare und Calderon," *Revue Hispanique,* LXXV (1929), 370–458.

40. In his *Four Stages of Renaissance Style* (New York, 1955).

41. For an excellent introduction to the history of Marxist aesthetics—especially Marxist literary criticism—see Peter Demetz' *Marx, Engels und die Dichter* (Stuttgart, 1959).

42. Karl Marx and Friedrich Engels, *Über Kunst und Literatur,* ed. M. Lifschitz (Berlin, 1953), p. 133, my translation.

43. *Der historische Roman* (Berlin, 1955), p. 163, my translation.

44. Quoted by Victor Erlich in "Social and Aesthetic Criteria in Soviet Russian Criticism" in *Continuity and Change in Russian and Soviet Thought,* ed. E. J. Simmons (New York, 1955), p. 408.

45. Such a position was taken by members of the movement

"Junges Deutschland" (Ferdinand Freiligrath in his poem "Hamlet" of 1844, etc.). The entire complex is treated by Hans Jürg Lüthi in *Das deutsche Hamletbild seit Goethe* (Bern, 1951).

46. Marx significantly discussed *Timon* in the work entitled *Philosophisch-Ökonomische Manuskripte;* see Demetz' *Marx, Engels u. die Dichter*, p. 209.

French school of comparatists: differences from American, 3–10; exclusion of literary criticism, 4; exclusion of influence studies, 4–5; exclusion of syntheses, 5; important contributions of, 6; attitude to comparisons between literature and other fields, 6–7; general attitude of, 283–84. *See also* American school of comparatists; Comparative Literature; Van Tieghem, Paul

Freud, Sigmund: works illuminating literature, 97–98; explorations of inner consciousness analagous with Stream of Consciousness technique, 98–102; influence on Thomas Mann, 103; on Kafka, 103; Oedipus complex theory of Hamlet's madness, 104; Ernest Jones's biography of, 109; use of symbolism by followers of, 112; on Hamlet's version of Oedipus complex, 275; mentioned, 9, 67, 96, 110, 113, 114, 115

Friederich, Werner Paul: on Comparative Literature in U.S.A., 28; on danger of common denominator for Romanticism, 228; (with D. H. Malone) work on Romanticism, 254. *See also* *Bibliography of Comparative Literature*; *Outline of Comparative Literature*

General Literature: examples of, 15; Van Tieghem's definition of, 15–18; no rigid division between Comparative Literature and, 18; misleading term, 18; mentioned, 284n7. *See also* Comparative Literature; National Literature; World Literature

Goethe, Johann Wolfgang von: and "werthérisme," 47; and Dostoevsky, 67; and A. W. Schlegel, 74; *Faust*, as translated by Bayard Taylor, 74–76;

and by others, 75–76; and content of fiction, 97; followed by Henry James, 100; on classical and romantic, 230; on Hamlet's "impossible" task, 273; mentioned, 12, 48, 129, 237, 246, 248, 249, 297n2

Gothic: change in meaning of term, 38–39; Diderot's use of term, 39; studies on term, 52–53; mentioned, 43

Guyard, M.-F.: against influence studies, 4; against large-scale literary syntheses, 5; *La Littérature Comparée*, 22; mentioned, 6, 283n2

Hamlet: Freudian views of Hamlet, 104–5, 274–75; illustrates most types of literary criticism, 262; need to ascertain the text of, 262; earlier versions of, 262; *Urhamlet*, 262, 263, 265; mastering Elizabethan English for study of, 262–63; mastering Elizabethan cultural history for study of, 263; stories parallel to, 264; literary models for, 264–65; and *Der bestrafte Brudermord*, 265; archetypal relationships of, 265–66; mythological extensions of, 266; and Orestes parallel, 266; and *Hamletisme*, 266–67; and folklore, 267; Hamlet as type of Western man, 267–68, 270–71; as allegory, 268; historical setting of, 268–69; as *drame à clef*, 269–70; doctrine of humors in, 270; considered as tragedy, 271; Voltaire on, 271; complexity of plot of, 271–72; "failure" of, 272; psychological and psychoanalytical study and, 272–75; study of Hamlet's character questioned, 274; as Shakespearean autobiographical material, 276; study of imagery in, 276–78; as verbal structure, 278; political, philosophical or socio-economic ideas in, 278–80; Marxist criti-